The Future

改變未來的 100 件事

2020 年全球百大趨勢

+ WUNDERMAN
THOMPSON

書　　名 / 改變未來的100件事：2020年全球百大趨勢

作　　者 / Wunderman Thompson Intelligence

協作作者 / MayYee Chen, Wunerman Thompson Intelligence

Marie Stafford, Wunerman Thompson Intelligence

Elizabeth Cherian, Wunerman Thompson Intelligence

Sarah Tilley, Wunerman Thompson Intelligence

Maeve Prendergast, Wunerman Thompson Intelligence

Nina Jones

Jessica Rapp

助理編輯 / Hester Lacey

Katie Myers

Harriet O'Brien

設計總監 / Shazia Chaudhry

視覺研究員 / Farrah Zaman

協作編輯 / 李冰捷 Maggie Lee　張雅帆 Yafan Chang

陳宜佳 Irene Chen　黃昱嘉 Chia Huang　劉昀欣 Vik Liu

江詠延 Yongyan Jiang　徐慧真 Pin Hsu　陳鈺云 Tina Chen

中文版團隊 / 香港商台灣偉門智威有限公司台灣分公司

翻譯 / 林庭如 Rye Lin

出版者 / 香港商台灣偉門智威有限公司台灣分公司

地址 / 台北市南港區市民大道7段8號13F之五

電話 / (02)3766-1000

傳真 / (02)2788-0260

總經銷 / 時報文化出版企業股份有限公司

地址 / 桃園市龜山區萬壽路2段351號

電話 / (02)2306-6842

書籍編碼 / Z000128

出版日期 / 2020年5月

定價 / 500元

ISBN / 978-986-98992-0-8

序言

歡迎閱讀《改變未來的100件事：2020全球百大趨勢》這是我們針對2020年所做的年度預測報告，以淺顯易懂的內容介紹100種年度趨勢。

在邁向新的十年之際，我們看見了許多關鍵的正向變化。由於2010-2019這個年代從2010-2019這個年代的尾端逃開，將日光放到新的十年。大眾開始團結一心，全球的倡議行動也跟著增加，社會規範和魁儡領袖開始為更廣大的社會和環境責任做出貢獻。

2010-2019這十年之間，政治、經濟、環境都動盪不安，所以消費者和企業都亟欲從2010-2019這個年代的尾端逃開，將日光放到新的十年。科技巨頭的主宰權已來到尾聲，過去不負責任的企業和魁儡領袖開始為更廣大的社會和環境責任做出貢獻。

那麼2020有什麼值得期待的呢？消費者受到道德標準啟發，品牌也因此有了全新的價值觀。他們開始保護消費者、保存文化、帶來希望（詳見第1章《前景樂觀》）。領導品牌的目標不僅只是達成碳中和。他們更宣布了對提升氣候正效益有幫助的計畫，希望其他品牌也能跟進提升他們對環境的承諾。

健康與永續議題密切相關，消費者對地球健康、已不亞於自身健康。在飲食方面，食譜的走向也開始以整體生態系的未來發展為考量：在服務業中，飯店將健康概念直接納入建築物的本體之中。

而企業也開始注意健康與人際連結的正向關聯，並以旗下的產品及服務來建立有意義的人際連結，以回應人口增加及整體壽命延長的新型現象，孤單被視為社會和公共健康議題的一部份，因此大都市的新型態社區開始加強社會福祉，甚至連社群媒體也開始推廣有意義的生活，而非多重的關係。

數據也開始放到顯微鏡下檢視，各行各業因此受到影響，消費者對品牌的信任度，與品牌使用消費者數據的方式以及相關款的透明度息息相關。保護消費者的規範也緩慢地被納入法條中，而品牌也爭相確保他們以負責任的態度使用個資（詳見第17章《隱私時代》）。

消費者已是促成改變的基石，而擁有前瞻思考的品牌也開始為大眾打造樂觀且讓人安心的未來。

Emma Chiu
偉門智威智庫全球總監
JWTintelligence.com

新世代不僅有了永續環保的概念，健康意識同時也大幅提升。

無酒精飲品風潮開始席捲世界各地的餐廳與酒吧，使用蔬菜做成的漢堡肉而製作出的不可能漢堡 (Impossible Burger) 不僅讓蔬菜更為各色的漢堡健康更友善地球，就連過去以販售比較不健康的速食為名的速食漢堡王 (Burger King) 都開始販售。

在動盪不安的世代人們開始有了許多不同的反思，危機或許就是轉機，對於過去一直以來所知的信念似乎開始有了很大的反轉，而這些新的趨勢必會在下個十年深深地影響每一個人。

「我們活在一個需要信任和信念的時代，今年的年度代表色『經典藍』正是要反映人們對於穩定、自信的渴望。不具侵略性的『經典藍』是我們開始終可以信賴、堅實且可靠的藍色。」彩通色彩研究所 (Pantone Color Institute) 於 2019 年年底公佈了 2020 年度代表色，凸顯了在這平靜的時代中，人們對於穩定與心安的渴望。

在新型冠狀病毒肆虐之後，2020 的你，對未來將有什麼渴望？

這本由偉門智威智庫 (Wunderman Thompson Intelligence) 所出版的《改變未來的 100 件事：2020 全球百大趨勢》同樣包括了「文化」、「科技與創新」、「旅遊與觀光」、「品牌與行銷」、「食品與餐飲」、「美容」、「精品」、「零售」、「醫療保健」、「金融」十大領域，將用最淺顯易懂的方式帶您一起面向未來、掌握趨勢。

鄧博文
台灣偉門智威 董事總經理

序言

回顧已知，掌握新知，探索未知。

《改變未來的100件事：2020全球百大趨勢》——
寫在新型冠狀病毒發現之前，發行在新型冠狀病毒蔓延之際……

希望大家一切康健平安。

回顧 2019 年，似乎充滿了大風大浪，不論是政治、經濟上的動盪不安，還是全球環境的劇烈變化。2020 年的一開始，新型冠狀病毒便在全球肆虐，緊急狀態下各大城市的繁華與喧鬧早已被空無一人的街道所佔代，另一次的金融危機已無可避免。病毒改變了數以平計人們的生活習慣，造成的影響難以計以計，面對未知的未來，人類正遭逢重大考驗。

氣候變遷所產生的問題也刻不容緩，全球氣溫不停上升，極端氣候所造成的洪水、森林大火、旱災等天災不斷發生，這似乎都是大自然對於人類的反撲。人們開始反思且環保意識漸漸抬頭，也開始慢慢影響到品牌對於永續環保的關注。從家具龍頭宜家家居 (IKEA) 到精品業者古馳 (Gucci)，品牌企業開始為他們造成的環境衝擊承擔更多責任；全球各知名景點紛紛祭出新的政策，目的就是為了防止遊客對於環境的破壞，奢華旅遊不再只是物質上的享受，人們開始有意識到航空與開車旅行對於環境帶來的負面影響，用更環保且更隨意緩慢的方式旅遊已成為最新的生活型態。

WUNDERMAN THOMPSON

文化

01

前景樂觀

各品牌對於2020年及往後的發展抱持樂觀態度。

過去幾年中，全球社會中充斥著不穩定的政治、經濟、環境問題中載浮載沉，消費者也比過往更加焦慮，2018年蓋洛普公司（Gallup）的一則調查顯示，美國人是世界排名最焦慮的一群人。今日，渴望擺脫荒涼光景及反烏托邦主義的廠商和消費者，終於能開始以謹慎、寬心的視角看望向未來。

奧多比公司（Adobe）的創意潮流總監布蘭達‧米莉絲（Brenda Milis）向偉門智威智庫表示：「雖然多數人認為目前處於一個焦慮的時代，但我已經開始抱持謹慎、樂觀的態度了。目前有越來越多的創意專案和宣傳企劃，都把焦點放在最真實的情緒表現上。傳達人的情感和人際連結，而這些就是那種能夠建立信任、凝聚社群，並且讓世界變得更理想的視覺設計。」

2019年9月，樂高公司推出了有趣的宣傳企劃試圖啟發下一代，希望他們能接下載帆並「重新創造世界」；普拉達（Prada）的2020春夏男裝「樂觀飾奏系列」展現了「自信、享樂、無限的積極和機

Top: Scenic view of Aegean Sea with Athos Mountain
By Gencho Petkov/Stocksy/Adobe Stock
Bottom: Portrait of androgynous young man in blue velvet dress
By Alexey Kuzma/Stocksy/Adobe Stock

「經典藍」（Classic Blue）訂為年度代表色，更完美地詮釋了經過深思熟慮後展現的樂觀精神，彩通認為這個顏色「能讓人想起浩瀚無垠的夜空」，進而開展充滿機會的世界。

且繽紛，展現了我們對正向思考及向上提升的決心。」而彩通公司將

值得關注的原因：

處無主義的時代已經結束，擁有前瞻思考的公司在審慎評估後，也以踏實且樂觀的前景預測來一掃過往陰霾。

會」。這些品牌發揮創意，透過充滿希望和能量的辭藻以及視覺瑩語彙，來傳達向善發展的改變，對消費者展示充滿希望的未來。

彩通色彩研究所（Pantone Color Institute）也發表了代表自信、猛烈的「火餘燼紅」（Flame Scarlet）以色票展現他們對 2020 年春夏的正面期待。整體色盤帶有明亮、溫暖的調性，使用大膽且理智的色彩。該色盤也被其行政總監莉雅翠絲‧艾斯曼（Leatrice Eiseman）形容為「一個多采多姿的故事」。艾斯曼認為「這季的色盤顏色強烈

02

女性運動革命

隨著女性職業運動員受到越來越多的社會關注，
女人在運動界的遊戲規則也開始有了變化，她們
聞名全球，成為下一代眼中有影響力的人以及
模範，也促成代言模式的改變。

女性運動員打破往年紀錄，吸引到前所未有的媒體關注。美國短跑
運動員艾莉森·菲利克絲 (Allyson Felix) 在 2019 年 9 月時打破了
「閃電波特」(Usain Bolt) 的紀錄，成為贏得最多面世界田徑錦標
賽金牌的運動員。來自肯亞的冠軍選蓋 (Brigid Kosgei) 在 2019 年 10
月的芝加哥馬拉松上刷新了世界紀錄；當月在斯圖加特的世界競技
體操錦標賽中，西蒙·拜爾斯 (Simone Biles) 表演了兩種全新的動
作，那些動作後來也以她的名字來命名。

女性運動賽現在已經能號召到廣大的觀眾群，而這也代表著更高
額的贊助，因為品牌往往亟欲簽下頂尖的運動女將。Visa 公佈了一
份針對 2020 東京奧運及殘障奧運贊助的運動員贊助名單，諸如拜爾斯、
足球球星梅根·拉皮諾 (Megan Rapino)、游泳健將凱蒂·雷德琪
(Katie Ledecky) 等頂尖的女性運動員都在其中。Barclays 公司的
三年贊助計畫中，有高達 1,000 萬歐元的資金投入英國女子超級聯

If they think your dreams are crazy,
show them what crazy dreams can do.

Just do it.

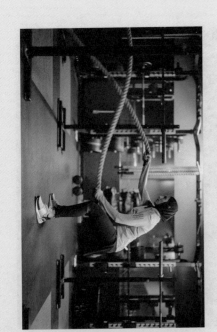

筆，而該贊助也被足球總會形容為「英國女子運動界中，單一品牌投資金額最高的贊助」。愛迪達（Adidas）推出了一項計畫，打圖「打破女性在運動場上所面對的藩籬」，並帶來一系列的「她」打破藩籬」（She Breaks Barriers）宣傳短片。

隨著女性運動賽事得到更多的社會關注。因性別偏見所造成的高調差別待遇也成了眾人的目光焦點。2019 年 3 月，美國女子足球隊控告美國足球協會刻意地「性別歧視」，以致酬勞不公。跑者瑪麗．凱恩（Mary Cain）在「Nike 奧勒岡計畫」中除了需忍受惡劣的女性文化；她的身體也受到羞辱，而此消息曝光後，Nike 也成為鎂光燈的焦點。該公司在其宣傳企劃「更瘋狂的夢想」（Dream Crazier）中，展現了女人的勇氣和力量，但他們的內部行徑，卻與廣告不甚相符。也有女性運動員表示，該公司在她們懷孕期間砍掉她們的酬勞，而該公司的女性員工也對公司違反同工同酬的法條提出訴訟。

女性運動員除了在其專業領域發光，在運動領域促成大幅變革，她們同時也展示了對於性別平權的態度以及女性的力量，樹立了讓人稱羨的典範。

值得關注的原因：
運動界的女性為女力做出全新的詮釋。她們精力充沛、熱情、充滿影響力。她們揮灑汗水、綻放勇氣。這些都成為女性特質的全新標誌。但任在這個領域，信譽也同時代表著品牌的行徑，尋求踏入女性運動革命的品牌，就像那些想透過宣揚女性精神，進而提倡鶴立雞群的品牌或公司一樣，需要謹思考他們在個層級的實踐方式。

"She Breaks Barriers' campaign by Adidas

NDERMAN
OMPSON

03

新型態社群聚落

年輕的社會企業重新定義了傳統居住模式，
以數位建設、再生資源、社會福祉為核心，
打造全新的社群結構。

在全新的共居型態中，居民不僅僅只是共享居所，最新類型的城市居概念將未有的大都會社群轉化成能夠自給的能源聯盟，共有的合作企業「跨世代社群集散地」，以及在地農產業團。

2019 年 6 月，宜家家居 (IKEA) 的 Space10 在其「城市聚落計畫」(Urban Village Project) 中，開發了「共同居住的全新方式」，為長們重新思考了未來住家的設計，財務管理、共享共用的方式，達一生的跨世代居住模式提供各項共享設施及服務，包含集體晚餐、公有日間照護、城市園藝、公眾健身器材、共享交通等等。關於永續發展的議題，則是讓社區能自給自足，生產自身所需的水源、綠能，以及在地良品。

該計畫也為屋主建立了全新的財管模式。居民可根據其中持有的法規，每月購入股份並逐步取得所有權，亦可以將股權重新賣回給聚落。最終，該社群的所有成員會全權持有聚落的所有權，成為革命性的新型民主共居集團。

此社群也將透過手機應用程式來互動、內建房租支付、監控股市資產、洗衣服務排程、預約腳踏車或小客車、預訂辦公室、飲食外送、追蹤能源用量、預約團體晚餐、以及與鄰居線上聊天等服務。

這個計畫奠基於 Space 10 於 2019 年 3 月推出的「太陽能城鎮」(SolarVille) 計畫。該計畫以太陽能為驅力，透過微電網共享能源。這種鄰戶間的交易型態是召集型的集區塊連技術以及太陽能板來共同達成的，除了創造出可循環使用的綠能系統，也讓居民能自行生產及交易這種平價的再生能源。

2019 年 8 月，TC Plus 發表 G-Lab 實驗空間，模糊了私有住宅以及社

The Urban Village Project by Space10 and Effekt Architects. Images courtesy of Space10

JNDERMAN
HOMPSON

我們打造了全新的物產來提倡社會福祉，讓我們的居所變成更健康、更快樂的地方，同時，對於居住於此的人來說，也更容易負擔、更有效率。

Space10 的建築總監｜傑米‧威廉斯 (Jamiee Williams)

居活動中心的界線。G-Lab 實驗室同時是家庭住宅，也是鄰居共享的空間，入口以 8 公尺寬的窗簾取代傳統的門設計，拉上以後即能保有隱私，室內則同時包含公共空間及私人領域，將移動式的隔板和床鋪藏身於木製屏風之後。

值得關注的原因：

城市居民已準備迎向一種對當地居民及地球環境皆友善的全新住型態。Space10 的建築總監傑米‧威廉斯 (Jamiee Williams) 說道：「很顯然，除非我們重新思考我們所建立的環境，否則我們的城市會變得越來越不永續，讓人更無力負擔，社會也越發不平等。」

這些計畫讓未來的共居樣式能與其理念對話，如同威廉斯所說，「我們能打造了全新的物產來提升社會福祉，讓我們的居所變得更健康、更快樂的地方，同時，對於居住於此的人來說，也更容易負擔、更有效率。」

玩轉數據的創意人才

由一批新的人工智慧藝術家所引領的
現代文藝復興。

機器將參與創意計畫的討論過程，將數據重新轉化成可供利用的
「未來創意素材」。為科技注入創意因子後，這些「創意人才」更彰
顯了人類在數位時代中的角色。

2019 年 11 月，人稱電音教父的尚米歇爾・雅爾（Jean-Michel
Jarre）發表了「無限的專輯」《永世》（Eon），以其時長七小
時的音樂作品，創造出不斷演變的動態音樂聆聽經驗，讓每次的聆
聽感受都不盡相同。成為雅爾在個人網站中解釋的那種「永不終
止、永不重複，會永遠蔓延下去的有機藝術品，恆常存於聆聽者自
身的時空連續介質中。」

雅爾向英國廣播公司（BBC）表示：「人工智慧的出現是一種革命，
有史以來第一次，我們終於可以讓機器加入創意開發的過程。在未
來 10 年或 15 年內，機器會開始擁有懷舊情懷，也會開始流淚，我
覺得這滿酷的，也很讓人興奮，這代表著全新的創意發展模式。」

藝術家勒菲克・安納多爾（Refik Anadol）也對機器的情緒和心理
狀態深感著迷，他以視覺需圖像詮釋出機器的記憶和夢想，藉以探討擁

AI: More Than Human exhibition at the Barbican, London

THE FUTURE 100

THE FUTURE 100

> **數據之所以讓我雀躍，是因為他們不只是數據，他們有點像像記憶，一段關於生活中某個時點的記憶。**
>
> 藝術家｜郭菲兒・安納多爾（Refik Anadol）

有許多人類共同文化記憶的機器，他們的潛意識究竟為何？安納多爾告訴韋博智威智庫：「數據之所以讓我雀躍，是因為他們不只是數據，他們有點像像記憶，一段關於生活中某個時點的記憶。」

他近期的創作計畫「機器幻覺」（Machine Hallucinations）以仿於機器中的意識來探索紐約。這項創作計畫於 2019 年 9 月在紐約 Artechouse 藝文空間公開，成為這個位在曼哈頓雀兒喜市場（Chelsea Market）內藝文空間紐約的開幕展演作品「為了籌備這個展，安納多爾影像搜集了上千萬備紐約市的建築圖像及城市景觀圖，透過已接受受影像辨識訓練的機器學習模型、人工智慧、演算法，以機器的視角來將「與紐約相關的潛意識轉化成視覺影像」。

這些影像被投影往牆壁、天花板、地面上，帶給觀眾沈浸式的體驗，安納多爾將這種影像格式稱為「潛在劇院」（latent cinema），他認為這是一種「全新的探索方式」，能用來探討由機器意識所創作出的敘事，而這種探索方式也能自行編造出本身所處的現實。」

> 藝術家賦予科技和機器自由發展
> 創意的能力，讓新時代能透過人工智慧的創意，
> 成為不只是人類的時代。

他向偉智威智庫表示，在《融化的記憶》(Melting Memories) 展覽中，他以人工智慧結合記錄腦部電位活動變化的腦波圖，創作出「能將瞬間的記憶行為轉化成視覺影像的一種數據形態的動態雕塑。」

倫敦的巴比肯藝術中心 (Barbican) 也在探討浸淫於數位世界中的人性和創意模式。該藝術中心以 2019 年的展覽《人工智慧：不只是人類》(AI: More than Human)，對此現象提出質疑：「在科技可以改變一切的時代裡，身為人類究竟意謂著什麼？」

值得關注的原因：
藝術家賦予科技和機器自由發展創意的能力，讓新時代能透過人工智慧的創意，成為不只是人類的時代。

05

重新定義時間

非線性敘事時代來臨，越來越多人運用彈性節目開放的方式，來體驗不同的敘事方式和娛樂。

串流內容大受歡迎。消費者的娛樂模式也隨之改變，串流服務讓消費者可以隨心所欲地觀賞影片。不受過往那種轉播時刻或常帶狀播放方式的限制。根據尼爾森（Nielsen）的市調顯示，有 56％的美國成人透過電視機收看串流平台的非線性內容。而 Hulu 公司也發現 35 歲以下的消費者收看非線性節目的比率高達兩倍之多。非線性電視節目讓使用者能用自己的步調分配時間，可以選擇自己方便的時間，不須配合轉播時刻表。

或許正因如此，才會讓社會大眾開始認為時間是不可預測的。大都會博物館（Metropolitan Museum of Art）也許也是因為相同的原因，才會決定將 2020 年的春季展覽聚焦在這個廣泛的主題上。然而，這樣的主題卻讓位在 2019 年 11 月的記者會上手足無措，不知如何解釋這個主題。《時尚》（Vogue）的頭條標題「晚了 24 小時發布，網路鄉民還在努力釐清今年大都會博物館慈善晚宴（The Met Gala）的主題是什麼」，《美麗佳人》（Marie Claire）也寫道：「大都會博物館慈善晚宴 2020 年的主題讓很多人感到困惑。」

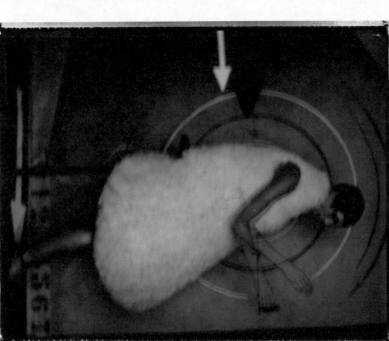
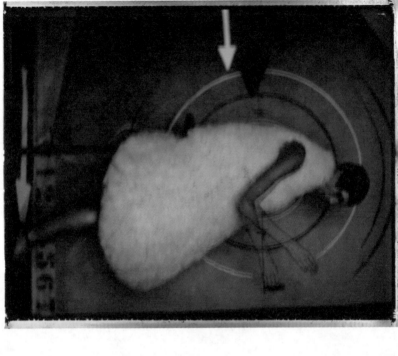

那麼大都會博物館的「關於時間：時尚與存續」（About Time: Fashion and Duration）究竟代表什麼意思呢？官方的新聞稿指出：這個主題是受到維吉尼亞·吳爾芙（Virginia Woolf）與時間有關的小說，以及法國哲學家亨利·柏格森（Henri Bergson）的「時間綿延」（la durée）概念所啟發，但柏格森認為：「流動的時間會堆疊起來，且是不可分割的。」嗯，讓人有點摸不著頭緒，但或許也不會。因為消費者正處在非線性敘事的時代中，使用可調整時間速度的產品（見第 15 章〈可調控速度的娛樂模式〉），他們配置時間的方式已不同以往，不須再受到時針的限制，時間已經變成一種更自主的概念了。

該時裝秀會在 2020 年 5 月對外開放，以「精密、開放的方式」處理時間，任職大都會博物館服裝館的「安娜·溫圖大獎」主策展人」安德魯·波頓（Andrew Bolton）說道。他也向《時尚》表示：「這是對原先破碎、不連貫且異質的時尚史的全新想像。」

值得關注的原因：
隨著消費者越來越熟悉隨選用的模式，也越來越能自由地支配時間後，與時間相關的討論不斷演變。對於有意挑戰此一概念的創意品牌來說，要為 2020 年的消費者重新定義日常以及重構現代生活模式有其機會。

06

新一代超級英雄

娛樂產業正在改寫「超人」的定義。

根據韋氏字典 (Merriam-Webster dictionary) 的定義，超級英雄是「虛構的英雄角色，有著不平凡的超能力」，也或者是「極有能力或威極為成功的人士」。超級英雄是人類文化中、大眾對於力量、勇氣、無私的形象投射，也是粉絲心中的模範人物。隨著 LGBTQ（女同性戀者 Lesbian、男同性戀者 Gay、雙性戀者 Bisexual、跨性別者 Transgender、與酷兒 Queer 的英文縮寫）的超級英雄出現，新一代的英雄將展現定義上更為廣泛的英雄氣概。

LGBTQ 的角色比例在電視劇創了有史以來的新高。根據媒體監察機構「同性戀者反誹謗聯盟」(GLAAD) 2019 年 11 月的統計，在這些 LGBTQ 的角色當中，有 10.2% 的人物重返電視螢幕，比起前一年的 8.8% 更高了一些。美國 Showtime 影視公司的《金錢戰爭》(Billions) 和網飛影音平台 (Netflix) 的《漢娜的遺言》(13 Reasons Why) 皆由非二元性別的演員演出，而美國國家廣播公司 (NBC) 的《乖乖女》(Good Girls)、網飛的《莎賓娜的顫慄冒險》(Chilling Adventures of Sabrina)、美國廣播頻道 (ABC) 的《實習醫生》(Grey's Anatomy)，則都由跨性別演員演出跨性別男性角色。

化

值得注意的是，這當中有許多角色都是戰鬥或超級英雄，他們擺脫過時的性別認知，重新定義了超人的力量。2019 年 7 月，女武神瓦爾基麗（Valkyrie）確定會在 2021 年 11 月釋出的《雷神索爾 4：愛與雷霆》（Thor: Love and Thunder）中現身，成為漫威宇宙的首位女同性超級英雄。漫威的首席製作人維多利亞・阿隆索（Victoria Alonso）告訴《綜藝報》（Variety）：「我們的成功全來自這些人物在性格上的美妙差異。如果我們不想聚面向歧異，就無法保持成功。我們的目標是為那些觀看我們電影的人，提供這樣的東西。」

CW 電視網為非二元性別及 LGBTQ 的超級英雄打了頭陣，2019 年 10 月，由擁有流動性氣質的演員露比・蘿絲（Ruby Rose）所飾演的蝙蝠女俠，成了電視影集中的首位同志超級英雄。《超女》（Supergirl）在 2019 年一月播出時，美劇第一位跨性別戰鬥英雄「夢者」（Dreamer）也由跨性別運動倡議者妮可・梅因斯（Nicole

Maines）飾演。該電視網的《綠箭俠》（Arrow）也加入這個行列中有多位同性戀和雙性戀超級英雄，包括地下英雄卓越先生（Mr Terrific）、白金絲雀（White Canary）、刺客妮莎・奧古生（Nyssa al Ghul）。

值得關注的原因：
Z 世代與千禧世代的消費者拋下載帶有性別歧視的過時偏見，從服裝打扮到日常對話，在在體現了他們的思想，而形象狹隘的超級英雄，也因此受到重新審視。在新一代的觀念下，英雄們將展示「身為人類的意義」，並以更廣泛的眼角呈現人物形象，不再為固定性別認同、固定性傾向等無稽之談買單。

THE FUTURE 100

The Tele-mental Health
Platform for Southeast Asia

07

逐步解禁的東方人

長期存在亞洲世界的禁忌正逐漸開放，雖然步調緩慢，方向卻很明確。

亞洲看待心理健康、性健康、性別議題的態度，開始追上當地急速發展的經濟進程，而科技也在旁扮演了重要的一角。

在泰國，以心理健康為主的科技新創公司 Ooca，在其網站和手機應用程式上推廣視訊治療，使用者可以選擇困擾他們的問題，不管是工作壓力或是戀愛煩惱，都能在查看醫生學經歷後預約看診。為了讓員工更快樂、生產效率進一步提升，大公司的雇主也準備加入這個行列，其社會觀感也隨之改變。他們的其中一項訴求便是以該應用程式的內建功能來分析匿名數據，並偵查初出顯露的問題，例如超時工作或其他壓力源。

Ooca 的創辦人艾克斯（Kanpassorn "Eix" Suriyasangpetch）本身即有憂鬱問題，他對偉門智威智庫表示：「這有點像公司內部無聲的熱鬧畫面。」

性健康也開始逐步受到重視，且被認為是影響整體健康的一項重

UNDERMAN
HOMPSON　　Images courtesy of Ooca

要因素。在中國，多數的性健康教育資源都面向男性受眾，而 Yummy 社群平台則提供女人一個可以自由討論性事的地方，從親密關係到高潮，再到乳癌預防等健康議題，據說其使用者已超過 200 萬人。

與性別歧視相關的討論也浮上檯面。受傳統標教堡壘束縛的日本開始出現對抗性別不平等的「#KuToo 運動」，呼應西方世界的「#MeToo 運動」，這項運動由日本自由作家及演員石川優實（Yumi Ishikawa）發起，起因為她在葬儀社工作時，被迫穿著高跟鞋工作。

石川將日文中表示靴子「kutsu」和痛苦「kutsuu」的單詞並置，提出 #KuToo 一詞，公開譴責要求日本女性穿著高跟鞋的文化，認為這是性別歧視且會導致實質的傷害，包括拇指外翻、退水泡、流血等等。她在 2019 年發起了線上連署，要求政府取締此種強制員工穿著跟鞋的規定並列入違法條。共有超過 31,000 人簽署此案，但政府仍未改變相關法條。2019 年 10 月，石川被英國廣播公司列入全球百大最有影響力的女性名單中，她也推出了自己的平底鞋品牌「KuToo 追隨者」（KuToo Followers），以男性的綁帶鞋為基礎，提供較小版型給女性使用。

日本女性也對職場上與髮型相關的層規則感到憤火。2018 年，洗髮精品牌潘婷（Pantene）祭出口號，意圖解放女性求職者需要紮起乾淨馬尾的造型規定，鼓勵女性把頭髮放下來，繼「自由選擇求職髮型」（More Freedom in Job-Hunting Hair）的口號之後，潘婷表示，性別已經不像過去那樣重要也不再是定義一個人的重要指

也推出了「一起出髮：我的頭髮帶我前進」（Hair We Go: My Hair Moves Me Forward）企劃同時針對求職者及人資專員，希望終結被迫彰顯一致性的職場形象。

值得關注的原因：

亞洲的調查數據和社會輿論都顯示了對傳統禁忌和性別束縛轉趨開放的態度。一份由偉門智威智庫針對五個國家（中國、日本、印尼、泰國、澳洲）2500 名消費者所做的調查顯示，心理健康對各個世代來說都是重要的議題。受訪者當中，有 38% 的人認為性健康與整體健康狀況有關，且男性做出此陳述的比例比女性還高，新的世代已帶著新的期計進入職場。偉門智威智庫在「亞洲Z世代」報告中，調查了九個國家、4500 名消費者，其中有八成的受訪者表示，改變全然降臨。

亞洲看待心理健康、性健康、性別
議題的態度，開始追上當地急速發展的經濟
進程，而科技也在勇於扮演了重要的一角。

08

分手數據

新型服務進入市場，為談戀愛的現代人
提供心痛的解藥。

根據偉門智威獨有的研究工具 SONAR™ 收集的數據照示，86% 的
美國單身人士認為單身代表他們享有更多自由，83% 的人認為他
們得身為讓他們有更多時間做他們喜歡的事，77% 的單身人士覺
門的選擇。不過，要如此滿足現狀，還是要先透過一些難關。隨著
越來越多人選擇單身，有更多人也開始欣然接受單身這個選項，新
型服務已不再將重點放在尋找另一半，而是著重於如何幫助結束
一段戀情的人們撫平情緒，並讓他們能夠享受脫離情侶狀態的生
活。

2019 年 11 月，針對剛剛失戀的人提供的全新旅遊服務「失戀旅行」
(Breakup Tours) 開始上線，針對各個案情況和個人喜好客製旅程，
安排「療癒心靈和洗滌靈魂」的行程，也可開啟旅行交流圈 (Circle
of Travelers) 功能來交友，還為每位旅客特製一組專屬的「急救
箱」，內含治療型寫作療程。

共同創辦人鐘振傑對《CNN 旅遊頻道》(CNN Travel) 表示：「分手
很難，因為改變很難，在你習慣某種生活方式之後，你會放大檢視
和以往不同的生活習慣。旅遊可以讓你戒斷這樣的思考方式，它會
給你全新的視角。」

Did you meditate, take a bubble bath, or get outside today? Self care is major for your mending.

log self care activities

Read advice specific to your breakup and connect with a global community of Menders in your shoes.

real advice

合用），每位客戶都會分發到一名服務專員，他們會為客戶準備一份「客製化的流程圖」來解決當下的痛點，並為下一步做好準備。」梅克如此解釋。

值得關注的原因：

有越來越多派別的消費者都在單身後狂歡作樂，而這些服務重新定義了從情侶到單身的轉換期，根據梅克的說法，他們「針對傳統僵化的敘事，創造了全新的對話空間」。

Curated training plan of 3-5 minute daily audio trainings written by mental health & wellness experts.

audio trainings by experts

Was it Commitment? Distance? Incompatible lifestyles? You let us know about your breakup.

choose breakup reason

「也許你的分手不是毀滅，而是一種突破，一個迎向更好人生的機會？」Onward 的執行長暨共同創辦人琳賽‧梅克（Lindsay Meck）如此提問。分手善後服務 Onward 於 2019 年 2 月推出，梅克告訴偉門智威報庫，他們的服務旨在「協助你從一段長期戀愛關係中失戀的人，實際抽離那個環境，並從心出發，開始新的人生。」

該服務為為客戶處理後勤類型的工作（例如搬家、找房、地址變動、家居裝潢），也處理他們各方面的挑戰（身心健康、財務健全、法律

09

驚駭科技帶來的影響

面對即將到來的2020美國總統大選，政治人物和科技公司都在找尋辦法管理政治言論在網路上的走向，尤其是西大荒地區的社群風向。

2019年10月，推特（Twitter）的執行長傑克·多爾西（JackDorsey）在一系列的推特貼文中宣布，該公司「決定停止全球推特平台上的政治廣告。因為我相信政治曝光應該是贏來的，不是買來的。」

他還補充：「我們很清楚知道自己只是大型政治宣傳環境中的一個小小部分。有些人可能會驚訝，我們今天的作為是對現在政治人物有利的作法，但我們也見識過許多社會運動擴及了大量的人群，他們都沒有做政治廣告，所以我相信這種現象會是有增無減的。」

《美聯社》（Associated Press）強調，推特的做法可能會對使用者帶來「預料之外的結果，且可能不只一種結果」，文章也同時提及「在那些可能會受影響的人當中，可能跟現在政治人物對抗的候選人；且正想要拓展受眾的非營利機構；有還跟現在政治人物對抗的候選人；顯然他會有以投放政治廣告維生，為候選人下單買廣告的政治顧問。」

2019年11月，英國曾因此已發強烈的抗爭，當時正準備迎接12月的英國大選。保守黨卻在兩黨電視辯論期間，將他們其中一個推特

jack @jack · Follow

We've made the decision to stop all political advertising on Twitter globally. We believe political message reach should be earned, not bought. Why? A few reasons...🧵

1:05 PM · 30 Oct 2019

103,666 Retweets 428,707 Likes

jack @jack · Oct 30
A political message earns reach when people decide to follow an account or retweet. Paying for reach removes that decision, forcing highly optimized and targeted political messages onto people. We believe this decision should not be compromised by money.

jack @jack · Oct 30
While internet advertising is incredibly powerful and very effective for commercial advertisers, that power brings significant risks to politics, where it can be used to influence votes to affect the lives of millions.

jack @jack · Oct 30
Internet political ads present entirely new challenges to civic discourse: machine learning-based optimization of messaging and micro-targeting, unchecked misleading information, and deep fakes. All at increasing velocity, sophistication, and overwhelming scale.

jack @jack · Oct 30
These challenges will affect ALL internet communication, not just political ads. Best to focus on the root problems, without the additional burden and complexity taking money brings. Trying to fix both means fixing neither well, and harms our credibility.

jack @jack · Oct 30
For instance, it's not credible for us to say: "We're working hard to stop people from gaming our systems to spread misleading info, buuut if someone pays us to target and force people to see their political ad... well...they can say whatever they want!" 😬

jack @jack · Oct 30
We considered stopping only candidate ads, but issue ads present a way to circumvent. Additionally, it isn't fair for everyone but candidates to buy ads for issues they want to push. So we're stopping these too.

官方認證帳號改名為「英國事實查核網」（factcheckUK）。隨後，推特發表聲明：「就像大家在英國大選辯論上看到的，任何有意以更改認證帳號資訊的方式來誤導民眾的人，將要面對重大的矯正措施。」

2019 年 11 月下旬，谷歌（Google）聲明，他們會對美國大選的選舉廣告投放做出限制，僅可利用年齡、性別、郵遞區號等大分類來篩選受眾。以往在政治宣傳人員可以依照過去公開的投票記錄和普遍的政治傾向（例如左傾或右傾），來瞄準美國的合適廣告。（合歌已對歐盟和英國提出相同的限制，以遏止這樣的情形發生。）合歌廣告的產品管理副總史考特·史賓賽（Scott Spencer）在 2019 年 11 月發布了一篇部落格文章，在文章中說明了這項變革：「由於對近期的政治廣告感到擔憂，我們想讓選民對在我們平台上看到的政治廣告有信心。不管成本、效應，或者花在我們平台上的金錢多寡，我們都相信這些改變會讓選民對數位政治文宣更有信心，也更信任世界各地的選舉過程。」

他也簡要說明了這個網路巨擘如何訂定政策，遏止「內容明顯不實，且在民主選舉過程中，會嚴重損害選民參與率或選民信心的廣告」。

Spotify 是最新一個針對政治廣告發表立場的公司，他們在 2019 年 12 月宣布，從 2020 年開始，會停止接受政治廣告在該音樂串流平台上投放。

UNDERMAN
HOMPSON

Elizabeth Warren at SXSW 2019.
Photo by Amy E Price/Getty Images for SXSW

我們相信

政治曝光應該是贏來的，不是買來的。

推特執行長｜傑克‧多爾西（Jack Dorsey）

總體來說，民主黨候選人伊利沙白‧華倫（Elizabeth Warren）早已將打破科技巨頭的壟斷現象列為其選戰的一項中心原則。根據《彭博商業週刊》（Bloomberg）的說法，她的計畫包含「鬆動過往的收購案」，（例如臉書收購 Instagram 和 WhatsApp），「確保亞馬遜（Amazon）不得在其網站（Amazon.com）上販售自有品牌或第三方的產品。

250 億美金，且有經營網路交易平台的科技巨頭，不得和平台使用者競爭」，提供使用者相同的服務。也就是說，「亞馬遜彷如他小公司在該平台上販售的產品。接著將自己推出的產品賣給消華倫於 2019 年 3 月在一則 Medium 文章中寫道，「亞馬遜與使者，打垮了這些小型公司」。該文章也進而帶動該計畫。

Instagram 在全球用戶帳號上測試隱藏「讚數」的功能，意圖處理某些元素在該平台上的負面觀感。2019 年 11 月，Instagram 領導人亞當‧莫瑟里（Adam Mosseri）在推特中寫道：「我們要隱藏某些數，是為了要減緩 Instagram 年輕用戶的壓力。這可能會影響某些人在我們平台上和他人互動的方式，可能會比較少按讚，或張貼更多貼文，但我們主要還是想知道，這到底會讓大家有什麼感受。」

值得關注的原因：

社群媒體野火燎原般地將政治和社會議題帶往全新的階段，不管是傳播速度、內容或是真實性都是。現在，無論政治人物或是科技巨頭本身，都發現了這個現象，也想扭轉這些惡意的影響，在接動法規和守護言論自由兩大方向上，2020 年將更聚焦資訊（尤其政治類資訊）在這些平台上流通的方式。

10

走進多重宇宙

受到相信世界末日的反烏托邦思想啟發，藝術家、設計師、創新實驗家創造了變化無窮的替代世界，讓時空、能量、物質能在其中相互碰撞。

2020 年 8 月的火人祭（Burning Man），相信在地球之外仍有其他宇宙，而舉辦活動的臨時城鎮將以多重宇宙為主題。同時參照平行宇宙、超現實主義、古物理學，探討「可能選項的量子萬花筒」。主辦方也提供參加者一個遇見「另一個自己」的機會。量子糾纏和多重宇宙理論面對許多有啟發意義的詰問，而2020 年的火人祭也將成為多維創意的實驗場，讓參加者得以脫離現代生活中的焦慮壓力，將自我放逐到每一個無限的宇宙中。

2020 年 6 月，英國的維多利亞與亞伯特博物館（the Victoria & Albert Museum）邀請觀眾「進入奇幻世界體驗一段心靈交融的旅程」，深度探討路易斯‧卡羅（Lewis Carroll）所作的《愛麗絲夢遊仙境》（Alice's Adventures in Wonderland）。展覽名為《愛麗絲：好奇寶寶與好奇寶寶》（Alice: Curiouser and Curiouser），聚焦這個有 155 年歷史的故事源頭，改編版本再創作，呈現出奇幻世界的樣貌，以反其中歷久不衰、持續引人省思的人物角色。

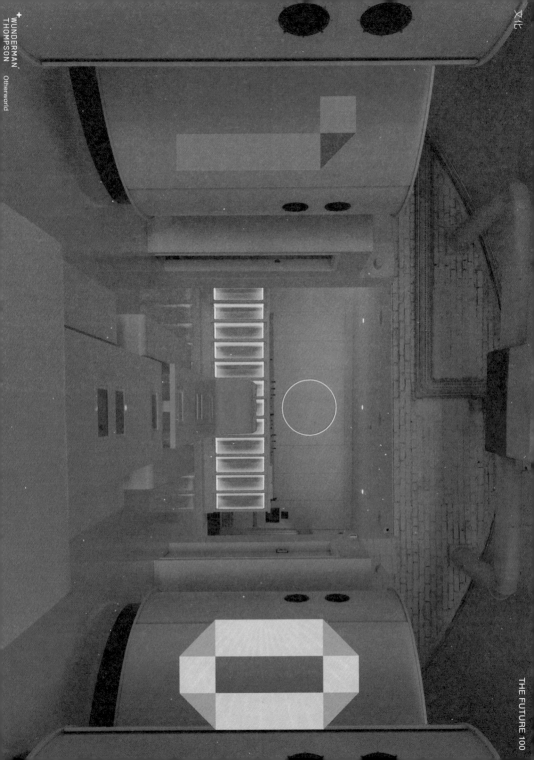

沈浸式裝置也帶領觀眾進入另一個時空維度。紐約市的 ZeroSpace 於 2019 年夏天開立，以世界頂尖新媒體藝術家所做的大型藝術裝置「沈浸式藝術遊樂場」，將觀眾帶向「藝術、科技、人文匯流的多重宇宙」。倫敦的 Otherworld 藝文空間利用虛擬實境技術，鼓勵觀眾離開現實世界，進入「擁有無限可能的平行宇宙」。

值得關注的原因：

雖然在談及地球時，現實世界的近期論談往往指向反烏托邦式的無望未來，但藝術家卻創作出另一個擁有無限可能的替代時空。厭倦現下平凡生活的消費者，正努力尋找逃避現實，投入冒險的管道，同時也想窺望其他地方的生活，會是什麼樣子。

科技 & 創新

11

防護科技

世界充斥著憂慮，品牌為此打造新的產品來舒緩焦慮、提供慰藉並帶來安全感。

面對讓人懼怕的環境、政治、經濟動盪、大眾比以往更加焦慮。由美國心理學會（American Psychological Association）於 2019 年 4 月所作的一份調查指出，有 32% 的美國人比前一年更加焦慮。而先前由美國心理學會所做的另一份調查，也發現千禧世代是目前為止最焦慮的一代。隨著焦慮和不安的提升，消費者開始尋求針對周遭世界提供防護以反慰藉的產品和服務。

2019 年，華麗的年度科技展示會「消費電子用品展」（Consumer Electronics Show）中，展出了大量的防護型產品。Listtot 是形似鑰匙圈的攜帶式水質檢測器，可以立即檢測飲用水的水質及安全。智慧濾水器 Mitte 保證可以濾出現代污染源，例如塑膠微粒、生物激素、化學物質等等。得過創新產品獎的 Larq 自動淨水壺，使用 UVC LED 殺菌燈，可消除飲用水中 99.9999% 的細菌和病毒。

在一則 2019 年的研究中，麻省理工學院（Massachusetts Institute of Technology）的研究人員發現，快樂程度和空氣品質有直接的關聯，污染越高的地區，群眾的快樂指數就越低。2019 年 11 月，新德

JNDERMAN　& 創新

THOMPSON　Larq self-purifying water bottle

我們除了要讓大家可以在家中呼吸到較好的空氣，也希望Gunrid空氣淨化窗簾可以提高社會對室內空汙的關注，藉此改變所作所為，為地球的清淨空氣盡一份力。

英特宜家集團的永續發展國際負責人，蓮娜．普里普－科瓦奇 (Lena Pripp-Kovac)

里因嚴重霧霾而發布了公衛緊急事件，隨著空汙指數創下新高，品牌也致力於發展相關的個人防護用品。

三星集團 (Samsung) 利用消費者對於肉眼看不見的有害環境因子的恐懼，打造了全新產品 Bot Air。於2019年的消費電子用品展上曝光。Bot Air 是自動空氣淨化機，會在住居中巡邏，以藍控空氣品質。宜家家居 (IKEA) 計畫於2020年推出 Gunrid 空氣淨化窗簾。在布料中加入獨特的技術，在光線照射下可破壞空氣中的污染粒子。英特宜家集團 (Inter Ikea Group) 的永續發展負責人蓮娜．普里普－科瓦奇 (Lena Pripp-Kovac) 說道：「我們除了要讓大家可以在家中呼吸到較好的空氣，也希望 Gunrid 空氣淨化窗簾可以提高社會對室內空汙的關注，藉此改變所作所為，為地球的清淨空氣盡一份力。」

值得關注的原因：

污染和現今的負面環境問題引發越來越多擔憂，也因此催生了新的產品浪潮，有多項產品和服務應運而生以期減輕大眾對周遭環境的不安。

Captured from PS4 Pro

Captured from PS4 Pro

12

電玩遊戲反霸凌

遊戲設計師正努力翻轉因轉困擾遊戲社群許久的負面文化。

2019 年 10 月，微軟（Microsoft）在 Xbox Live 中新增一項功能，讓玩家可以過濾遊戲中的聊天訊息。微軟新解釋，這個更新讓玩家可自行決定「出現在 Xbox Live 上的文字訊息中，哪些是他們可以接受的，哪些是他們不能接受」。

微軟的 Xbox 營運總監戴維‧麥卡錫（Dave McCarthy）在一次接受科技媒體平台《Verge》採訪時說道：「女性玩家在競爭激烈的環境下，被喚以各樣的稱呼，這讓她們在現實世界中感到被騷擾。我們旗下擁有 LGBTQ 社群，也覺得他們無法在 Xbox Live 上用自己的聲音說話，因為怕被人趕出遊戲。如果我們真的打算釋放這個產業的潛能，讓這個美好的科技可以接觸到所有人，這樣的現象就是理所不容的。」

2019 年 11 月，巴西三星（Samsung Brazil）跟線上遊戲《要塞英雄》（Fortnite）共同在當地推出一項對抗網路霸凌的企劃。玩家可在這款熱門的遊戲中獲取「皮膚」，那是一種圖形屬性，可以改變角色的外貌，但是這款要價 50 美金的「皮膚」，在玩家群中變成

階級象徵。無法負擔這種造型的人常被嘲笑。戲手。為了打擊這個現象，該企劃創造了一種新款購買，稱為極光（Aura Glow），玩家可以送給其他人，強化友情點數和遊戲包容力。

其他款遊戲也在發展更有建設意義的行為模式。谷歌（Google）的全新遊戲平台 Google Stadia 於 2019 年 11 月上線，同時推出一款獨家的原創遊戲，聚焦反霸凌議題。遊戲製作公司 Tequila Works 解釋，該遊戲會帶領玩家進入一場面對最深恐懼，且會受到戰鬥後情緒衝擊的冒險。

2019 年 10 月推出的《壁中精靈》（Concrete Genie）為遊戲玩家帶來全新視角，鼓勵玩家以藝術創作為對抗霸凌的解方。此款遊戲由索尼（Sony）旗下的 Pixelopus 遊戲工作室所開發，希望啟發玩家以創意對抗消極。為遊戲社群提供一個新的正向框架。Pixelopus 的設計師李靜（音譯自 Jing Li）解釋道：他們的目標是讓玩家「覺得自己代表世界的光明面，同時也是世界的魔法師。我們希望讓他們感受到自己正在以藝術、創意、正向能量來填滿世界。」

值得關注的原因：

遊戲社群長期以來都被批為鼓勵暴力、霸凌負面文化的一群人，現在，他們聚在一塊，想建立更正面、安全、友善的空間。

13

全新數位社群

社群媒體開始有了私領域的界線，新世代的使用者棄守毫無上限的好友清單，追求和自選受眾共享更親密的社群連結。

為追求個人隱私、真實自我、身心健康等目標，年輕的消費者尋求數位時代中能夠只與最親密摯友互動的方式，或許是像 Instagram 開發的 Threads 這類小型通訊群組、也或者 Discord 上的小眾同好團體。在我們以社群媒體安全為主題所發表的文章中，曾提到由英國皇家公共衛生學會針對 1,500 名 Z 世代和千禧世代的使用者所做的調查，這些用戶想在網路上提到像 Instagram 這類的平台帶給他們大多壓力了，因為他們想在網路上展現完美的形象，也有很多人漸漸看清網紅文化對他們心理健康帶來的影響。

Threads 於 2019 年 10 月推出，希望用戶更能順暢地和他們的摯友溝通，分享他們不願和其他數以百計的追蹤者一併分享的個人資訊。Threads 上的好友即便受限於自動模式（Auto Status）而無法交談，卻可以在一天當中輕易地和朋友保持聯絡，開啟「自動模式」後，系統會自動公開用戶是否正在移動或者出現資訊。

WUNDERMAN THOMPSON　　Instagram Close Friends feature. Images courtesy of Facebook

隨著消費者轉向
小型、緊密、志同道合
的群組發展,品牌有
全新的機會打造
網路世界中更直接、更聰明
的連結方式。

2019 年 7 月,Snapchat 以其首支全球形象廣告展現該平台的
理念。他們要讓散布在全球各地的家庭成員和三五好友可以緊密地
連結在一起。Snap 的行銷總長肯尼·米切爾 (Kenny Mitchell)
向《廣告週刊》(Adweek) 說道:「真正的朋友」(Real Friends)
這個企劃,是想展現 Snapchat「確實是一種解決社群媒體當前
挑戰的管道。它讓大家可以暫時逃開社群媒體,讓大家可以做自
己。」2019 年初,Snap 推出一款多人手遊「位元表情派對」(Bitmoji
Party),讓用戶以虛擬影像身份的互動,使用者能在這種情況下和
最好的朋友互動。

另外,就連以小眾創意社群聞名的 Tumblr 網路平台,都在尋找讓
公開群組成為標配的方法。2019 年 11 月,Tumblr 開始在手機版介
面測試傳訊功能,讓思想相近的愛好到特別的愛好與興趣為
核心,開啟一個個討論空間,從寵愛自我到龐克音樂都包括在內。

值得關注的原因:
《叛逆行銷》(斷譯自 Marketing Rebellion) 的作者馬克·謝佛
(Mark Schaefer) 對偉門智威智庫表示:「目前需要一個新的商業
思維。但這也是行銷的未來。」隨著消費者轉向小型、緊密、志同道
合的群組發展,品牌有全新的機會打造網路世界中更直接、更聰明
的連結方式。「為了達成這樣的目標,你必須先被邀請進入這些群
組,不要把他們當成機會,而是把他們當成朋友來對待。」

韓國汽車製造廠 Kia，正打算將解讀情緒的技術導入駕駛的日常生活。在 2019 年的消費電子用品展（CES 2019）上，Kia 發表「即時情緒調適駕駛」（Real-time Emotion Adaptive Driving "Read" System），可利用生物辨識技術來監測駕駛的情緒。該系統會分析臉部表情、心跳速率、膚電活動、聲電活動或音樂，來幫助駕駛找回平靜狀況，例如切換燈光或音樂，來幫助駕駛找回平靜。

值得關注的原因：

長期以來，科技產品因為對心理健康造成影響而備受譴責，而今，科技則提供全新的方式，讓我們過得更幸福。

技 & 創新

14

感知科技

品牌利用新科技來辨識和回應人類的情緒，希望能紓解用戶的壓力和焦慮。

2019 年 3 月，瑞典清晰頻道（Clear Channel）推出情緒展（Emotional Art Gallery），利用斯哥爾摩運達站內的 250 個數位告示板展示數位藝術作品來紓解乘客的壓力。系統從各品牌提尋紀錄、社群媒體、新聞報導、交通資訊等管道收集資料，再將系統選取的藝術圖片以實況方式展示在螢幕上，即時回應這座城市當下的情緒。這些作品都任為乘客灌輸正能量，讓他們能感到慰藉、平靜、快樂、活力。

2019 年 10 月，微軟（Microsoft）的駐村藝術研究員珍妮·莎賓（Jenny Sabin）於微軟雷德蒙德園區（Redmond campus）發表作品《艾妲》（Ada），一件能回應人類情緒的人工智慧雕塑。艾妲整體積龐大，黏細胞般的結構可以將人類的情緒轉譯為繽紛的色彩，一旦有人靠近建築物，並接觸到攝影機做出即時回應。越多人和這件雕塑互動，表情和聲調，以色彩變幻做出即時回應。越多人和這件雕塑互動，它就會變得越活潑，在不同情緒下變幻流動出各式各樣的色彩。

技公司 (Hewlett Packard) 的梅格·惠特曼 (Meg Whitman) 擔任執行長。

惠特曼對《洛杉磯時報》(Los Angeles Times) 表示:「我們內部在討論的是,我們想要兼有 HBO 的品質和 Spotify 的便利。我們不是臉書影音平台 Facebook Watch,不是 Snapchat,不是 Instagram TV,不是 YouTube。我們是 Quibi。我完全沒有要貶低這些平台的意思,但我們的立足點比他們的更好。」

這項服務每月大約收費 5 美元或 8 美元,前者會有廣告置入;後者則無。洛杉磯時報的報導顯示:這個平台提供「由得獎導演所拍攝的絕佳影片,例如史蒂芬·史匹柏 (Steven Spielberg) 和凱薩琳·哈德德威克 (Catherine Hardwicke),並且會以精簡的影集形式來呈現。」

值得關注的原因:

由於注意力長度下降,娛樂公司開始極力探求以簡短影片吸引青年輕消費族群的全新方式,但彼此同時,創作者們的反對這個做法。希望保留沉浸式的文化體驗。既然科技已能提供量身定做的文化體驗,時間便會證明這種模式何種模式更勝一籌。

15

可調控速度的娛樂模式

隨著注意力時間縮短,科技業也發展出加速文化體驗的解法,但這會讓創意產業付出什麼代價呢?

網飛影音平台 (Netflix) 於 2019 年秋天,開始測試旗下影片於安卓 (Android) 裝置上可快轉調慢播放速度的功能,這讓許多電影導演和演員驚駭不已。身兼電影製作人與演員的賈德·阿帕托 (Judd Apatow) 表示:這種行為非常「荒謬又污辱人」,導演布萊德·柏德 (Brad Bird) 則推文說道:這種功能「又是一個非常爛的主意。在已經嚴重失血的觀影經驗上再補一刀。」他質疑向要「一邊支持並資助電影製作人的願景,又一邊動手摧毀他們想呈現的效果呢?」

也許網飛這麼做的其中一個原因,是來自一組常被提起數據:千禧世代的注意力長度還有 12 秒鐘,但 Z 世代用戶只剩下 8 秒。媒體內容加速呈現並壓縮總長度,和某些社群平台的興起有關,例如抖音。抖音的影片時長只有 15 秒,在 Z 世代中大受歡迎。

Quibi 是另一家進入串流服務市場的公司,在 2020 年 4 月上線後,會在該平台上推出「快播式」的八分鐘影片。該平台由自資深製作人傑佛瑞·凱森柏格 (Jeffery Katzenberg) 創立,並由先前領導惠與科

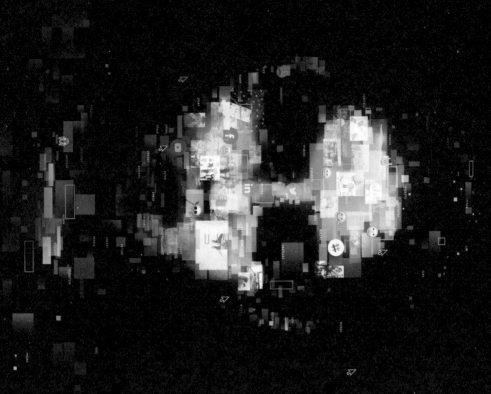

16

臉部辨識的全新規則

在臉部辨識的世界裡，隱私已開始凌駕於便利之上。

運用這項科技的品牌，如果要在公眾反彈和法規緊縮情況下繼續生存，只有改變策略一途。

2019 年 11 月，印度咖啡連鎖店 Chaayos 強制顧客用臉部辨識技術來付款，沒有提供其他替代方案。這件事在推特上掀起了一陣狂怒風暴，無數的美國公司也因為使用相同技術而引發不滿，其中包含美國售票公司 Ticketmaster 的母公司理想國欲發展以臉部辨識取代傳統演唱會票券的意圖，曾對已岌岌可危的社群造成更多傷害。（詳見我們針對臉部辨識技術進行的相關報導）

2019 年 11 月... Live Nation Entertainment）。抗議者認為，理想國欲發展以臉部辨識取代傳統演唱會票券的意圖，曾對已岌岌可危的社群造成更多傷害。

縱使品牌開始注意到臉部辨識技術的發展潛能，消費者卻還沒準備好全面迎接這樣的技術。根據偉門智威獨有研究工具 SONAR™ 的報告顯示，約有 60%的美國消費者認為，品牌及企業留存他們臉部照片的行為非常詭異。

2020 年，我們將有機會看到立法人員針對臉部辨識技術所做出的變革，尤其是在個資和隱私這兩方面。品牌將會面對更多

值得關注的原因：

臉部辨識技術提供品牌無數個機會來收集消費者相關數據，藉以改善並高度客製他們的消費體驗，也帶來前所未有的便利。然而，企業必須要公開透明的表明，他們打算以何種方式收集數據，才能保留消費者和立法人員對他們的信任。凱瑟說：「如果他們不想被干擾，他們就會跟你講清楚，你就不用再浪費你的行銷資源在他們身上。最後，這對整體商業模式來說其實是好的，因為不想看到廣告的人就被你剔除了，接著你就能為想跟你互動的消費者，提供最真實、最即時的資訊，讓他們能有更好的體驗。」

規章，裡面會寫明在什麼情況下才可以使用這些資訊。布特妮・凱瑟 (Brittany Kaiser) 除了是劍橋分析 (Cambridge Analytica) 的前業務總監、也是資訊透明的倡導者，她對偉門智威智庫表示，透過臉部辨識技術一類科技所收集的數據，有機會以財產權相同的方式來處理。

「這個概念是：在未來當我們有更多的使用權，更清楚要哪些數據時，我們就可以自由選擇和分享這些數據的方式，我們要和哪些機構分享，盈利或非盈利組織？政府機構？或者任何對這些數據有興趣的人都能使用？」凱瑟如此答道。

但這些全都有個例外——中國。《TechNode》的總編輯約翰・阿特曼 (John Artman) 對我們說：「到頭來，和生物測定有關的隱私疑慮，在中國的情形會和美國大不相同，臉部辨識被視為某種歐威爾《一九八四》(1984) 式的『老大哥正在看著你』但在中國，就只會是『嗨，可以刷我的臉喔』，『喔好吧』，為何不行？」

**到頭來，在中國的情形會大不相同的
隱私疑慮，在中國的情形會和美國大不相同。**

《TechNode》總編輯｜約翰・阿特曼 (John Artman)

技 & 創新

Privacy. That's iPhone.

11

隱私時代

維護數據隱私的日子，正式到來。

一開始使用數據是為了以最不費力的方式，讓消費者的生活更便利，讓他們可以輕鬆地接觸他們有興趣的資訊、產品、服務，但後來，品牌淪為數據採擷下的犧牲品，這樣的初衷也就快速地被遺忘了。今日，品牌使用的數據資料多半被認為是以不正當或不道德的管道取得的，依據偉門智威獨有的研究所以下正當來看，有89%的消費者認為企業收集資訊、使用資訊的方式是「見不得人的」。從影響鉅額的劍橋分析（Cambridge Analytica）風波，到信用報告業者艾可飛（Equifax）大量信用資料外洩，再到2019年9月的可口可多個資外洩……消費者距離引爆隱私越來越近，達法使用數據的情況越來越嚴重且普遍，於是品牌開始當試多方改善這個現象，並以品牌政策和實行計畫來闡明這樣的舉措。

布特妮．凱瑟（Brittany Kaiser）除了是劍橋分析的前業務總監，也是資訊透明的倡議者，她對偉門智威智庫表示：「品牌開始察覺到，要培養忠誠度，就要以公開透明的方式運作。但這不等於品牌要一直努力攫取消費者的注意，而是要培養對話空間和信任基礎。」

技 & 創新

> 掌控自己的數據資料和數位身份並非只是空想，也不是對於未來的狂妄想像，這是真的有可能達到的事。
>
> 資訊透明倡議者｜布特妮‧凱撒（Brittany Kaiser）

科技巨頭（大概是達法最嚴密的單位之一）爭相推出新的隱私權權相關辦法，希望重新贏回消費者的信任。

蘋果（Apple）2019 年的宣傳大幅地往隱私看護這靠攏，並喊出「隱私，就是 iPhone」（Privacy. That's iPhone.）和「在你的 iPhone 裡出現的東西，就只會在你的 iPhone 裡出現。」（What happens on your iPhone, stays on your iPhone.）等口號。2019 年 11 月，蘋果重新設計了與隱私權相關的網頁，讓它們能和產品頁面一樣好讀。

以簡單、直接、易懂的方式傳達其隱私權政策。依據偉門智威獨有的研究工具 SONAR™ 的數據來看，蘋果之所以這麼做，是因為有 68%的消費者覺得他們的交易條款那些交易條款。隨後，蘋果在 2019 年 9 月推出 iOS 13，在這個新版作業系統中大力加強對隱私的關注，其中一項功能便是封鎖背景執行的設定，限制應用程式在未開啟的狀態下，不能於背景執行網路語音傳輸協定（VoIP），以防止應用程式在使用者不知情的情況下竊取資訊。

2019 年 10 月，谷歌（Google）在資安考量下，發布了一項密碼與安全檢查工具（Password Checkup），會自動檢查使用者的密碼，在密碼強度過低或者被第三方入侵的時候，會對用戶提出警示。

2019 年 5 月，谷歌在歐洲成立了隱私工程中心，該中心的執行長桑德爾‧皮察（Sundar Pichai）解釋道，這座新的谷歌資訊安全工程中心（Google Safety Engineering Center）之所以成立，是因為在「世界上的每個人都應公平享有隱私和資訊安全」，他們也努力了「讓隱私和資安成為谷歌旗下產品的價值核心」。

值得關注的原因：

雖然這樣的倡議，已為修補數據隱私漏洞跨出了第一步，但未來還有一段路要走。凱恩說：「掌控自己的數據資料和數位身份並非只是空想，也不是對於未來的狂妄想像，這是真的有可能達到的事。任何品牌只要能用受信賴、符合道德標準的方式來實現這樣的目標，就能贏得消費者的青睞。」

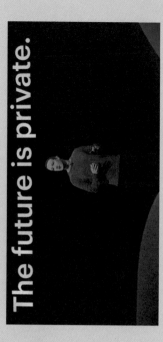

The future is private.

觸覺科技

2020年，觸覺科技即將大舉流行，讓企業能在虛擬環境中提供觸覺體驗。

觸覺科技指的是任何可以誘發觸覺感知（例如如何碰觸或移動）的技術，在結合擴增實境和虛擬實境之後，可以在視聽風景之外，額外帶來體感互動體驗。多款於 2019 消費電子用品展（CES 2019）中激起火花的觸覺科技產品，將於 2020 年進入市場，在而將全球各大市場的 5G 技術輔助下，觸覺技術即能順利運作，從阿里巴巴（Alibaba）到迪士尼（Disney），無不爭相探索觸覺技術以擴增他們現有產品的體驗。

零售業很快就適應了這項創新。來自全球最大市場中國的阿里巴巴推出 Refinity 觸覺技術，為線上購物帶來多重感官體驗，消費者自行想像產品觸感的日子已經過去，曾與觸覺科技公司 Tanvas 合作過的美國線上零售平台 Bonobos，其體驗型手機總監多明尼克．艾席格（Dominique Essig）解釋道：「在智慧型手機和平板上模擬質感和布料材質，是線上購物體驗中的一大突破，讓購買質感和數位世界產生連結。」

教育界也以創新的方式應用了這項技術，科技讓他們可以在訓練

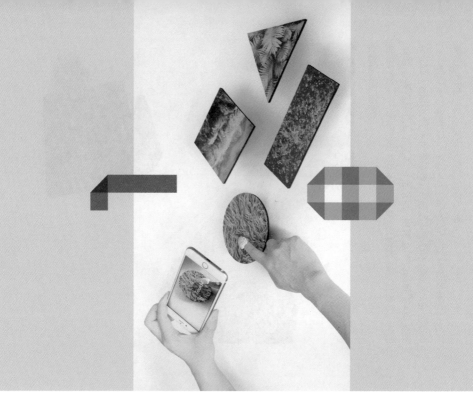

過程中測試自己的技能，即便犯錯也不會對他人或自己造成傷害。舉例來說，英國一間名為 Generic Robotics 的醫事訓練軟體公司，使用觸覺科技和虛擬實境技術，在模擬實境中訓練醫事人員，讓他們不需要在病人身上練習這些技巧。

品牌也很快認知到，觸覺科技能為擁有 1,500 億美元產值的遊戲產業帶來效益。臉書（Facebook）的研發實驗室正在開發一款名為 Tasbi 的感知型腕帶，而迪士尼也以觸覺技術為核心，創造出「力量夾克」（Force Jacket）的原型。為虛擬環境帶來新的觸覺感受，是上述兩項產品的共同目標。

除了讓數位體驗更真實之外，觸覺科技也可以實現更基本的事情。就像倫敦教計師多田亮（Ryo Tada）在 Fulu 網站上說的，「觸覺感知對於建立信任和憐憫是很重要的，就像嬰兒和母親的第一個連結，就來自於一次輕輕的碰觸。」Fulu 是戴在指尖的觸覺介面，類似多田亮在皇家藝術學院所開發的 EPFL 人工皮質。

對許多品牌來說，誘發消費者的情緒反應，能帶來明顯的效益，所以觸覺科技被應用在多項產業中，從遊戲到廣告，再到其他行業。2017 年，「IPG 媒體實驗室和 Immersion 公司做了一項名為「摸得到的廣告」（Ads You Can Feel）的研究，發現利用觸覺科技完成的廣告在許多指標上的表現都比傳統廣告更加優異。也許這當中最重要的指標是，運用觸覺技術的廣告，在潛在的新顧客當中，表現大勝傳統廣告。

WUNDERMAN
THOMPSON

Tanvas haptic technology

值得關注的原因：

觸覺科技將會在各方面引發劇烈的變革，從娛樂到教育皆然。它讓

3D 數位環境能提升接持互動效果更佳、情緒更強烈的層次。隨著產

品在加入觸覺科技後持續改良，消費需求也會開始增加，研發單位

可以加入更多的資金投入其中。現在就是品牌評估觸覺科技可以

為他們的產品帶來何種創新的絕佳契機。

觸覺感知對於
建立信任和聯繫是
很重要的，就像嬰兒和
母親的第一個連結，
就來自於一次
輕輕的碰觸。

Fulu設計師｜多田亮（Ryo Tada）

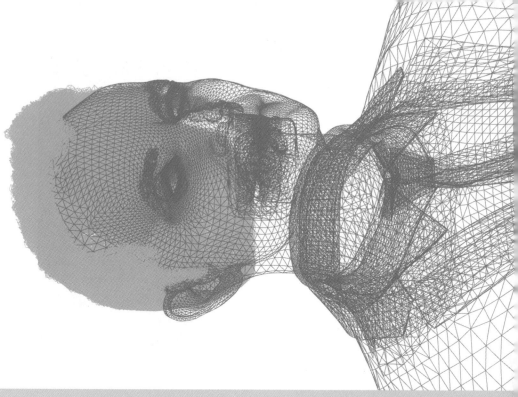

技 & 創新

19

人工智慧職場導航

職場上的人工智慧應用，已從簡單的自動聊天機器人，進化到認知程度更廣的領域。

全球企業都在將虛擬人格和人工智慧軟體納入徵才的一環。雖然省時又省錢，但在這項技術的肆虐下，許多酸民開始出現。大眾對此也相當擔憂。英國皇家文藝學會（Royal Society of Arts）的數據顯示，有 60% 的消費者反對在徵才過程中使用自動決策系統，部分律師事務所也準備好要應付與人工智慧相關的官司了。

HireVue 已為 700 多家客戶提供徵才軟體，包括聯合利華（Unilever）、希爾頓集團（Hilton）、摩根大通集團（JP Morgan Chase）、達美航空（Delta Air Lines）、沃達豐集團（Vodafone）、宜家家居（IKEA）、高盛集團（Goldman Sachs）等。除了有視訊面試的功能，也包含了求職面試的用詞習慣。可以擷取讀面試者的用詞習慣，從主動、被動語態，到語調、語速，全都包含其中。該軟體也會分析面試者的表情，例如皺眉、微笑、睜大眼睛。

這樣的徵才模式已非常普遍，有些大學甚至開始提供針對這種人工智慧面試模式，提供學生相關的訓練。

雖然有些人讚許，使用人工智慧可以撤除人為偏見，但這類平台的效率，卻也引來大量擾臺。波特蘭州立大學的電腦科學系教授

梅蘭妮・米歇爾（Melanie Mitchell）在 2019 年 10 月發布了新書《人工智慧：為會思考的人類提供的參考指南》（暫譯書名 Artificial Intelligence: A Guide for Thinking Humans）當中提及許多當前系統的缺陷。人工智慧很容易上當受騙，也無法抵禦駭客，而且臉部辨識技術在面對有色人種時，極易發生誤判。

全球皆有據點的盛衛律師事務所（Paul Hastings）在 2019 年 3 月引進了一批人工智慧訓練師，協助客戶使用人工智慧相關的產品及服務，幫助客戶應對集體訴訟，並提供多方面的法律建議，例如法規合用、隱私議題、人工智慧管理和道德準則。該公司其中一名人工智慧訓練師布來佛德・紐曼（Bradford Newman）向美國人力資源發展協會（Society for Human Resource Management）說道：「人工智慧將會員責做出決策，決定誰可以升遷，誰要被遣散，在

你把工作這類嚴重影響人類生活的相關決策，交給演算法裁定的時候，在公正、公開、以及法治層面上，會引發爭議，而關於法律層面的問題，我相信很快就會開始顯現了。」

相反地，認知型人工智慧對決策的影響較小，所以顯得較為合適。加州科技公司偶邦（Oben）旗下的人工智慧虛擬人格，在中國已經漸受到歡迎，眼前的關卡似乎也減少了一些。

2019 年 1 月，由中國最大傳播平台央視所製作的春晚，觀看次數高達到 18 億人次，節目中有四個真人比例的「個人化 AI 人物」，以四位節目表演者的樣貌現身，並以 3D 全息投影的方式出現在節目上，會走會動會說話，甚至會演唱歌曲，製作出這些個人化 AI 人物的偶邦公司，最終的目標是要發展出可供大眾使用的技術，潛在機會包括名人替身，或者提供給工作場合中的遠距會議使用。

中國的新華社亦開始在 2018 年底的播映期間使用虛擬人格。他們利用搜尋引擎搜狗的合作，讓「致敬不倦」的 24 小時新聞播映成為可能。

值得關注的原因：
米歇爾在她的書中問到，人工智慧還有什麼問題都還沒解決？而她最終的答案非常簡潔，所有問題都還沒解決。職場上，讓人工智慧作為決策者已讓許多人感到不自在，也引起許多人的擔憂。偶邦和道德相關的問題出現後，更深入的法規也不遠了，品牌對此需要謹慎而行。

20

更年期科技

數位導向的全新資源和以科學技術改良的產品，
讓越越來越會使用科技產品的消費者，
在更年期期間仍能感受生命活力。

聯合國表示：在 2025 年前，更年期的女人將占全球人口 12%，但目前因為舊有污名的關係，進步的科技產品市場仍未大量開發，而眾領導品牌也正在努力在改變這個現象。

蘋果（Apple）希望能在與女人健康相關的知識上有所進展，並致力於發展「新一代創新健康產品」。2019 年 11 月，蘋果推出全新的健康管理應用程式，內有女人健康報告可供選用，讓消費者和醫師能更了解女人在更年期的轉變以及其他婦科症狀。數位健康平台 Gennev 的執行長吉爾・安潔洛（Jill Angelo）告訴偉門智威智庫，這件事之所以重要是因為以目前來說「更年期的狀況是無法預先得知的，而科技卻讓我們能開始為此建立資料庫。」

Gennev 利用數據和科技，改善更年期女人的生活經驗。安潔洛透露，「我們正在利用科技，建立全世界最大的更年期健康數據庫，假以時日，我們可以為更年期的女人推薦並創造一份目前尚未出現

Rory menopause health vertical

科技 & 創新

Three ways to start feeling better.

Get your personalized plan
Tackle your symptoms with a 6-week course. From hot flushes to fatigue, have access to an action plan.
Get your plan

Speak with a doctor
Amazing menopause-trained practitioners and OB/GYNs are now just a click away. It's simple and convenient to get the care you need.
Book an appointment

Shop solutions for relief
Designed specifically around common menopausal symptoms, our growing menopausal product line was created to help you feel better, from hot flushes and vaginal dryness to insomnia.
Shop menopause relief!

的理想藍圖。這個平台以科技為核心，重新為女人賦權，並讓更年期成為更易懂的事。

2019 年 3 月，以男性健康為主的新創公司 Ro，推出為女人更年期前後階段所設計的全新產品 Rory。整合遠距醫療和直接面對客的產品模式，讓數位健康成為這個世代女人的選項之一。透過 Rory，女性可以直接與健康管理者溝通，並可連結療程、資訊、社群等項目。

安傑洛說道：「我希望對更年期相關科技產品的關注，可以讓更年期在大家心中成為正常現象，不會像現在這樣讓人支吾其詞。看著科技使很多事物成為可能，看著科技改變了我們對於教育、金融、個人財務、健康照護的想法，我相信更年期科技也會加入這個行列，而我們也正準備開始這趟旅程。」

我希望對更年期相關科技產品的關注，
可以讓更年期在大家心中成為正常現象，不會像現在
這樣讓人支吾其詞。

Gennev執行長｜吉爾．安傑洛（Jill Angelo）

值得關注的原因：

5-7 字頭的女人並未受到品牌和行銷人員的高度重視，但是這個多采多姿的族群已日漸推翻既有狀態，推翻期待也拋棄陳腐的刻板印象，市場充滿機會，等待科技品牌以創新的方式，改寫更年期前後婦女的生活方式。

WUNDERMAN THOMPSON

Gennev announces launch of gendered digital health platform

旅遊 & 觀光

21

環保觀光計畫

旅遊業開始改邪歸正，訂出一波波削瞻策略，從以往將不造成環境損害定為目標，跨向為減碳正效益做出實質貢獻。

挪威在 2019 年末開工動土，想要建立世界第一座正能源機場城。

奧斯陸機場城將餘能全面使用再生能源，也會開始為當地社區供應綠能，該城試驗場，在此嘗試創新的綠色科技，包括無人電動車、街道及建物的自動照明系統、智慧廢物管理及安全維護方案。

發展不只在機場城裡實現，這座城市也會成為減少碳排放的裝置，讓永續

建築事務所 Haptic Architects 的總監湯瑪士・斯托克 (Tomas Stokke) 向設計網站《Dezeen》表示：「這是一個從頭開始設計一座城市的獨特機會，藉由最新的科技發展，我們將能創造出環保、永續的未來城市。」

這項由挪威政府支持的發展計劃，是該國全國計畫的延伸，挪威打算將能源從石油轉向綠能。

由挪威政府所擁有的奧斯陸機場，計畫在 2025 年以前，將一列機場運輸工具改為電能，且在 2040 前將進出挪威的短途班機，全面改為電動飛機。

在距離奧斯陸北方 300 英裡的特隆赫姆鎮，建築事務所 Snohetta 於 2019 年 9 月公開了位於北緯 63 度線上，所以四季日光極為劇烈，呈現挪威城鎮位於北緯 63 度線上的「一個要在極北地區的情況下，收集和儲存太陽能的獨特構造」。這棟建物名為 Brattørkaia 電廠（Powerhouse Brattørkaia），能生產比其日常用電多出一倍以上的電量，而未用完的剩餘能則會透過區域微電網供應給鄰近建物的巴士、電動車、電動船使用。

Snohetta 如此形容這個專案：「為明天的建築訂下全新標準的專案，讓建築物在其一生中（包含搭建和拆除過程）能生產比其所需耗能更多的能量。其中也包含建材中的內含耗能（embodied energy）。」

Snohetta 也將這項標準應用於斯伐特特飯店 (Svart Hotel) 之中，該飯店在 2021 年對外開幕後，成為世界第一間正能源飯店，含建物本身的用電在內，這間飯店能產生比其耗電量更多的太陽能。

儲相關注的原因：

單單不造成環境的危害已經不夠了，這些專案證明了未來的旅遊、觀光業和服務設施，會更有意識地對未來的減碳正效益做出貢獻。

旅 & 觀光

Oslo Airport City renders

22

旅遊管制

熱門觀光景點因被遊客擠爆，限制人數的新法規也開始出現，為未來的豪華旅遊立下基礎。

重要的文化景點因人流過量而遭受破壞，守門員訂計畫前在的遊客，立下更嚴格的法規，甚至完全不再對公眾開放這些景點。

烏魯魯是澳洲原住民族阿南古人（Anangu）的聖地，長久以來，這塊遙遠在北領地的巨石，每年都吸引了成千上萬的觀光客圖登頂，即使附近有計多告示牌，基於尊重阿南古人及安全考量下，一再懇求旅客不要靠近這塊巨石。阿南古族人，前任烏魯魯－卡達族國家公園董事會主席山米‧威爾森（Sammy Wilson）對英國廣播公司（BBC）說道：「這是一個非常重要的地方，不是遊樂場或迪士尼那類的主題公園。」

2019 年 10 月，該景點開始全面禁止遊客攀爬聖地，但在封閉關令來臨之前，遊客數量大增，據澳洲國家公園處（Parks Australia）統計，該景點在 2018 年下達禁令後，遊客量比前一年多出 7 萬人。

2019 年 3 月據《華盛頓郵報》（The Washington Post）報導，南加州小鎮埃爾西諾湖市發布了一件公共安全危機，有一群「跟迪士尼差不多大的群眾」湧入該鎮，來欣賞稀有的野花綻放奇觀。

為了保護該地景並同時維護當地居民的安全、生計、居住環境，許多景點已設立新的進場規則。2018 年 12 月，位於尼德蘭首都阿姆斯特丹國家博物館前的知名文字地標「I Amsterdam」遭政府移除，以遏止觀光人潮過多的情形。隨後這座尼德蘭首都也定下目標，要以吸引頂級奢華旅客為觀光主軸。位於北美把尼德蘭觀光局，其局長安東尼亞·庫代克（Antonia Koedijk）說道：「以往的遊客數量讓當地居民感到擔憂。聚焦這類旅客，能讓當地居民敞開心胸擁抱地迎接旅客的到來。」

其他世界遺產也訂下高難度的進場資格。2019 年 10 月，印尼提出會員制度。限制知名的科莫多國家公園（Komodo National Park）遊客人數。頂級會員會費為 1,000 美金，可以進入整座國家公園，包含科莫多等多領地；其他非頂級會員只能進入特定區域。比比往還嚴格的售票規定也於 2019 年 1 月出現在馬丘比丘。當年四月，菲律賓長灘島在旺季期間禁止郵輪進入。2019 年 5 月，冰島宣布該地熱門的羽毛峽谷（Fjaðrárgljúfur canyon）每年將只對遊客開放五個禮拜。

值得關注的原因：

為保存具指標意義的景點和生態景觀，人流過量的景點紛紛立下限制。隨之而來的品質門票和有限使用權，讓這些景變成排外的頂級旅客招待所。

過度擁擠已是全球現象，2019 年 4 月，尼德蘭（荷蘭）一知名的鬱金香季中架起圍欄，以防止遊客為了拍出美照而破壞花田。當時《衛報》（The Guardian）上出現一則譯自尼德蘭《大眾日報》（Algemee Dagblad）的訪談，鄰近尼德蘭西南方球莖地區（the bulb region）的諾德韋克豪斯特農業鎮長，佩尼斯（Simon Pennings）說道：「這些遊客都很不小心。」雖然很多人來訪可以是很有趣的事情，但他們踩平了所有東西。「很遺憾，去年我有一塊價值 1 萬歐元（約台幣 33 萬）的田地遭到破壞，所有東西都被踩爛，他們不管怎樣就是要拍一張自拍照。」

除了鬱金香花田被圍了起來，尼德蘭觀光局也發布了一份花卉拍攝行為守則。當地觀光局也組織了一隊觀光大使，與遊客分享花田歷史以及花田維護作業。

23

科學探險

探險家走向世界盡頭，追求永生難忘的體驗和探索科學新發現的機會。

2019 年 12 月，Airbnb 發起「南極學術計畫」（Antarctic Sabbatical），召集 5 位無畏旅者進行一場長達 1 個月的研究探險。此計畫與美國海洋保育協會合作（Ocean Conservancy），由環境科學家克莉絲蒂・瓊斯威廉斯（Kirstie Jones-Williams）領軍。希望能更了解塑膠微粒對南極生態系的影響。參與者無須具備科學背景或相關經驗，在前往南極之前會先提供速成教學，教授冰河學、野外採樣、研究規範等知識。

出發之前，瓊斯威廉斯會讓參與者瞭解：這不只是一般的旅行而已。我們希望可以找到有熱情、有全球公民意識的人，除了熱情參與我們的團隊之外，也能在返家後向世界分享我們的發現。

「這次的探險會很辛苦，會在嚴寒的天氣下做實驗的科學計畫：

Luxury Action 旅行社也即將在 2020 年 4 月推出為公民科學家舉辦的北極旅遊行程。創辦人詹恩・洪卡寧（Janne Honkanen）接受美國有線電視新聞網（CNN）訪問時表示：「設備我們都會提供，但你必須具備探險家或科學家的精神。」他們宣傳這是地球上最北邊的旅館，有能力容納超過 10 萬美金費用的參與者，就可以住進有暖氣的冰屋，還有極地

旅 & 觀光

JNDERMAN   Airbnb Antarctic Sabbatical. Image courtesy of Airbnb.
HOMPSON   Photo by Christopher Michel

嚮導與私人保全團隊陪同。

「我們不只是提供體驗而已，我們還想把這裡發生的事，說給別人知道。」洪卡寧表示：「氣候變遷如何影響當地文化、飲食、北極圈的動物—這些我們都親眼見識到了。」

蓄華郵輪公司 Polar Latitudes 將在 2020 年 3 月發起第二次遠征鯨探險活動，並與 Woods Hole Oceanographic Institution 海洋研

究所合作，在海洋生物學家、環境學家、地理學家、歷史學家的陪同之下，公民科學家可以追蹤鯨魚並研究鯨魚的行為。

值得關注的原因：
蓄華放程與物質享受不再劃上等號，對新興的冒險精英來說，以科學目標為導向的旅程，才是蓄華放程的終極指標。

我們不只是提供體驗而已，我們還想把這裡發生的事，說給別人知道。

Luxury Action 創辦人｜盧恩·洪卡寧 (Janne Honkanen)

24

慢活旅行

近來的旅行風潮不再是急著抵達目的地，
而是活在當下，享受旅程。

現在的旅行者重視心理健康，因而崇尚更長的旅程並視之為享受當下的好時機。旅程曾經只是到達終點的沿途風景，但現在，旅程就和目的地一樣值得細細品嚐。人們也開始意識到航空和開車旅行對環境帶來的負面影響，於是鐵路旅行的浪潮也再度興起。

環保倡議者格蕾塔．童貝里（Greta Thunberg）非常反對坐飛機，所以在巡迴歐洲期間，她選擇搭火車。如今隨著搭乘飛機運動的情勢越來越高漲，許多全球風潮領導者也開始支持浪漫的火車旅行。

超模艾迪．坎貝爾（Edie Campbell）從倫敦出發到到米蘭參加 2019 年的秋冬時裝週，她不搭飛機，而是選擇搭 12 個小時的火車。2019 年 10 月，在坎貝爾為《Elle》雜誌所撰寫的文章中，她提到時尚產業的碳足跡，並形容自己的旅程如同「天堂」，還不容地穿著籠罩著陷在座位中、掠過眼前是閃閃發亮的湖光山色，還不經意瞥見穿著經典條紋的義大利老奶奶。」

2019 年 10 月與 11 月時　模特兒兼倡議人士艾德娃．阿波亞（Adwoa

Aboah）在 Instagram 上張貼了一連串在英國 Belmond British Pullman 火車上拍的照片，高揚火車旅行的美好。她在貼文中寫道：「和媽咪優雅地搭火車已成為我的最愛。」

時尚指標品牌香奈兒（Chanel）在 2020 的度假系列（Resort）中，也車申了火車旅行的極致享受。這個系列並未在傳統火車站內走秀，而是讓模特兒在香奈兒特別打造的美術風格火車站台上發表。而這個系列的後繼行銷活動展現了現代火車旅行的優雅，並回應了「投身冒險的承諾」。

坎貝爾寫道，「以往我們所認知的奢華旅行是快速的生活型態，例如搭乘私人飛機，在 4 萬英尺的高空中享受香檳。」但她接著表示，這樣的定義已經過時了。「奢華旅程是跟隨自己的步調，以更緩慢的速度前行。」

值得關注的原因：

消費者渴望能放慢腳步，脫離日常壓力，並專注在身邊的人事物上。於是即奢侈懶的火車旅行重新崛起，翻轉了奢華旅行的定義。

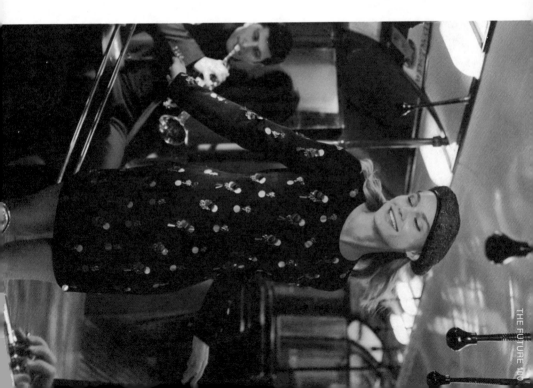

WUNDERMAN
THOMPSON

Above: Chanel Resort 2020. Image courtesy of Chanel
Right: The Outnet FW19 holiday campaign. Image courtesy of the Outnet

25

菜園直送的飛機餐

航空公司開始把鮮採收的食材列入機上飲食清單中。

飛機的諸存空間少，備餐空間也很小，要提供佳餚美饌絕非易事。但是當健康、迎合注重健康與永續的乘客，為乘客提供超新鮮的現採農作呢？就是在機場跑道旁種植蔬菜。

新加坡航空（Singapore Airlines）與水耕蔬菜公司 AeroFarms 合作，打造健康飲食計劃的「菜園直送機艙」菜單。從 2019 年 10 月開始，在紐澤西紐華克自由國際機場（Newark Liberty International Airport）飛往新加坡樟宜機場（Changi Airport）的班機上，就可以享用到由航空菜園的「紐華克垂直水耕系統」所生產的芝麻葉、小白菜、綜合生菜。

「想像你可以在飛機上享用起飛前一刻才採收製作的沙拉，這真的是全世界最新鮮的飛機餐了。」新加坡航空全球飲食總監安東尼·麥克尼爾（Antony McNeil）表示：「擁有超新鮮蔬果的唯一途徑，就是從自己的菜園裡採收蔬果。」

但是健康、迎合消費者的首要考量，航空公司也開始提供不一樣的餐食。那麼最近一次的壯舉是什麼呢？

ANDERMAN
THOMPSON

Farm-to-plane dining program by Singapore Airlines.
Images courtesy of AeroFarms

想像你可以在飛機上
享用起飛前一刻
才採收製作的沙拉，
這真的是全世界最新鮮
的飛機餐了。

新加坡航空（Singapore Airlines）
全球飲食總監｜安東尼・麥克尼爾（Antony McNeil）

WUNDERMAN
THOMPSON

Farm-to-plane dining program by Singapore Airlines.
Images courtesy of AeroFarms.

Crop One 是一間位於矽谷的水耕蔬菜新創公司，這間公司提供大量的新鮮食材給航空公司，並與阿聯酋航空（Emirates Flight Catering）合作，在杜拜成立全球最大的垂直水耕生產系統。杜拜

曾名列 2017 年與 2018 年國際旅客最多的機場（截至撰稿時的最新數據顯示），而從 2019 年 12 月開始，這個機場生產系統所生產的良材將走出杜拜，躍上其他班機的餐盤之中。

芝加哥的歐海爾國際機場（O'Hare International Airport）是水耕蔬菜的先驅，自 2011 年開始，就在其中一樣航廈中設立垂直菜園。這間菜園的蔬菜直送航廈餐廳與咖啡店，為準備起飛的旅客供應全年性的新鮮餐點。

值得關注的原因：
這些新興計畫將新現採用的食材直送天際，讓旅客在空中也能像在地面上一樣吃得健康。

因為我们每做出来一个产品都是独一无二的
Everything we make is one of a kind

最重要的是我们不知道接下来体验的东西会呈现出来什么样
But most importantly we can't predict exactly how it will turn out

26

文化資產保存

旅客和企業開始清楚地意識到旅遊可能會威脅歷史遺跡與傳統文化的未來。

「超跟旅遊」（overtourism）已成為流行語。2018 年，《牛津英語辭典》（Oxford English Dictionary）將該詞收錄至辭典的年度詞彙中。現在旅遊勝地和各企業都開始反擊，意圖減少超跟旅遊的情況，並提供一些能夠為當地景點和社區，產生正面影響的導覽行程和觀光活動。

目前已經有許多國家開始採取行動，讓遊客成為維護旅遊景點的一份子，如威尼斯針對短期蠢動的旅客，徵收 10 歐元（約新台幣 340 元）的費用；阿姆斯特丹則拆除知名文字地標「I Amsterdam」，因為這座地標會吸引大批的 Instagram 使用者前來拍照（詳見第 22 章〈旅遊管制〉）。英國旅遊業公會（Association of British Travel Agents）執行長馬克・坦澤爾（Mark Tanzer）表示：「旅遊業能帶來可觀的收益，這是旅遊業應該感到驕傲的。而旅遊帶動經濟和就業發展，不僅能保護文化提升文化交流的機會，也維護了自然環境和文化遺產。」

2019 年 10 月，Airbnb 中國分部也發起保護文化資產的計畫，名為

「失物招領」（Lost & Found）。《Marketing Interactive》雜誌於文章中寫到，此舉是為了「保存中國的文化遺產，因為傳統技藝面臨消失的困境。」而中國 Airbnb 網站提供遊客學習的機會，讓他們能向 40 位大師學習中國傳統技藝。中國 Airbnb 行銷總監陳黛儒（Mia Chen）表示：「我們想將旅遊和文化體驗結合。」她還補充，Airbnb 公司希望能鼓勵年輕族群探索並關注珍貴的中國傳統文化。

另一方面，Airbnb 也贊助了一項名為「義大利學術假期」（Italian Sabbatical）的計畫，獲邀請者將成為南義村落格羅托托（Grottole）的短期居民。Airbnb 表示，這個計畫將「振興這個正面臨消逝危機的村莊」，因為這個村莊正面臨人口老化與青壯人口流失的困境，並進行 3 個月的志工服務。Airbnb 會從 28 萬報名者中選出 5 位，到格羅托托來生活，並進行 3 個月的志工服務。Wonder Grottole 與 Wonder Grottole 的網站上寫道，遊客並非被動參觀或享受當地人提供的體驗，而是成為改變的一份子。

若要說明保存文化地標能蘊藏多少的情感，可以看看巴黎聖母院（Notre Dame）。2019 年，巴黎聖母院因火災嚴重損毀，對於修復聖母院一事也在法國國內引發劇烈爭論。根據 Odoxa-Dentsu 2019 年 5 月公開於《費加洛報》（Le Figaro）的數據顯示，有 55% 的法國人民認為應要重建聖母院，回復至以往的面貌。然而當代建築，取而代之，法國政府也已經邀請建築師針對推動「當代建築」提案。《衛報》（The Guardian）報導，推特上的「#別碰聖母院」

（#TouchePasANotreDame）標籤風潮，負責監督聖母院重建的尚一路易斯·喬治林（Jean-Louis Georgelin）上將表示，聖母院的尖塔設計預計會在 2021 年底定案。

值得關注的原因：
旅客和品牌端都已經注意到當地旅遊會對當地文化和景點有多重要。這些新行動採取積極的做法保存文化遺產，希望可以將利他主義帶入旅遊業，並符合年輕消費者的旅遊期待，也就是在旅遊的同時，也能帶有正面影響，期待未來看到更多不同旅遊體驗，以更全面的方式改變旅遊景點的風貌。

21

社交型住宿

獨自旅遊日漸盛行，許多飯店紛紛投入資金
為獨遊的旅客提供現成的娛樂活動。

有越來越多人選擇獨自旅行。英國旅行社協會（Association of British Travel Agents）的調查發現，在2018年有15%的人選擇獨自度假，比前一年多了12%。為因應這些獨遊者的需求，許多旅館紛紛轉型為社交與文化據點。

史特拉福旅店（The Stratford）是這領域的其中一個實驗場。它是一家旅館，並兼營樓挑高的飯店式公寓，於2019年春季開始在東倫敦營運。他們提出的Happenings計畫，正試圖「將生活風格、流行、健康、藝術、文化、娛樂帶進史特拉福」，此旅館在2019年提供的養生課程，包括了藝術家亞歷山德里雅‧柯伊（Alexandria Coe）開設的寫生課程，調酒大師班以及替狗狗與飼主開設的人寵瑜珈課。

旅遊網站《Skift》在2019年1月時刊出一篇文章，指出奢華旅館想要「讓人與文化產生連結」，報導中也提及2018年底開業於英格蘭漢普敦的赫克菲爾德廣場飯店（Heckfield Place）。這棟喬治亞式建築式飯店舉辦了「集會活動」（Assembly

Events) 計畫，內容包含由策展人策畫的藝術收藏品導覽，由羅素．布蘭德 (Russell Brand) 主講的康復講座，以及名為「泥巴與勇氣」(mud and guts) 的兒童戶外體驗活動。「這場「集會活動」的靈感其實來自我們老闆。」赫克菲爾德廣場飯店的總經理奧莉維亞．李奇里 (Olivia Richii) 這麼告訴《Skift》：「他是一位學者，所以非常希望你不僅僅是奢華飯館體驗，也希望你在離開時能有所收穫。」

這項計畫承襲了莫克西飯店集團 (Moxy Hotels) 提出的知名社交計畫，莫克西飯店在時代廣場的分館引進編織課程，並於 2018 年與交友軟體 Bumble 合作，也獲得 Bumble 認證成為「和不同

Bumble 網友見面的全包式環境，可以約會、交友，或拓展專業人脈關係。」

Life House 連鎖飯店開發了專屬的應用程式，讓旅客在入住時能夠和其他旅客互動。生活屋的執行長暨共同創辦人拉米．齊丹 (Rami Zeidan) 對偉門智威傳統說道：「旅遊業具有獨特的機會能為新客與其他人配對交流。現在大家都在旅行，但旅遊時創不一定有固定的住所就是安全的交友網路。飯店具有獨特的機會，能夠讓這些人產生連結。」

值得關注的原因：

旅館面對 Airbnb 等業者的競爭，紛紛將自身定調為「不只是住宿」的地方。未來有望看見更多飯店推出社交與文化活動，供旅客與當地人參與，以強化旅館之於旅客與社區中心的有力地位。

28

機場再進化

機場體驗開始升級，
而機場也搖身一變成為令人雀躍的文化地標。

對新新機場來說，綿延不絕的隊伍、難吃的食物、陰森的航廈，這些恐怖的事都已成為過去。許多城市紛紛規畫了大型的機場空間，提供順暢愜意相當吸引人的互動體驗。

新加坡的星耀樟宜機場在 2019 年 4 月正式啟用。這裡有著全世界最高的室內瀑布，高達 40 公尺，水源來自航廈巨大甜圈狀屋頂所收集到的雨水。天井由玻璃板構成，讓自然光充能夠照耀在旅客與多層結構的花園上。花園中種植了 2,000 多棵樹與 10,000 多叢灌木。旅客可以參加導覽探索花園，也能在超過 280 間的商店中購物、用餐、享用飲品。負責設計機場的 Safdie Architects 建築事務所表示：空間的設計同時考量到旅客與非旅客，希望讓機場不再只是個轉運站，更能建立「機場的新典範」成為獨立的購物、娛樂、社交活動地點。」

北京最新的大興國際機場於 2019 年 9 月 25 日啟用，其海星狀的造型運用了動線法則，並採最新科技加速機場內的程序。這些設計相當必要，因為該機場在 2025 年前，希望其旅客吐量能達到

JNDERMAN
HOMPSON

Jewel Changi Airport, Singapore. Image courtesy of Jewel Changi Airport Devt

許多城市紛紛規畫3大型的機場空間，提供順暢甚至相當吸引人的互動體驗。

7,200萬人次。無論你是否要搭飛機，札哈·哈蒂（Zaha Hadid）設計的這座機場都會是一個值得造訪的地標。

瑞士格施塔德的薩嶺機場是 Tarmak 22 畫廊的所在地。2019 年，該畫廊舉辦了德國藝術家安德烈斯·古爾斯基（Andreas Gursky）的展覽，也展出其他家收藏的墨蓋勒藝術（Alex Hank）的作品。畫廊對外開放供大眾與旅客參觀，成為旅客與當地居民共享的藝術場所，既能欣賞當代藝術滑雪勝地的常設展場，也能參加文化講座或觀賞演出。這家畫廊是安東尼雅·克里斯皮·本納薩爾（Antonia Crespi Bennàssar）告訴偉門智璞智庫：「透過 Tarmak 22，我們希望能夠創造與文化相關的對話，並且讓格施塔德成為計多好奇的遊客與當地人帶來啟發。」

值得關注的原因：

機場藉由提供這類新型的設施來啟發或創造的娛樂訪客，而不再單單只是協助旅客南來北往的設施，機場擴充服務內容之後，不僅只是吸引了新的客群，機場本身也能自成獨特的文化景點。

29

防災建築

高瞻遠矚的建築師開始
設計各種能夠抵抗重大天災的房屋。

從五級颶風到不斷延燒的森林大火、異常氣候逐漸變成常態，而建築師也紛紛開始設計更能抗災的建築物，以便能夠應受日漸多變的氣候。

勒布朗・拉奇（Lebron Lackey）位於佛羅里達海岸的住宅在 2018 年 10 月麥可颶風來襲時一戰成名，是當時少數毫無損傷的建築物。拉奇據說花了普通建築兩倍的造價，來興建這間能抵擋時速 250 英哩暴風與洪水的房子。拉奇告訴《紐約時報》（New York Times）：「我們想要建造能夠抵擋大型天災的房子，只不過我們不知道大災難來得那麼快。」

建築師採用了海事建築工法來抵擋豪雨、洪水、海岸的暴風雨。美國紐澤西州 Raad Studio 設計的海灘屋（Beach House）於 2018 年完工，能夠抵抗海邊房舍經常遭遇的暴風雨及洪水。該事務所表示：「我們設計了一組流體動力土丘，讓水能夠透過地面排出，同時將房屋升高至歷史最高水位以上，房屋下方有類似溝槽的小徑環繞著水泥擋土牆，在豪雨來襲時能夠作為排水道，以此工法所

INDERMAN
OMPSON

Raad Studio Beach House. Image courtesy of Raad Studio.
sPhoto by Eric M Townsend.

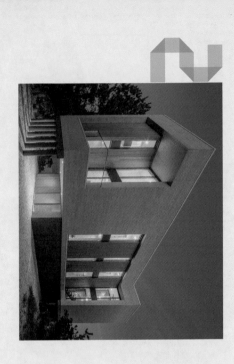

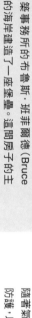

創造的建築物正効我阿德工作室的設計師醫總監查姆士 · 拉姆齊 (James Ramsey) 所說：「與土地及洪水夫生，讓建築得以生存下去。」

美國紐澤西長灘島上，一棟由 Specht Architects 建築事務所建造的海邊住宅在 2012 年時捲過了珊迪颶風的襲擊。這棟建築物的設計靈感來自船舶的建造工程，使用最高級的防颶風窗戶、不鏽鋼零件、玻璃纖維屋頂來抵擋惡劣的天氣。

Beinfield Architecture 建築事務所的布魯斯 · 班菲爾德 (Bruce Beinfield) 在康乃狄克州的海岸建造了一座堡壘。這間房子的主要特色，是當中有幾個特別設計的構造，能夠抵擋極端的氣候。

該事務所說明，這棟房屋利用回收木材製成的木頭側版以及鋼材捲門，創造了「橫向支撐的防暴風捲門分殼」，能夠保護大面積的玻璃美窗不受暴風雨的侵害。這棟房子搭建在高於海平面十五呎的水泥柱上，比聯邦緊急事務管理署 (Federal Emergency Management Agency) 的洪水規範還還高，地面的車庫別建造於鋼筋混凝土的地面上並設有排水口，讓洪水能夠進入，以達平衡水壓的效果。

值得關注的原因：

隨著氣候變遷日益提升，下一代的豪宅都提供了升級的防護，以免受到極端氣候的侵害。

30

健康招待所

新一代的旅館將健康招待的概念提升到新的高度，將增進健康的元素直接納入建築設計當中。

全球健康研究所（Global Wellness Institute）提供的最新資料顯示，2017 年保健旅遊在全球健康經濟中貢獻了 6,390 億美元。於是，洞燭先機的飯店開始以促進健康為目的打造特別的環境，意圖搶攻這塊市場。

位於加州恩希尼塔斯的月光海館（Inn at Moonlight Beach），在 2019 年 7 月成為第一間獲得「健康建築」認證的旅館。國際健康建築機構（International WELL Building Institute）在 2014 年開始進行標準認證，希望能「改善人類在建築物與社區中的健康與幸福指數」，並且「透過我們所居住、工作、遊樂的建築空間，來提升人類的健康與福祉」。該機構目前共收到來自 58 個國家的 3,880 個建案，其中以工作場所居多。

為符合認證的標準，月光海灘旅館重新審視了建築物本身及館內提供的服務，以符合健康認證於七個領域中的標準，包括空氣、水、營養、光線、舒適、健康、心靈。該旅館的特色包含了生態農場、冥想花園，以及頂級的空氣過濾系統。

在月光海灘旅館成為第一間獲得「健康」認證的旅館後，其他幾間旅館也紛紛跟進，包括了日本京阪京都飯店（Keihan Kyoto hotel）、西班牙亞利坎堤（Alicante）的禪 健康養生飯店（Zem Wellness Retreat），以及美國加州的史丹利農場（Stanly Ranch）。

值得關注的原因：

熱衷於保健旅遊的人已開始尋找各種新方式來護自己能夠充分休息與放鬆。他們開始關注活動以外的事物，仔細選擇以健康與保健為標準所興建的場或。

UNDERMAN
HOMPSON

Inn at Moonlight Beach, Encinitas, California

品牌 & 行銷

31

遊戲網紅

全球數據公司 (GlobalData) 預測在2025年前，遊戲產業將會擁有高達3,000億美元的產值，而品牌也想從這塊千億大餅分一杯羹。

蘋果遊樂場 (Apple Arcade) 於 2019 年 9 月推出後，提升了手遊的標準與取得便利度，而谷歌 (Google) 也試圖改變遊戲取得的方式，因此在 2019 年 11 月推出了 Stadia。

遊戲的世界越來越多元，使用者的數量也持續攀升，品牌開始瞄準了遊戲網紅，希望能受到這群不斷成長的觀眾群所青睞。《要塞英雄》(Fortnite) 遊戲中的超級明星泰勒·布列文斯 (Tyler Blevins) 以「忍者」的名號廣為人知，他在 2019 年 8 月與愛迪達 (Adidas) 簽了好幾年的合約。而 Nike 則在 2019 年稍早，與中國英雄聯盟職業賽 (League of Legends Pro League) 的選手簽約，成為他們服裝與鞋類的獨家合作夥伴。甚至還邀請英雄聯盟選手 Uzi (本名簡自豪) 於品牌廣告中現身。K-Swiss 則是在 2018 年贊助了 Immortals 電競隊的專用鞋款。

美妝品牌則開始與女性玩家攜手合作。2019 年 3 月，《要塞英雄》與《英雄聯盟》的直播主 Pokimane (本名為 Imane Anys) 與美妝品牌 Winky Lux 合作，推出聯名眼影盤。2019 年 2 月，Mac 彩妝 (Mac Cosmetics) 也與騰訊的手機遊戲《王者榮耀》(Honor of Kings) 建立策略聯盟，推出限量版唇彩，據聞 24 小時內便銷售一空。

路易威登 (Louis Vuitton) 也曾瞄準遊戲內的品牌商機。這個精品品牌曾在 2019 年 9 月與銳玩公司 (Riot Games) 合作，替《英雄聯盟》冠軍賽設計兩款獨特的「尊絕不凡造型」。這兩款造型是由路易威登女裝部的藝術總監尼古拉‧蓋斯奇埃爾 (Nicolas Ghesquière) 操刀設計。其中，姬亞娜 (Qiyana) 的造型先於 2019 年 11 月發表，珊娜 (Senna) 的造型也預計於 2020 年初推出。

值得關注的原因：

遊戲產業逐漸成為品牌行銷的下一個場域，電競明星也成為新興的名人階級。「過去品牌接觸遊戲產業時都相當謹慎，因為其中多少存在一些未知的因素。然而現在遊戲業選手都聚眾的能力卻已不容忽視，其中手遊玩家更是如此。」電競媒體公司 Ampverse 的共同創辦人查利‧巴利 (Charlie Baillie) 如此表示。

WUNDERMAN THOMPSON

32

音效品牌策略

從財經到時尚，各行各業的公司
都以量身打造的音效來強化品牌形象，以期與當今
的消費者達成更多維度的連結。

正如2019年《改變未來的100件事：2019全球百大趨勢》中提到的聲
音帝國趨勢一樣，視聽娛樂及大量音響系統的出現，讓耳朵成為通
向受眾的關鍵通道，品牌也開始注意到這點。

2019 年 9 月，Coach 在 Instagram 上一連分享了許多篇貼文，並要
求觀眾打開音效觀看。影片中強調了與 Coach 有關的聲音，並說明
這些「總是讓人感到療癒的聲音」有轉扣包（Turnlock）嵌上金屬
扣的聲音，也有縫初機車種皮件的機台運轉聲。同月，三宅一
生包（Bao Bao Issey Miyake）邀請了倫敦設計節的與會者參加
「包包之聲」（Bao Bao Voice），那是一場「互動式多重感官活動」，
收錄 100 種以上由該品牌知名的幾何圖形包包所發出的聲音。

在汽車界，聲音的創新則是讓電動車不再靜默，因為在過去，過於
安靜的電動車引發了安全上的疑慮。歐盟已經制定了新的法規，
要求新的電動車款必須加裝發聲裝置，並從 2021 年 7 月起，歐盟
所有的車輛都必須安裝汽車聲響警示系統。BMW 決定要更上一

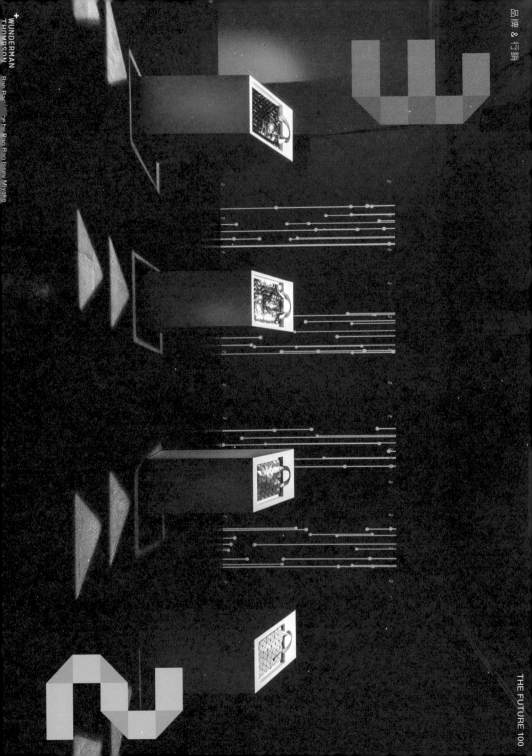

+
WUNDERMAN
THOMPSON

Bag Bag by Bao Bao Issey Miyake

Hans Zimmer composing BMW IconicSounds Electric

層，他們屏棄傳統的汽車引擎聲，並找攬作曲家漢斯‧季默 (Hans Zimmer) 以及音響工程師倫佐‧維塔萊 (Renzo Vitale) 替 BMW Vision M Next 電動車操刀，創作專屬音效。BMW 與季默，維塔萊的合作在 2019 年 6 月時公布。目前也已經開發出 BMW IconicSounds Electric 系列音效。BMW 表示，這麼做的目的是為了在駕駛近乎無聲的電動車時，填補「駕駛經驗中的情感空缺」。

匯豐銀行 (HSBC) 與萬事達卡 (Mastercard) 在 2019 年初也紛紛發表了新的識別音效。匯豐銀行與作曲家尚‧米歇爾‧雅爾 (Jean-Michel Jarre) 合作，創作「量身打造的音樂，讓大家立刻就能認同該銀行」。萬事達卡則設計了聲音商標，並聘請音樂學家與資料庫當中現有的音樂比對，確認音樂的原創性。

美國音樂平台《潘朵拉》(Pandora) 在 2019 年 6 月推出名為 Studio Resonate 的品牌聽覺識別顧問服務。《美國商業資訊》(Businesswire) 表示，這項服務能夠「推動品牌進入聽覺的新紀元」。同月，iHeartMedia 以及 WPP 集團聯手推出「聆聽專案」(Project Listen)，提供聲效行銷相關的全新內容與研究服務。

隨著客製聲效的需求增加，與聽覺相關的品牌策略需求也日益增加。「消費者比過去更注重聆聽，我們也已經得知音樂、聲音、音效創造人類情感連結的力量，」WPP 執行長馬克‧雷德 (Mark Read) 如此表示。「隨著消費者行為的演進，從他們聆聽的媒體，到這些媒體如何與品牌產生連結並影響購物決策，所有媒體的創意和決策，都要以現代的方式執行，聽覺媒體也不例外。」

值得關注的原因：

企業紛紛利用聲音科學來強化品牌識別，與消費者生產生更好的共鳴，畢竟聲音是我們最敏捷的感知。聽覺神經科學家賽斯‧霍洛維茲 (Seth Horowitz) 表示：視覺辨識的過程至少要花大腦四分之一秒的時間，但處理聲音只要 0.05 秒。如果品牌想讓消費者留下持久的情感印象，那麼就應該訴諸聲音商標。

33

單身詞彙庫

可以稱呼他們與己為伴、自願性無伴者、或是自婚者，但就是不要以他們單身狗。

現在逐漸出現一套詞彙，用以描述各種面向的無伴侶生活，重新形塑令人厭煩的刻板印象與污名。

美國女演員葛妮絲・派特蘿（Gwyneth Paltrow）與英國樂團主唱克里斯・馬汀（Chris Martin）在 2014 年因為他們的「自願性分手」（conscious uncoupling）而成為頭條新聞，這個新詞開啟了一扇門，讓大家以新的方式談論與思考無伴侶生活，而社會文化也緊跟在後。

演員艾瑪・華森在 2019 年接受英國《時尚》（Vogue）12 月號的專訪時，描述自己的生活型態為「與己為伴」（self-partnered），這個詞彙就像派特蘿與馬汀創造的詞彙一樣，在各大媒體颳起一陣炫風。

在這股熱潮當中，有件顯而易見的事情：形容單身生活的傳統詞彙已經不再適用了。

「在艾瑪・華森與葛妮絲・派特蘿站出來使用『與己為伴』以及『自願性分手』等辭彙時，便挑戰了『單身』與『離婚』的心理暗示與論述。」洽療師崔維斯・麥克納提（Travis McNulty）對國家廣播公司新聞（NBC News）如此說道。

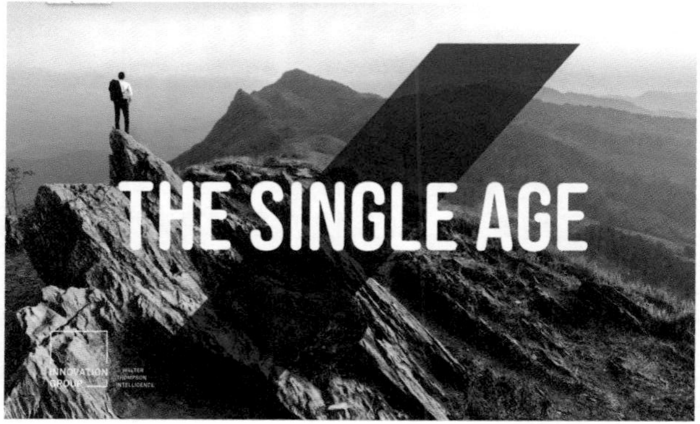

近期的文化正面臨著重塑單身者形象的驅力：他們的形象應是自信、滿足，且充滿力量。

達頓（Joe Staton）告訴偉門智威智庫，一旦有品牌把當成單身人士來行銷，那「他們會立刻被我從考慮名單中剔除。我會覺得那些品牌自認高人一等，也不會引起我的共鳴。雖然我覺得單身很快樂，但我不該被歸入單身的類別當中。」

由於這樣的對話不斷增加，媒體上描述單身的修辭也正在轉變，擺脫了不成熟、可憐、絕望的形象，而變成了獨立自由的象徵。一份利用偉門智威獨有的研究工具 SONAR™ 針對美國、英國、中國 3,000 位受訪者進行的調查，發現美國有 82% 的單身者認為現今的社會變得比較能夠接受單身，77% 的人則認為社會過度著重戀愛關係。大多數的受訪者，無論年齡、性別、國籍為何，都表示他們喜愛單身，超過 70% 的人說單身是他們自己的選擇。另外也有超過 50% 的美國人喜歡單身勝過戀愛，而這個數據來源並不限於單一世代。

值得關注的原因：

近期的文化正面臨著重塑單身者形象的驅力：他們的形象應是自信、滿足，且充滿力量。不斷演化的對話反映出典範的劇烈變化。有在成年時期處在有伴侶的狀態中，社也成為一種典型狀態。有了更微妙與精確的詞彙作為武器，社會便能夠以這群人真正的樣貌來面對他們，而這群人的數量仍不斷上升中。

THE SINGLE AGE

這些高調的女性為了自我實現以及自由，加入了擁抱單身的行列，這群人的數量日益增加，力量也越發強大。作家葛林妮絲·梅克尼可（Glynnis MacNicol）在 2018 年出版了《沒人告訴你的事》（暫譯自 No One Tells You This），這是一本關於單身生活的回憶錄。她告訴偉門智威智庫，訴她意圖「在有關女性生活的故事當中，加入一些新的語彙。」

她說「我們描述女性生活的方式，沒有一種和婚姻或小孩無關」，

她也繼續補充：「但現在的情形是這樣：我們正開始創造有關女性生活的新語彙。這種情況不時出現，有時候看來不錯，有時候則像是：哇，他們真的做得很棒爛，根本是一團亂，這是相當困難的事，也是全新的事。」

在我們的「單身時代」（The Single Age）報告當中，受訪者喬·史

34

新一代超級創意人才

數位工具為下一代的消費族群提高創造力，
並賦予他們強而有力的聲音。

年齡在 13 至 22 歲的 Z 世代，是第一個從小就生活在科技之中的世代。他們善用數位的能力與超高網路使用率，賦予了他們無與倫比的流暢創造力，而這種超級創造力正被用在更為公眾的利益上。創新集團（Innovation Group）與 Snapchat 合作發布的報告「進入 Z 世代的未來」（Into Z Future）顯示，在 Z 世代被要求為他們同一代人喊出口號時，他們一開始說要「做自己」，隨即又說要「拯救地球」。

2019 年 11 月，由勇於發聲的女性生育權倡議者 —— 19 歲的黛婭 · 福克斯（Deja Foxx）所共同創立的「Z 世代女子幫」（Gen Z Girl Gang）與三星公司（Samsung）合作推出「人人都能讀大學」（College Access for All）企劃。這是三星 Galaxy 新創會議（Samsung Galaxy Innovator Sessions）的一部分，他們使用自有平台，討論了教育的包容性和新的顧問指導機會，並與關注青春期健康的品牌 Blume 合辦自我照護工作坊。

Z 世代還有其他傑出的創作者，包括原住民維權人士兼詩人金塞爾 · 休斯頓（Kinsale Hueston），最近與時尚網站《Refinery29》和 Target 合作，共同發起「未來追求者」（Future Seekers）企劃；馬特 · 伯恩斯坦（Matt Bernstein）則以化妝為說故事的手法，表達 LGBTQ 的權利。還

有 19 歲的姆‧奧德瑟（Em Odesser），她憑藉自己的創造才能，為年輕人消除了與心理健康和性健康有關的污名，並因此被列在 2019 年《青少年時尚》（*Teen Vogue*）的「21 位 21 歲以下的新秀榜」。

她告訴《青少年時尚》：「我不知道我是想當記者、假陽具鬥士、小說家、雜誌編輯、喜劇演員、造型師，還是其他職業，但我希望我還是可以真實地表達自我。」

值得關注的原因：

青少年正在為數位藝術表現方式開闢新的領域，他們個性積極並以不同的思維去溝通。由 Z 世代所經營的智囊團「不正常實驗室」（Irregular Labs），其共同創辦人莫莉‧洛根（Molly Logan）在《進入 Z 世代的未來》中，告訴譚門智威智庫：「你必須完全拋開所有的二分法和規則」，因為對 Z 世代來說，沒有什麼是矛盾的。眼前所見都是可發揮的題材。」獲得年輕消費者青睞的企業，將是那些把自身活動與 Z 世代所關心的事物連結在一起的公司，這些議題從從真實性、包容性，到環境問題皆涵蓋其中。

UNDERMAN
HOMPSON

Above: "Into Z Future" report
Right: Future Seekers, Refinery29 x Target. Photo by Heather Hazzan for Refinery29

你必須完全拋開所有的二分法和規則，
因為對Z世代來說，沒有什麼是矛盾的，
眼前所見都是可發揮的題材。

不正常實驗室（Irregular Labs）共同創辦人｜莫莉·洛根（Molly Logan）

35

類比復興

文化創作者轉向類比格式，藉以消除數位噪音。

有越來越多的藝人開始復興眼看似已被揚棄的類比格式。

2019 年 6 月，電台司令（Radiohead）的主唱湯姆・約克（Thom Yorke）在倫敦地鐵、義大利電話亭、《達拉斯觀察報》（Dallas Observer）的分類廣告中，刊登了一系列神秘廣告，預告他的專輯《阿尼瑪科技公司》（Anima Technologies）即將發行。

這些廣告還提供了一個電話號碼，撥打該號碼時會播放一則神秘的訊息：「當局已責令《阿尼瑪科技公司》停止運行，並終止其廣告業務。」

酷玩樂團（Coldplay）也以類比手法宣傳他們的第八張錄音室專輯《偉大日常》（Everyday Life），針對他們所選的報紙，在北威爾斯《北威爾斯每日郵報》（North Wales Daily Post）上，《偉大日常》的廣告和乾草捆和冰箱的銷售廣告放在一起。

酷玩樂團還藉此機會復興了一項備受喜愛的傳統，將看似客製過的相似的銷售廣告放在一起。

明信片透過平信寄給特定粉絲。

完成類比慶典後，該專輯也同時發行於不起眼的卡式錄音帶上，而卡式錄音帶本身即是一種新興的類比復興格式。卡帶儲存日（Cassette Store Day）是專門為此媒體格式所舉辦的年度活動，於 2013 年起源於英國，但今天在中國、印尼、美國、加拿大等地也都相當盛行。

在英國，卡式錄音帶的銷量達到 2004 年以來的最高峰。根據《衛報》（The Guardian）2019 年 11 月的文章，在美國，2018 年的卡帶銷售額增長了 23%，總計售出 21 萬 9 千捲卡帶。1975 樂團（The 1975）、瑪丹娜

在數位時代，類比格式伴隨懷舊情懷出現的新選擇，而除了懷舊，甚至還包括「對從未經歷的事物產生的懷舊感」(anemoia)。

(Madonna)、凱莉巴特爾 (Catfish and the Bottlemen) 等藝人也都發行了卡帶專輯，帶動了這波潮流。

青少年歌手怪奇比莉 (Billie Eilish) 雖然並不出生於錄音帶的全盛時期，她的首張錄音室專輯《當我們睡了，怪事發生了》(When We All Fall Asleep, Where Do We Go?) 也發行了限量版的米姆綠卡帶，其中還有螢光版本。

或許設計後者的收藏價值，和它能發在 Instagram 上的炫耀意義，大過了卡帶格式本身講究的價值。但是，懷舊情懷在卡帶銷售中確實喚起了重要的作用，因為卡帶讓許多樂迷回想起他們年輕時聽到的獨特特質音。

英國唱片業協會 (BPI) 的根納羅．卡斯塔爾多 (Gennaro Castaldo) 將這一轉變歸因於「懷舊元素」。他補充說：「在過去的幾年中，以卡帶作為故事一環的《星際異攻隊》(Guardians of the Galaxy) 系列電影，也重新喚起了大眾對卡帶的興趣。」

值得關注的原因：

在數位時代，類比格式是伴隨懷舊情懷出現的新選擇，而除了懷舊，甚至還包括「對從未經歷的事物產生的懷舊感」(anemoia)。

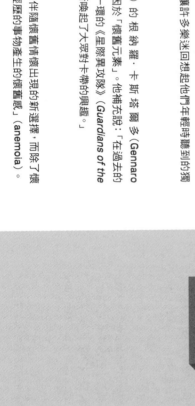

36

公正的互動介面

近年來，一直存在的性別偏見問題已滲透到媒體及演算法等各個領域中。

2019 年秋季風靡一時的蘋果公司信用卡（Apple Card）即為一例，其用戶坦稱，蘋果公司向女性用戶提供的信用額度低於男性，但發卡商高盛集團（Goldman Sachs）表示，他們的演算法「根本沒輸入客戶性別」。美國雜誌《連線》（Wired）則指出：「即使是沒有性別辨識力的演算法，只要在其中加入與性別相關的數值，最終還是會產生對女性有偏見的結果。」他們還補充道，有研究表明「可以透過使用 Mac 或他牌個人電腦作為種種信用預測信用額度的方法，而其他變量（例如住址）則可以代表種族。同樣地，某人購物的地方也可能指示其性別資訊。」

考慮到這一點，企業開始發想能將性別中立納入旗下界面的創新方法。

2019 年 5 月，Vice 傳媒有限公司（Vice Media）旗下的 Virtue 推出第一個無性別語音助理「Q」。Virtue 表示：「Q 是我們理想中的未來典範。一個具有理念、包容力、定位、多樣表現形式的未來。」他們也指出「科技公司通常會覺得區分性別，以為這會讓大家更願

German's can now choose third gender option on legal records.

Colorado becomes fifth state to allow third gender on licenses.

ENDERMAN
OMPSON

Q, the first genderless voice assistant, by Virtue. Images courtesy of Vice Media

意採用這樣的技術，不幸的是，這反而加強了對二元性別的觀點，並讓許多人致力於抗衡的性別刻板印象繼續延續下去。」

美德創意社鼓勵大家分享這項創新理念，讓蘋果 (Apple)、亞馬遜 (Amazon)、谷歌 (Google) 和微軟 (Microsoft) 在其語音助理中，採用這項創新技術。

MagicCo 是家將品牌配置到家用物聯網上的公司，而語音助理屬其中。其創始人兼執行長班·費雪 (Ben Fisher) 向偉門智威集團表示：他相信「將來消費者都能夠選擇各種聲音的語音助理，而無性別語音助理將是眾多選項之一。我認為無論有無性別的選項都會影響公司的銷售額，尤其消費者若有表明他們對無性別語音的偏好的話。」

費雪補充：「我對第一批的聲音究竟聽起來如何，某個程度上，還是讓人感到遺憾。我猜想這是因為很多科技業的決策者都是男性吧，但從長計議，我認為以後會有針對不同人設計的語音選擇。語音助理只是個可以安裝軟體的平台，而未來它們也一樣是如此。」

費雪指出，無性別的聲音究竟聽起來如何，某個程度上，還是讓人不太確定。他這麼說道：「很難做到百分之百正確，可能還需要一時間才能弄清楚。」費雪表示，由於目前的語音助理理會配為用戶所接受及信任，可供選擇及安裝。因此「這會讓語音助理為用戶所接受及信任。」

性別平衡改革的概念也開始出現在提尋引擎中。2019 年 4 月，寶僑集團 (Procter & Gamble) 旗下的品牌潘婷 (Pantene) 推出了 SHE 工具，三個英文字母分別代表搜尋 (Search)、人類 (Human)、

等化器 (Equalizer)，用以「揭示搜尋結果中的偏見」。寶僑集團指出，該搜尋工具在「在後端過濾資訊，以提供較無偏見和平衡的搜尋結果，並讓世上有偉大成就及發動偉大改革的女性，得到她們應有的知名度。」此次發表新的內容，跟潘婷的「變革之力」(Power to Transform) 企劃相呼應，該運動品牌旨在企劃中聚焦女性如何「改變世界」，同時昭示他們提出的 100 萬美元計畫，專注與女性會員俱樂部 The Wing 合作，透過投資競賽來資助企業家和女性所領導的企業。

偉僑關注的原因：

品牌號稱要解決性別不平等和偏見的問題，不僅僅在口頭上，而是致力以創新方式打造能積極推廣女性成就的產品。這些創新對於科技公司在性別偏見議題上的聲譽，或許也將因此有了變化。

People would not assume gender based on voices anymore in the future.

37

原創內容經濟

隨著串流媒體的競爭升溫，各品牌開始投資原創內容。

觀影習慣正在改變。民調公司 YPulse 在 2019 年 8 月的報告指出，「千禧世代的父母，不靠有線電視來撫養小孩。他們的孩子最有可能收看的是串流節目。而這也預示著：未來收看有線電視會被視為稀有的人。」該報告發現，在美國 13-18 歲的受訪者中，只有 33% 的人會每週看電視節目，73% 的人表示，他們用智慧型手機收看影片。另外，會每週每週或更頻繁地觀看有線電視節目的人，只有 18%。

在觀眾可隨選隨播的趨勢下，娛樂平台為了要提供獨特的產品而承受壓力。他們也為此開始投資原創內容，來跟競爭對手作出區別。

蘋果的 TV+（Apple TV+）於 2019 年 11 月首次亮相，推出一系列的獨家節目、電影、紀錄片，包括由海莉・史坦菲德（Hailee Steinfeld）主演的艾蜜莉・狄金生（Emily Dickinson）傳記電影，以及歐普拉（Oprah）和哈利王子（Prince Harry）合作的心理健康紀錄影集。

12 天後，迪士尼+（Disney+）也推出了一系列新片，包括星際大戰

For All Mankind sci-fi series on Apple TV+. Image courtesy of Apple

（Star War）宇宙中的新影集《曼達洛人》（The Mandalorian），以及一系列漫威（Marvel）電影宇宙的劇情片和紀錄片。為了進一步彰顯原創內容的重要，迪士尼於 2019 年 11 月底宣布了新設立的國際內容部副總裁一職，致力開發與生產全球原創內容。

美國國家廣播公司環球集團（NBC Universal）的串流影音平台孔雀（Peacock）將在 2020 年 4 月上線，該公司在 2019 年 9 月時表示，它將提供「世界級的原創內容」，以及美國國家廣播公司（NBC）麾下的熱門節目。華納媒體（WarnerMedia）旗下的 HBO Max 也將於 2020 年 5 月推出，並已與演員瑞絲·薇斯朋（Reese Witherspoon）和編劇葛瑞格·貝蘭提（Greg Berlanti）簽署了電影製作協議。

美國的 OTT 影片內收入將以10.3%的速度成長，並在2023年達到237億美元

資誠聯合會計師事務所（PwC）

娛樂業以外的品牌也希望透過原創內容吸引消費者的注意力。日用品公司寶僑集團（Procter & Gamble）與《國家地理頻道》（National Geographic）合作，推出一系列六集的紀錄片《行動》（Activate），於 2019 年 9 月首次公開播映。希望在全球喚起行動主義。《Fast Company》點評道：「這不是產品置入，也不是贊助內容，這是聲望很高的電視節目。」

2019 年 10 月，交友軟體 Tinder 發行了原創互動式影集《滑過夜晚》（Swipe Night），為用戶提供新的配對機制。2019 年 6 月，電子郵件行銷平台 Mailchimp 公開了旗下的 Mailchimp Presents 部門，是為大企業家和中小企業主製作原創劇集、電影、播客語音節目的新娛樂部門。2019 年 4 月，租屋平台 Airbnb 公司宣布了要製作原創

節目的計畫，用以推廣 Airbnb 房東、住客、旅遊景點。2019 年 1 月，電子商務平台 Shopify 與 Shopify 工作室（Shopify Studios）聯合跨足電視電影影集產業，將推出為企業家打造的紀錄片集和紀錄片形式的電影長片。

資誠聯合會計師事務所（PwC）預測，美國的 OTT（over-the-top，即透過網路直接向觀眾提供的串流媒體服務）影片收入將以 10.3% 的速度成長，並在 2023 年達到 237 億美元，且原創內容的重要度沒有減少的跡象。資誠指出：「事實證明，獨家和原創的內容，是吸引用戶訂閱串流媒體服務的關鍵因素。新舊平台投入內容市場的資金相當驚人，而且短期內也沒有減少的跡象。」

值得關注的原因：

品牌原創內容開始成為分拆解析的娛樂業支柱，同時也是吸引觀眾的新穎方式，因為觀眾正在尋求帶狀電視節目以外的娛樂模式。

氣候正效益品牌

38

先驅品牌正在整合商業模式與永續議題,並用以實際投資展現行動力。

根據偉門智威獨有的研究工具 SONAR™ 顯示,有 90% 的消費者認為企業和品牌有責任照顧地球及其居民。隨著對氣候問題的關注達到高峰,品牌開始為他們造成的環境衝擊承擔更多責任。

BJSS 公司的零售顧問麗茲·威利特 (Lizzie Willett) 向偉門智威智庫表示:「我們看到越來越多的品牌優先考量了永續議題。品牌不能只是以聰明的廣告來做做樣子,因為消費者會審視整個環節,不僅僅是行銷和廣告,整個公司的企業精神都要如此,也需要將溫度的理念實踐在產品中。」

2019 年 11 月,英國公司 Dame 成為第一個實現氣候正效益的生理用品牌。他們新推出的碳補償計畫與品牌的創立精神相符,可重複使用的棉條置入器能減少一次性塑膠的使用量。這項新計畫預計縮減大氣層中的碳排放量,且減少的幅度是該公司自 2018 年推行計畫以來所產生的碳排量的兩倍。他們的產品也成為英國第一個獲得碳足跡 (Carbon Footprint) 認證的碳平衡正效益 (Carbon Neutral Plus) 商品。

「作為一間企業,我們有很大的責任要盡力協助解決緊急的氣候問題，並為消費者提供更好的選擇。」Dame 的共同創辦人西莉亞‧普爾（Celia Pool）告訴《倫敦標準晚報》（*Evening Standard*）：「對我們來說，氣候正效益不是一種選擇，而是絕對必要的事。」

大眾消費品牌也對此需求做出回應。自 2017 年以來，時裝公司 H&M 一直努力在 2040 年前達成碳中和的目標，而聯合利華公司（Unilever）則承諾會在 2030 年前，實現減碳正效益，不僅從生產過程中淘汰所有化石燃料，也支持其供應商達成相同的目標。

2019 年 9 月，宜家居（IKEA）宣布將為旗下店面生產再生能源，日產量將高於店面所需用電量。這間家居用品公司還主計畫要在 2025 年前，於旗下所有賣場中開始販售太陽能能板，以幫助消費者自行達成碳中和的目標。

宜家的控股公司英格卡公司（Ingka）執行長傑斯珀‧布羅丁（Jesper Brodin）告訴路透社（Reuters）：「提高氣候方面的智慧並不是額外增加的成本，這其實是一門明智的生意，也是未來商業模式的樣貌。」

值得關注的原因：

減碳正效益已不僅只是拿來換取消費者忠誠度和建立信任的活動，此舉已開始改變為現代企業的當前要務。古馳（Gucci）的執行長馬可‧畢薩力（Marco Bizzarri）在 2019 年 11 月的公開信中，邀請眾執行長一同參加「碳中和挑戰」，他寫道：「我們正邁入企業責任面對眼前的全球氣候問題和生物多樣性危機。我們都有企業。作為企業，我們都有責任面對眼前的全球氣候問題和生物多樣性危機。」不過耐心才是關鍵，永續發展計畫需要 20 到 30 年的時間才能完全實施和擴展，因此品牌、消費者、利益關係人都需要把眼光放遠。

我們正邁入企業責任新的十年。作為企業，我們都有責任要面對眼前的全球氣候問題和生物多樣性危機。

古馳（Gucci）執行長｜馬可‧畢薩力（Marco Bizzarri）

39

非比尋常的品牌行動

最令人意想不到的品牌促動，是否最具影響力？

注重永續議題的品牌近日做出許多令人意想不到的舉動，以強調自己對環保的承諾。

舉例來說，REI（Recreational Equipment, Inc.）以及護膚品牌 Deciem 公司反對黑色星期五（Black Friday）的過度消費行為，於是選擇在這個美國重要的購物節關閉旗下商店。Deciem 宣布將在 2019 年的黑色星期五這天，關閉網路與實體商店，並表示他們「對參與這種過度消費的節日不再感到自在。」Deciem 作法是，在 2019 年 11 月份的一整個月裡，都提供顧客 77 折的商品折扣。

Deciem 公司表示：「我們堅信，保養決策應以教育學習為基礎，而非由衝動購物來驅使。我們想讓消費者有時間去研究、思索、考慮。」

2019 年，戶外服飾品牌 REI 在黑色星期五期間關閉了旗下商店，這是他們連續實施這項計畫的第五年。除此之外，他們還在感恩節前夕，在美國發起了「清淨社區」（任務：邀請消費者參與清掃社區。他們也推出「一起而行」（Opt to Act Plan）計畫，提供消費者一份行動清單，列舉 1 年共 52 週可以做的環保行動。「如果只是一間公司，

那我們的影響力很有限；但如果有一整個社群，我們就能在公司以外的地方，也推動有意義的行動，並帶來改變。」REI 執行長艾瑞克·亞茲（Eric Artz）在公司合作紀錄中寫道：「身為一個組織，我們得知道每個人只要做一些小小的行動，就能成就巨大的改變，集體意念能促成強大的集體作用。」

Patagonia、Lush、Ben & Jerry's、Seventh Generation 等品牌都在 2019 年加入了全球氣候變遷的抗爭行動，並於當年 9 月 20 日關閉旗下的商店，與氣候議題的運動人士站在同一陣線。

新創媒體《Vox》的一篇文章說道：「為了支持氣候變遷這個更大的理念而放棄某部分收入，此舉似乎些激進。」然而，《廣告週刊》（AdWeek）指出：「關閉商店的作法對消費者而言，表示這家公司不只是坐而言，更願意起而行。」

哈利特·沃金（Harriet Vocking）是倫敦 Eco-Age 永續顧問公司的品牌長，她接受當門普威智庫訪問時表示，這些非典型行動的重點「不在於犧牲銷售量，而是讓目標成為品牌的核心理念，讓企業能為續經營 20 年，而不懂僅是 5 年。」沃金舉客戶 Chopard 珠寶公司為例。在經過諮詢後，該珠寶公司決定使用公平採礦（Fairmined）認證的黃金來製作商品。Chopard 目前直接與哥倫比亞的責任採礦聯盟（Alliance for Responsible Mining）合作，認購該聯盟 4 座礦場的金礦。沃金表示：「使用公平採礦認證的黃金需要支付額外費用，但 Chopard 自行吸收，因此費用不會轉嫁給消費者。」

INDERMAN
OMPSON

Deciem closed stores on Black Friday 2019.
Image courtesy of Deciem

如果只是一間公司，那我們的影響力很有限；但如果有一整個社群，我們就可以在公司以外的地方，也推動有意義的行動並帶來改變。

REI 執行長艾瑞克·亞茲（Eric Artz）

「消費者想知道的是，他們付費支持的這個品牌，是一個值得信賴的品牌，也是個致力於不斷進步的品牌。」她補充：「並不是說品牌必須臻於完美，而是品牌要開始檢視自身的供應鏈與生產製程，並開始改變系統生態。」

另一個出乎意料的行動則是 Travalyst 計畫。該計畫於 2019 年 9 月發起，由哈利王子（Prince Harry）領軍，並由互為競爭對手的 Booking.com、Visa 信用卡、Ctrip、TripAdvisor、Skyscanner 共同創立，目標是「推動全新的旅遊方式，讓每個人在探索世界的同時，也能保護人類與環境，確保無論是旅遊景點或是當地社群，都能迎向永續與明朗的未來。」

零售顧問公司 MHE Retail 的執行長喬治·瓦勒斯（George Wallace）表示：「這一年來，永續議題從一開始的乏人問津，到現在成為發燒的主流話題。每個人對此都必須有一套自己的主張。」但他也相信「有些行動其實沒什麼意義或影響力。在氣候議題示威期間關閉商店，並沒有什麼實質貢獻，他們所表達的就只有『我站在你這邊』如此而已。」

瓦勒斯表示，大型經銷商普遍採用的作為才能造成較大的影響，例如英國的連鎖超市 Tesco。該超市於 2019 年 11 月時承諾，要在 2020 年底前減少十億件商品塑膠包裝。他說：「這才是重量級的改變，這才會造成真正的影響，我覺得消費者的反應不錯，這不只是噱頭而已。微小的行動仍然十分有價值，令人振奮的是，現在大型企業已開始採取推動永續的行動了。」

值得關注的原因：

消費者注重永續議題，而現在拜網路上的大量資訊所賜，消費者得以檢視公司的永續與環境承諾是否足夠透明。品牌願意背離資本主義以追求永續與打擊氣候變遷，顯示他們真的與環保站在同一陣線，而這些行動也讓大型企業開始將環保永續視為首要之務。

40

亞洲Z世代

亞洲Z世代在世界上發展最快的地區長大，
經歷了貿易戰與區域衝突、中國市場停滯、
越南改革開放、日本經濟長期停滯，這些實驗成熟
也形塑了Z世代的面貌。

即使歷經動盪，亞洲的Z世代仍對未來抱持樂觀的態度，並善用科技達成自己的目標。

整體而言，Z世代的社會意識較為先進。偉門智威智庫新版的「Z世代報告APAC版」（Generation Z: APAC Edition）調查了9個國家中的4500位Z世代，發現Z世代認為種族差異沒有以往那麼重要了。10個Z世代當中，就有7位願意包容與不同種族的人約會。有鑑於此，許多品牌開始強調包容性。菲律賓美妝品牌Sunnies Face就捨去亮白化妝品，推出適合各種膚色的暖色系產品。無獨有偶，中國流行彩妝品牌Hedone也推出男性的彩妝用品。

Z世代能在網路與現實世界之間來去自如，有76%的受訪者對網路購物和實體購物感到一樣自在，但62%的受訪者還是比較喜歡在實體商店購物。在泰國，由京東商城（JD.com）資助的快時尚平

INDERMAN
OMPSON

Sunnies Face beauty brand

品牌 & 行銷

無論是環境、社會、政治，Z世代都亞欲購這個世界變的更好，而為了因應這樣的消費者特性，各品牌也必須著手瞭解Z世代，並迎合Z世代的需求。

在 Pomelo，將網路購物和實體販售搭配的天衣無縫，消費者在手機應用程式下單後，便可到附近的取貨點取物。這個取貨點可能是咖啡店、共同工作空間、健身房，他們可以在取貨點試穿，並立即退還不想要的商品。

亞洲的 Z 世代與其他地區的 Z 世代一樣，都十分擔憂氣候變遷與環境污染等等議題，也願意身促成政治與經濟氣候的轉變。香港學生除了讀書之外，還要為更大限度的自由進行抗爭；而大批年輕LGBTQ 的倡議者也發起遊行，如越南同志遊行 (Viet Pride)、臺灣同志遊行 (Taiwan Pride)、新加坡粉紅點同志遊行 (Pink Dot SG) 等。

每 10 位受訪者中，就有 7 位受訪者認為，身為 LGBTQ 族群的一份子不再是什麼大事；只是在印尼、多數年輕人仍不這麼認為。

金蘭醬油的廣播選一則廣告，由兩個媽媽組成的家庭在廚房裡做菜，而旁白說道：「不同家庭有著不同味道。」

沒錯，家庭仍然佔有重要地位。印尼、菲律賓、泰國、新加坡、越南的 Z 世代，最有可能將家庭成員視為英雄，而老師則位居他們心中英雄排行的第二名：中國、香港、臺灣的 Z 世代則傾向顧名人為英

雄。此外，科學家、企業家、政治人物，受到中國 Z 世代仰慕的程度也比較高。

值得關注的原因：

即將成年的 Z 世代正面臨嶄新的挑戰，包括氣候變遷、政治動盪、性別認同變動，以及隨之而來的一套現代價值觀。這表示年輕程度上，每個人都是行動者。Gerda Binder，聯合國兒童基金會 (UNICEF) 東亞與太平洋區域性別顧問，她在聯合國智威智庫新版的「Z世代報告 APAC 版」中，她提到「這個族群質疑現存的規範，也不願受常規束縛」。無論是環境、社會、政治，Z 世代都亞欲購這個世界變的更好，而為了因應這樣的消費者特性，各品牌也必須著手瞭解 Z 世代，並迎合 Z 世代的需求。

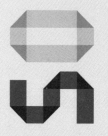

食品 & 飲品

47

永不過時的食譜

隨著減少食物浪費的壓力不斷增加，注重
氣候變遷的消費者開始接受新的食譜，這些食譜
不僅有益身體健康，也友善地球。

《Future Food Today》是一本食譜，主要是希望改造當今冰箱和
儲藏室中不符合永續概念的食物，並提供有益健康、環保的選擇。

本書於 2019 年 5 月發行，由宜家家居（IKEA）的 Space10 與創意機
構 Barkas 合作推出，食譜中介紹了為滿足未來消費者味蕾所量身
定製的食材，無論是含有可食用昆蟲的「臭蟲漢堡」、「藻類薯片」，或
是「微型菜園綠色冰棒」，未來食物的人們所熟悉的形式供應，由宰
見創可能拯救地球的美味和永續「健康的食材」，並以好奇以及更開明的
見創可能拯救地球的美味和永續，Space10 的共同創辦人賽門‧卡
斯帕森（Simon Caspersen）對這門智慧智重說：「我們的目標是激
勵大眾探索新的美味和永續「健康的食材」，並以好奇以及更開明的
態度去瞭解食物的多樣性。」

Space10 體認到，關於食品消費和生產的方式有必要做出巨大的改
變，他們認為「未來 35 年內，我們對食品的需求將增加 70%，若以
今日的飲食方式作估算，我們根本沒有資源來達成這種需求。」

創新的食品品牌正在善用技術、科學、食品，來應對食物對於環境的

WUNDERMAN THOMPSON

Future Food Today, by Space10 and Barkas. Image courtesy of Space10

47

衝擊，而消費者也樂意接受這些選項。以「不可能食品」（Impossible Food）的「不可能漢堡」（Impossible Burger）為例，這種用蔬菜為基礎食材所做的漢堡，像真肉一樣會流「肉汁」，現在在超市裡，甚至在漢堡王（Burger King）或白城堡（White Castle）的菜單上都可找到。

美國酪農公司 Dairy Farmers of America 的報告指出，2018 年的銷售額比前一年下降超過 10 億美元，而乳類替代品的銷售則持續成長。主流消費者似乎願意用同級或品質更優的永續概念產品，來取代不符合永續概念的飲食。

值得關注的原因：
消費者的飲食習慣正轉向「氣候飲食」（climate diet）模式，減少肉類和乳製品的食用量，並尋求環保的替代品。食品品牌需要開始生產健康並符合永續概念的食品，不僅要為消費者提供食物，還要能滋養地球。

Future Food Today, by Space10 and Barkas. Image courtesy of Space10.

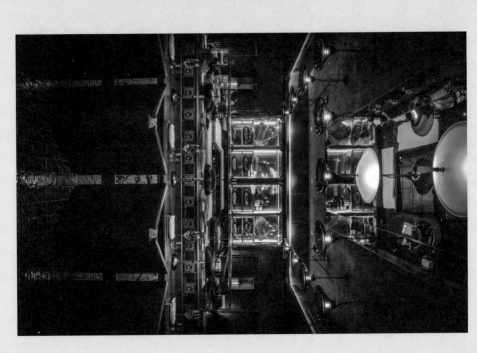

42

違反Instagram潮流的室內裝潢

最新的餐廳開始不再使用社群媒體所迷戀的
「單調又可預測」的設計風格

倫敦的 Lucky Cat 餐廳於 2019 年 6 月開業，業者有意識地避免了社群媒體 Instagram 上流行的飽和色調和吸睛美學。

餐館內，乞求顧客拍下照片的活潑色調、大膽壁紙設計，猶無數地時尚具掛飾等，形成鮮明對比的是，Lucky Cat 內採用深色調輔以昏暗的燈光設計，營造出餐館內部的陰暗氛圍，而這種氛圍並不適合在手機螢幕上呈現。

設計工作室 AfrodikiKrassa「故意將空間調調暗」，阻止大眾在 Instagram 上分享餐館內部的照片，並表示「我們試圖使用微妙而經典的材質和顏色，而不願顯得太過喧囂。」該工作室的創始人阿芙蘿黛蒂·克拉薩（AfroditiKrassa）對《Dezeen》如此說道。

「若某個地方在照片中看起來很棒，但現實生活中卻是令人失望的，你會去造訪幾次？」

Lucky Cat 餐廳的獨特環境將觸覺體驗置於視覺之上：透過質感產生深度，而不是依賴圖像來吸引目光。克拉薩如此解釋：「顏色、圖案、表面材質之間的對比度比較小，但質感和觸感卻非常豐富。

NDERMAN
HOMPSON

Lucky Cat • Photo by Afroditi Krassa

展望未來，消費者會更喜歡鼓勵他們活在當下的空間設計，而非透過手機鏡頭來體驗世界。

Lucky Cat 採用有層次的設計風格，每回顧客到訪都能有更多的發現。」

2019 年 5 月開業的加拿大蒙特婁四季酒店（Four Seasons Hotel）設有幽暗且重視感官體驗的 Marcus 餐酒館，為空間操刀的 Atelier Zébulon Perron 設計工作室受現場的氛圍激勵。庫里對《Dezeen》表示：「這個設計深深根植於親密的互動，特別的時光，深具魅力風情。」

2019 年春天，建築師伯納德‧庫里（Bernard Khoury）重新設計了貝魯特的 B018 空間，這是一間蓋在地底堡壘中的夜店，自 1998 年開業起，B018 一直以一間機構的形式存在。庫里採用單一的深灰色調做為室內裝潢的主色，以令人毛骨悚然的設計元素，增添其陰鬱驚悚之美。

值得關注的原因：

這些設計預示著一個華而不實的時代的終結。這個「看著我在幹嘛」的時代所推崇的體驗和空間設計，是為符合社交媒體發文所需而精心打造的體驗和空間。展望未來，消費者更喜歡能鼓勵他們活在當下的空間設計，而非透過手機鏡頭來體驗世界。

43

解決剩食問題

企業正在設計聰明的解決方案來處理食品包裝垃圾。

推陳出新的技術解決了食品包材相關的垃圾問題，讓消費者能更輕易地選擇零垃圾食物。新進場的競爭者為消費者的日用品和愛用品牌提供零垃圾的替代品，故消費者不必改變他們的日常習慣。

2019 年 9 月，關注食品浪費問題的瑞典應用程式 Karma 擴大了與家居日用品牌伊萊克斯（Electrolux）的合作，在斯德哥爾摩中央地鐵站測試了 Karma 智慧型冰箱，消費者可以在 Karma 應用程式中下訂打折食物，再從地鐵站的冰箱中取出商品。在返家途中更方便地取得食物。此概念是延伸自 2018 年在斯德哥爾摩 ICA Kvantum Liljeholmen 超市中試營的智慧型冰箱企劃。此賣點是，消費者可以在店內以較低的價格購買剩食。Karma 英國行銷經理查理・漢弗萊斯（Charlie Humphries）告訴偉門智威智庫，他們透過改變「日常行為模式中的微小行動改變現況。」

Loop 於 2019 年 5 月成立於美國，他們提供消費者耐用且可重複使用的包裝袋來購買日常雜貨、個人護理和家庭用品。消費者支付可退還的一次性押金來參與此計畫，Loop 則將他們所訂購的產品放在環保耐用的 Loop 托特包中，一一運送到他們家門口。等這些產

You love a saving,
don't choux?

Gander
JOIN THE CLUB

品用完以後，消費者再將產品包裝材料放回 Loop 托特包安排藏商取
件。最後運回 Loop 清理和將再利用。選擇自動補充方案的話，廠商則
會將顧客喜歡的產品，自動加入下一次的購物消單中。

在北愛爾蘭，新的應用程式 Gander 近來與亨德森集團（Henderson
Group）合作，協助他們的食品店面盡量減少浪費問題。該應用程式主動
通知當地用戶，讓他們可以在第一時間前往商店購買，在以色列，
SpareEat 這款應用程式為對抗食物浪費，借由幫助的使用者連線到當
地餐館、超市、咖啡館，讓他們可以買到過剩的食物，從而消除食物
浪費問題。這兩款應用程式皆於 2019 年秋季推出，為消費者和零售
商都帶來好處。

值得關注的原因：
藉由開發應用程式以及網路平台，善用現有食品和配送系統，企業幫
助消費者能更輕鬆便利地採用更環保的生活方式。品牌在這方面擁
有極大的機會，可以提供創新的方法來驅動消費者，並支持向永續生
活邁進的行動。

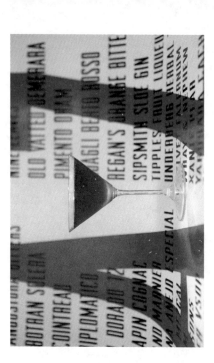

典雞尾酒。這些複雜的創作酒款，特色是將多種成分的冰塊投入飲用者所選的酒中。例如，老式立方體（The Old Fashioned Cube）將 23 種成分同時凍結在一起，以重現雞尾酒的辛辣、柑橘調、煙燻味。將這款冰塊加到少量的酒中，隨著冰塊融化，每口酒的風味都會隨之改變，帶來漸進式的獨特飲酒體驗。

值得關注的原因：

由於千禧世代和 Z 世代較少喝酒，酒類商品需要更多賣點才能吸引他們的注意。酒吧和餐館業正以更多花招因應，提供諸感官的吸睛飲調，激起消費客的興趣。並為他們提供無法在自家中複製的獨特體驗。

44

複雜的調酒

這些酒吧飲品中使用了 20 種以上的成分，對他們來說，多即是多！

Bompas & Parr 所調製的酒款 A-Z 雞尾酒，於 2019 年 1 月在時代廣場的 W 酒店推出，號稱每個字母對應一種內含成分。

哈利·帕爾（Harry Parr）是 Bompas & Parr 的共同創辦人，也是該款雞尾酒的創作者，他表示：「隨機地組合迷你酒吧的食材，很容易調出一些難以下嚥的飲品。目前的挑戰在於要創造不只新奇還要好喝的飲品。」

成分清單包括 8 款蘭姆酒、3 種白蘭地、1 種龍舌蘭酒、1 種琴酒、6 種利口酒、2 種苦精，以及苦艾酒和其他來自世界各地的開胃酒。

這樣做的目的是什麼？他們追求的是一種不尋常的飲酒體驗，一種消費者很難在自家裡調製出來的味道。帕爾表示：「混合這麼多蘭姆酒的想法是，想得到比簡單調酒更有趣的味道。」

布魯克林高檔墨西哥餐廳 Xixa 的飲品清單上，提供不同結構的經

JNDERMAN
HOMPSON　The A-Z Cocktail by Bompas & Parr. Image courtesy of Bompas & Parr

商品 & 飲品

WUNDERMAN
THOMPSON

Seesaw Coffee designed by Nota Architects. Photo by Shiyun Qian.

45

任意門般的室內設計

為了尋求菜單以外的優勢，咖啡館和餐館精心打造室內裝潢，把消費者送到異國風情的用餐場景中。

現在，喝一杯咖啡，可以同時在充滿禪意的庭園散步。點一杯調酒，可以把你推向外太空。

上海咖啡連鎖店 Seesaw Coffee 位於北京購物中心的分店中，建築師事務所 Nota Architects 創造出一條石頭砌的成的小徑，蜿蜒行過鬱鬱蔥蔥的樹葉和長滿青苔的巨石。小徑上抬頭可見櫻花樹，偶爾噴出白霧，瀰漫氣氛。空間中環繞著木製用板和長椅，而咖啡杯戲劇性地座落在燈光柔和的舞臺上。

在上海的愛探酒吧創意料理 (Icha Chateau) 中，Spacemen 設計工作室在天花板上掛了共 35,000 米長閃閃發光的分層黃金鏈，讓人聯想起中國傳統飲茶文化中的賜台設計。在這座擁有世界上最大星巴克的城市中，奢華的內部裝潢所突顯的是對室內設計越玩越大的賭注，讓走進咖啡廳有如置身劇院般享受。

東京也注重有如任意門般的室內設計。「肉の取り子」(Nikunoto-riko) 是一間日式燒烤餐廳，在東京與無數家開業餐廳相互競爭，而這裡之所以不同，是因為這是建築師家所亮二 (Ryoji Iedokoro) 之所以不同。

在山洞裡營造的用餐空間，採用低光光照，錫齒狀岩石牆面、半透明地板，讓人感覺好像站在水面上。

如果想要從注意門進入一個更遙遠的地方，可以前往東京有樂町的天文館酒吧（Tokyo's Bar Planetaria），酒吧經營者為柯尼卡美能達（Konica Minolta），他們建造了這個天文館，並在其中經營劇院，也定期舉辦飲食晚宴，讓東京居民可以在那幾小時中，躺在環形沙發上，在星空下喝酒。2019 年 8 月至 11 月期間，這座圓頂建築為訪客帶來夏威夷的夜空景致。

哥本哈根高檔餐廳 Alchemist 也設有天文館般的穹頂天花板。穹頂用餐區是客人到訪時會走向的區塊之一，整個體驗可能持續五小時之久。期間可能會有水母和塑膠袋的影像在頭頂上方游動，藉以提高大家對海洋污染的關注；也或者讓人有如置身於北極光閃爍的黑暗夜空下。Alchemist 的廚師兼創辦人拉斯穆斯．蒙克（Rasmus Munk）告訴《Food & Wine》雜誌，這家餐廳開設的目的「是要讓你感覺好像離開了外在世界，來到新的所在。」因而，誠如該餐廳網站所提醒顧客的那樣，這裡可能不是商務討論、成第一次約會這種緊張場合的理想去處。

值得關注的原因：

在咖啡館和餐館之間的競爭日漸升溫的時候，任意門型的室內設計漸漸嶄露頭角。談到如何吸引 Z 世代時更是如此。Z 世代歌頌體驗，並且渴望知道每杯茶或咖啡背後的故事，這些咖啡館和餐廳提供給消費者的，是無需實際登上火車、飛機或者快艇就能擁有暫時遠離生活的片刻時光。

WUNDERMAN THOMPSON

Top: Alchemist. Photo by Claes Bech-Poulsen
Bottom: Icha Chateau. Photo by Chen Xuan Min

品 & 飲品

46

生物多樣性飲食

以具有生物多樣性的美味料理，吸引關心環境議題的饕客。

自 1900 年代以來，美國已流失 90% 的原生種水果和蔬菜。根據聯合國糧食及農業組織（Food and Agriculture Organization）的資料指出，儘管全球有多達 30 萬種可食用植物，但在人類 75% 的飲食當中，僅包含 12 種植物與 5 種動物，而在現代的多數飲食模式下，從植物攝取的卡路里，有 60% 都被 3 種農作物佔據，也就是小麥、玉米、稻米。

只依賴少數幾種食物生活，會讓地球生態和食物安全都面臨極大的威脅。世界自然基金會（World Wide Fund for Nature）語重心長要維護人類健康、維持生態穩定、保育動物、生物多樣性具足輕重的地位。2019 年 3 月，這個野生動物保育組織與康寶（Knorr）合作，推出「50 種未來食物」（Future 50 Foods）活動，希望鼓勵民眾藉由多樣化飲食來保護瀕臨絕種的生物。

「50 種未來食物」報告中，列舉了 50 種可供大眾與廚師運用在料理中的植物。支持世界自然基金會的未來作物組織（Crops For the Future）亦參與了這項活動，該組織的研究顧問彼得．葛雷格利（Peter Gregory）解釋：「多樣化飲食不只對人類健康有益，也有利於保護環境。

WUNDERMAN
THOMPSON

Teranga restaurant, New York City

透過多樣化的生產系統，萬物得以生長，資源更能永續利用。」

2019 年 2 月，Teranga 西非料理餐廳在紐約開幕，經營者兼主廚皮爾·提亞姆（Pierre Thiam）十分注重能拓展飲食多樣性的食材。接受《富比士新聞》（Forbes.com）訪問時表示：「我選擇大家不常使用的食材做菜，讓我能對生物多樣性做點貢獻。以現在的狀況來看，設計菜單菜應是一項有意識且負責任的作為。」

Teranga 的特色食材有猴麵包樹、辣木、福尼奧米。在西方，這些食材常被忽略，但在西非料理中佔有重要地位。且還能維護生物多樣性。以古老的穀物福尼奧米為例，提亞姆表示：「這是一種對地球有益的植物，因為它耐旱，只需要兩個月就可以收成，而且升糖指數低，所以對健康也很有幫助。」

Lou 是一間於 2019 年 9 月在納許維爾開幕的餐廳。這間餐廳為了讓飲食多樣化，以椰棗與蕎麥等食材，取代一般慣用的精製糖與精製麵粉。

全球作物多樣性信託基金會（Global Crop Diversity Trust）是一個支持作物多樣性、維護全球食安的組織，執行長瑪莉·哈加（Marie Haga）接受《富比士新聞》（Forbes.com）訪問時表示：「透過積極提昌廚房中與廚房外的生物多樣性，可以提升大眾對不同食材的興趣，或者創造更多樣化的食材市場。在這當中，廚師扮演著關鍵角色。」

值得關注的原因：
近年純素主義與拒用塑膠吸管等風潮興起，表現出饕客為了保護環境改變飲食習慣的意願，而多樣化飲食讓饕客行動主義者多了一個選擇，也提供了一頓更美味的佳餚。

> 我選擇大家不常使用的食材做菜，讓我能對生物多樣性做點貢獻。以現在的狀況來看，設計菜單菜應是一項有意識且負責任的作為。

Teranga 經營者兼主廚｜皮爾·提亞姆（Pierre Thiam）

47

共享廚房

烹飪開始成為集體活動。

都市人口密集，所以必須更有效地運用空間，而初出茅廬的美食創業家最需要的就是精省的創業良方。受到共享工作空間爆炸性成長的影響，共享廚房也在世界各地如雨後春筍興起以迎合市場需求，不僅提供創新與交流的空間，更是烹飪與社交的場域。

沙米亞‧賓漢（Samia Bingham）為 Flavors Culinary Group 的創辦人兼執行長。2019 年 7 月，她帶領這間位於馬里蘭州的新興烹飪服務公司參加 UPS Store 和《Inc》雜誌在洛杉磯舉辦的小型企業挑戰賽（Small Biz Challenge），並贏得冠軍。她用挑戰贏得的獎金打造 Flavors, The Culinary Complex 風味料理基地，預計於 2020 年夏天開幕。廚師可以在此揮灑廚藝創意，也可以和烹飪社群的成員互相交流。

2019 年春天，WeWork 公司在曼哈頓創立 WeWork Food Labs 料理實驗室。最初以會員制為主，該料理實驗室的紐約旗艦店以及旗下第一個加速器計畫皆於 10 月啟動。

WeWork Food Labs 營運主管梅納罕‧凱茲（Menachem Katz）接受偉門智威專訪問時表示：「WeWork Food Labs 料理實驗室的目標，是培養這些在烹飪與農業領域中的創業家。我們提供工具與資源，讓他們能為我們的社群成為全球業界面對的挑戰，創造出可持續的解決方案。」申請成功以後，創業者除了會得到 WeWork Food Labs 的協助之外，還可以接觸業界專家、投資人、創業投資機構、參與相關活動與工作坊，並可得到研發廚房的空間使用權。

2020 年，Mission Kitchen 將於倫敦首次展店，開設兩間共享廚房，會員同樣能使用專業料理空間，並享有諮詢的服務，也可參與相關活動。

儘管如此，共享廚房並非專業人士獨有。在日本這樣公寓空間窄小的國家，共享廚房也比比皆是。位於東京的 Kitchen Studio Suiba 公寓可以租用的空間裡享用彼此烹煮的餐點，餐飲業人士也可以在這裡與消費者互動。

值得關注的原因：
共享的空間與廚房設備令計多人望之卻步，而共享廚房的興起，則同時為家庭料理和專業烹飪提供了一個既實用又能互相交流的空間。

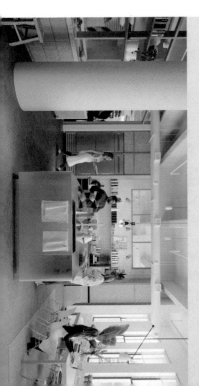

48

清醒酒吧

無精飲品風潮席捲無數餐廳與酒吧。

根據世界衛生組織（World Health Organization）的資料顯示，在2000年到2016年之間，全球飲酒者數量下降了5%，隨之而來的是消費者開始選擇禁酒或不再縱酒狂歡，而這群消費者要的不只是簡單的果汁或軟性飲料這類酒精替代品，而是開始尋找全新調製飲品。為滿足越趨挑剔的味蕾，餐廳和酒吧也開始設計無酒精飲品菜單，創造無酒精的飲酒環境。

Getaway 酒吧於 2019 年 4 月開幕，為布魯克林的禁酒者提供了時尚奢華的社交空間，菜單上的精緻飲品口感多變，還用了有趣的食材，如粉紅胡椒、杜松子以及香茅，但裡頭不摻一滴酒精。

紐約 Listen Bar 自 2018 年 10 月開幕以來，就一直是禁酒者的天堂。Listen Bar 每個月會舉辦一場主題派對，消費者可以享用無酒精的雞尾酒與精釀啤酒，甚至還有現場刻青等活動，證明沒有酒精也能嗨翻一整夜。無論用品版的真心話大冒險、杜松子以及香茅，但裡頭不摻一滴酒精。

位於都柏林的 The Virgin Mary 酒吧於 2019 年 5 月開幕，號稱全

WUNDERMAN
THOMPSON

Listen Bar in New York City. Photo by Tonje Thilesen

愛爾蘭第一間永久經營的清醒酒吧。這間酒吧完全遵守一般酒吧的營業時間,與正常酒吧的氣圍相比也絲毫不差。The Virgin Mary 提供精心手作且饒富變化的雞尾酒,甚至還提供從啤酒龍頭流出的氮氣咖啡,無論口感還是外觀都與健力士啤酒 (Guinness) 相差無幾。

倫敦的 Redemption 酒吧則專攻有健康意識的消費客群。這家酒吧提供豐富營養的無酒精飲料,原料包含活性炭、冷藏啤酒中的大麻二酚萃取物,以及使用啤酒龍頭供應的康普茶。宣稱飲品中的大對身體健康有諸多益處。

對於想投入無酒精市場的酒吧而言,Seedlip 這樣的無酒精飲品製造商讓一切都變得簡單許多。Seedlip 出產的無酒精以多種香料與草本製成,至今已在 300 間以上的米其林餐廳、以及超過 25 個國家中作為酒類替代品販售。Aecorn 出產的無酒精餐前酒,以黑皮諾 (Pinot Noir)、莫尼耶 (Meunier) 與夏多內 (Chardonnay) 這三種葡萄製成,可直接當作義大利開胃酒 (spritz) 飲用,也可作為調製雞尾酒的原料。

值得關注的原因:

隨著消費者的健康意識提升,酒吧和飲料品牌也開始順應潮流,讓消費者不會因為這樣錯過社交的機會。

WUNDERMAN THOMPSON

Top left: Redemption bar, London. Photo by Jessica Allegretti
Top right and bottom: The Virgin Mary bar, Dublin

品 & 飲品

JNDERMAN
HOMPSON   Getaway bar, Brooklyn

49

再生農業革命

食品公司以再生農業迎向氣候變遷帶來的挑戰。

集約農業對土壤的耗損十分嚴重，以致聯合國（United Nation）發出警告，認為人類可能只剩下 60 次的收成。為了處理這個問題，許多食品公司開始要求供應商轉型為再生農業，再生農業技法能幫助土壤恢復從前的土質，還能增加碳封存量，減少溫室氣體，進而創造雙贏——生產對環境有益，也對健康有幫助的食物。

英國 Riverford Organic Farmers 有機農產公司創辦人蓋·辛格一華森（Guy Singh-Watson）接受《Pebble》雜誌訪問時表示：「種在健康土壤裡的食物就當比較健康，營養較為均衡，毒素也更少。所以如果你有自己種菜的話，你就要開始注意菜園裡的土質。我曾經看過有農夫不願意吃自己種的作物。」

達能集團（Danone）目前帶領 19 家大型食品公司，包含雀巢（Nestlé）、聯合利華（Unilever）和家樂氏（Kellogg）等，與他們一同推廣再生農業，希望可以重塑人類的飲食系統，並找回食物多樣性。根據聯合國糧食及農業組織（Food and Agriculture Organization）的資料指出，全世界的農產總量中，有多達三分之二的產量僅由 9 種作物組成，這是土壤之所以耗損的關鍵影響因素。

> 種在健康土壤裡的食物就會比較健康，營養較為均衡，毒素也更少。
>
> Riverford Organic Farmers 創辦人｜蓋‧辛格－華森（Guy Singh-Watson）

品牌。這款啤酒以一種十分新奇的穀物凱恩札（Krenza）製成，而這種成分也成為該品牌的獨特標記。凱恩札擁有如品牌名稱所宣示的「長根」，所以相較於其他穀物，它可以吸收更多大氣中的碳，種植所需的水利和農藥卻更少，也有助於防止土壤侵蝕。

值得關注的原因：

未來，實行再生農業的食品公司，將會成為對抗氣候變遷、減少溫室氣體、促進土壤保育的最大助力。

通用磨坊（General Mills）也發表聲明，強調會全力支持再生農業，並承諾在 2030 年之前，將再生農業運用到美國近 1 百萬英畝的通用磨坊所屬農地上。此外，通用磨坊也捐贈 65 萬美元給 Kiss the Ground 親近土壤組織。這個組織會教導農民使用農地的技能，增強土地的復原力。通用磨坊旗下的 Annie's Homegrown 天然食品公司為了提升民眾對土壤健康的關注，也推出了「土壤很重要」（Soil Matters）這項企劃，以再生農業製作商品，並以限定版包裝販售。

戶外服品牌 Patagonia 抓緊對抗氣候變遷的機會，與位於奧勒岡的 Hopworks Urban Brewery 酒廠合作，推出 Long Root 啤酒

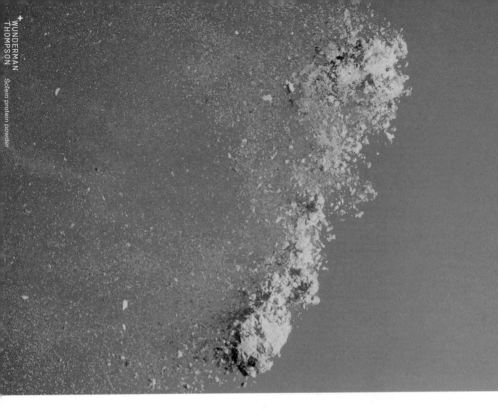

熱門新食材

人們對氣候變遷的關注讓原本默默無聞的食材
有了新的風貌。

索林蛋白粉

位於芬蘭的 Solar Foods 正在研發一種由空氣、水、電力就能製成的蛋白粉。索林蛋白粉（Solein powder）預計於 2021 年上市，裡面含有約 65% 的蛋白質成分，與黃豆和海藻相當。根據太陽能食品公司的網站說明，此產品為「一種全新的食物種類，不僅天然，而且不會造成碳業與水產養殖業的負擔。」

隨著可耕地逐漸減少，以及食肉的倫理問題一再浮上台面，全球都開始積極研究未來的蛋白質來源，包括實驗室的人造肉、酥炸蟋蟀或是麵包蟲泥。以上每一種食物都有缺點，例如人造肉造價不菲，而食用昆蟲讓很多人覺得噁心。

索林蛋白粉沒有任何上述的問題。其釀造過程類似釀酒的發酵過程，酒是將酵母放進含有糖分的液體中，而索林蛋白粉的微生物則是由氫氣和二氧化碳餵養成。無論外觀或味道都像是一般小麥做的麵粉，可以用來製作優格、奶昔、義大利麵等食物。

Solar Foods 的科技引起某族群的關注：這群人期待可以在缺乏（有

食品 & 飲品

些是極度缺乏）可耕地與陽光的地方生產食物。執行長帕夕・范倪卡（Pasi Vainikka）接受彭博新聞台（BNN Bloomberg）訪問時表示，目前公司正與歐洲太空總署（European Space Agency）合作，發展火星任務所需的相關科技。

西瓜籽

西瓜籽是中國新年和亞洲節日常出現的傳統點心，現在更脫胎換骨，躍上全球健康食品市場。

根據 Grand View Research, Inc. 的資料指出，全球西瓜籽市場預計於 2025 年成長到 7 億 5 千 1 百萬美元的產值。市場上將以未精製的西瓜籽為大宗，這類種籽富含營養成分，可成為脂肪的絕佳替代品。

除此之外，也有人用十分新潮的方式運用西瓜籽。Atomo 是一家位於西雅圖的新創公司，致力於咖啡的逆向工程，希望能不使用咖啡豆就煮出更永續的咖啡。

根據氣候研究中心（Climate Institute）的資料顯示，到了 2050 年，適合種植咖啡的土地可能會因氣候變遷而縮水將近一半；而該機構的研究員也指出，到了 2080 年，野生咖啡樹這類對咖啡農十分重要的基因來源也可能絕跡。Atomo 公司的咖啡，使用來自西瓜籽、葵瓜子殼、阿拉伯樹膠，以及瑪黛茶的咖啡因混合而成。共同創辦人賈萊特・史托福斯（Jarret Stopforth）接受全國廣播公司商業頻道（CNBC）訪問時表示：他們的目標是「模仿咖啡的核心特色──包括稠度、口感、香氣和味道。」Atomo 希望能在 2020 年將

人們對永續
和氣候議題的關注
帶動飲食產業的創新，
也讓先前默默無聞的食材
有了新的風貌。

第一批冰釀咖啡送達 Kickstarter 募資平台的贊助者手中，並於年中開始零售。

西瓜籽也二度躋身全食超市（Whole Foods）2020 年十大飲食趨勢名單中，因為它本身即是可以替代黃豆醬成分的純素食品，同時也能被做成西瓜籽抹醬。

蝶豆花

全世界的主廚和調酒專家都開始嘗試用蝶豆花鮮豔的靛藍，以及色彩多變的特性開發新品。這種在東南亞糕點與米食料理中常見的花，開始在全球市場綻放，因其營養價值與獨特的色彩而廣受歡迎。

《Thirsty》雜誌於 2019 年 5 月發表了一篇文章，介紹美國 8 種不同的藍色蝶豆花調酒，如紐約維格爾 Geist 酒吧推出的「v小紫羅蘭」(the Little Violeta)。其中還包含琴酒、鳳梨和蕎麥食材。聖地牙哥 Madison on Park 推出的「紫雨」(the Purple Rain) 還添加了水蜜桃利口酒、檸檬、蛋白，還有幾滴大麻籽油。《Food & Drink》雜誌也推出適合在 2019 年夏天自製的 3 種蝶豆花飲品，只要利用檸檬酸就可以讓蝶豆花的色澤由藍轉紫。

在孟買克拉巴（Colaba）的 Woodside Inn 旅店，使用蝶豆花為義大利龍蝦細扁麵增添色彩；澳洲的 Hunter Distillery 酒廠也出產了蝶豆花利口酒。

值得關注的原因：

人們對永續和氣候議題的關注帶動飲食產業的創新，也讓先前默默無聞的食材有了新的風貌。

> Z世代重新定義了美妝能做什麼、應該用來做什麼，他們推崇完全自由的表達方式，並挑戰美和美妝相關的規範。

化妝師｜多尼艾拉·戴維（Doniella Davy）

是 Vinylic Lip 唇蜜能打造超閃亮漆光效果，而 Glitter Gelée 眼影蜜則能創造如寶石般閃耀的眼妝，這些都是畫出《高校十八禁》仿妝的必需品。

風格極致強烈的大膽妝容，在過往的認知中僅專屬於高級時裝場合，但現在因為《高校十八禁》而開始趨向大眾化了。戴薇表示：該劇的創作者山姆·萊文森（Sam Levinson）鼓勵她「引進一種全新的美妝語言。」她也因此為 Z 世代和其他人開關了美妝實驗的全新可能。

值得關注的原因：
《高校十八禁》已經挖掘出 Z 世代對於美妝的渴望，並向他們傳達「美妝刷具可以描繪出故事」這層含義及概念。品牌應該重新思考如何以美妝品回應今晝愛自我表現和期望打破成見的青年世代，讓他們利用美妝傳達自己的感受，且在品牌的創意啟發之下，進行更多美妝實驗，更重要的是讓他們從中找到樂趣。

NDERMAN
OMPSON

Euphoria. Images courtesy of HBO

52

分子美容會館

奢華保養品牌開始投入 DNA 分析，目標是打造量身定做的美麗配方。

遺傳護理公司 EpigenCare 於 2018 年贏得強生創新公司 (Johnson & Johnson Innovation) 舉辦的生技美容競賽，於 2019 年 2 月開始試驗新產品 Skintelli，利用表觀遺傳學來分析皮膚，並計劃在 2020 年全面推出。這個以消費者導向為需求的個人化服務，使用了新一代 DNA 定序技術，為消費者提供更深層的膚質和遺傳基因的相關解說。

英國奢侈品零售商哈洛德百貨 (Harrods) 將 DNA 分析服務，納入旗下美容診所 The Wellness Clinic 的服務項目之中，該診所於 2018 年開業，是一家綜合美容養生會館。若要使用這項基因辨識 (Gen Identity) 服務，客人需提供唾液樣本，並完成生活習慣的相關評估，檢測結果將用於皮膚診斷和療程規劃。該診所的賈西亞·安東 (José María García Antón) 解釋：「我們根據每個人的 DNA 分析結果，為他們的肌膚檢測結果、診斷會打造一套獨特且個人化的美容護理療程。」依據肌膚檢測結果、診斷和遺傳基因，為其定製專屬面霜，並針對個人特定需求以及遺傳基因，為客戶量身定製方案。

人膚質相關的遺傳性需求，並為六成以上影響膚況的因素提出解釋。」

值得關注的原因：

像 23andMe 這類的服務已經使 DNA 檢測成為大眾的選項之一，而消費者也開始尋找新的方式，將基因分析融入日常生活之中，未來從飲食層面到美容習慣，都將徹底改變。

流行美容品牌 Biologique Recherche 也利用 DNA 的概念，打造最新的頂級產品。My Beauty DNA 試劑盒藉由分析口腔細胞採樣，來評估個人遺傳傾向和皮膚問題，例如膠原蛋白分解、糖化狀況（導致深層皺紋的糖類生產過剩）、發炎、敏感、自由基損傷和色素沉澱⋯⋯等。

Biologique Recherche 品牌經理拉斐爾·法雷（Raphaëlle Faure）表示：「瞭解遺傳傾向可以幫助患者和皮膚科醫生，讓他們更清楚這個

53

超人類之美

設計師開始尋找傳統之外的美貌標準，嘗試超越人類的造型，這樣的作為正如大眾所見，將會讓美的概念更進化。

趨勢預測家和設計師潔拉汀‧惠里（Geraldine Wharry）為美容雜誌《Dazed Beauty》撰寫了〈預示超人類的未來〉（The transhuman future is here）一文，文中指出：「世界各地的手術房、實驗室、藝術家、科技、設計師的工作室都展開了變革。」惠里所描繪的是一個由科學、科技、設計師匯聚一堂，共同崇尚超人類美學的前景。她預測：「新的美貌標準將從這個超人類的情景中產生，突變創作將殖民現今的傳統玩實感。」

隨著科學界用將人和機器穩定地結合在一起，美容和時尚產業也藉此概念，來創造超越傳統美學的形式和特色。2019 年秋冬季，巴黎世家（Balenciaga）將模特兒送上巴黎時裝週的伸展台，並展現以具有變形特徵、容戴誇張、雕塑型顱骨、過度豐滿的嘴唇等為特色的 2020 年春夏新品。這家高級時尚品牌解釋：這種造型的主旨為「玩轉現在，過去、未來的美麗標準。」

NDERMAN
OMPSON

Balenciaga SS20 ready-to-wear collection. Images courtesy of Filippo Fior/Gorunway.com

世界各地的手術局、實驗室、藝術家及設計師的工作室都展開了變革，超人類的未來已然到來。

趨勢預測者、設計師｜潔拉汀‧惠里 (Geraldine Wharry)

瑞克‧歐文斯 (Rick Owens) 在他 2019 年的秋冬系列中，以假角、黑色凸眼，以及其他能改變容貌的特徵來取代傳統妝容的美學。

2018 年 10 月《時尚》(Vogue) 為自稱「超人類」的 Instagram 網紅 Fecal Matter 雙人組做了專題報導，並於 2019 年 3 月在《時尚》的網站上充分展示這對情侶長達三小時的極致美容妝扮流程。這兩位藝術家已經做出了一雙與人類皮膚融為一體、要價 10,000 美元的靴子。他們以這款長跟鞋取代了傳統的細跟高跟鞋，並計劃在未來發行更便宜、更好入手的版本。

值得關注的原因：

超人類美學演變自 2018 年的「怪誕美妝」(Grotesque Beauty) 及傳統美學運動。這項新的美學態度代表人類在根除傳統美貌標準的過程中，又向前邁進了一大步。而在自然生態和人類生存的層面上，因為消費者和設計師預見了未來可能會發生的重大變動，因此開始重新審視美的定義。

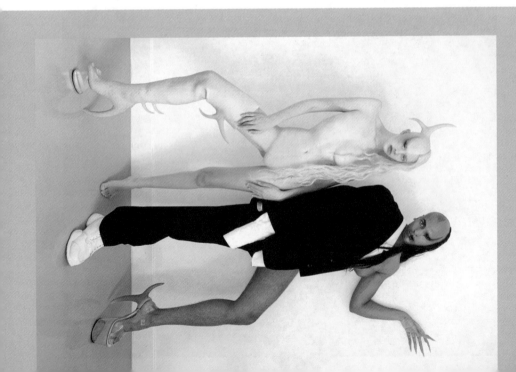

54

肌膚情報員

保養愛好者轉而求助科學專家，以期推出具有技術成分且功效精確的產品。

2016 年諾貝爾化學獎得主佛瑞賽·史多達爾爵士（Sir Fraser Stoddart）開發了高級保養系列—Noble Panacea，並於 2019 年 10 月推出。從他的研究衍生而且有註冊商標「有機分子容器」（Organic Molecular Vessels）比皮膚細胞小 10,000 倍，因此能為肌膚提供一個新的產品交付系統，提高產品的滲透率和吸收率。這位科學家說：「精準選擇和封裝活性成分是為了達到前所未有的結果。」

美國護膚公司 Atolla 於 2019 年 8 月成立，其使命是讓消費者成為自己皮膚的保養專家。該品牌由麻省理工學院（Massachusetts Institute of Technology）的畢業生所創立，利用機器學習和數據分析並快速精確且高度個人化的產品配方。從藥物、飲食、到當地空氣品質、污染、以及每個人皮膚油脂、濕度、pH 值狀況等，全面納入考量。每個月用戶都會進行一次皮膚測試，並收到新的精華液，精確的成分解析配方一同附上，詳細說明各成分的作用。

因此，如同 Atolla 的演算法可以從數據中學習而提高。Maelove 為皮膚健康的知識也會隨著使用產品次數的增加而提高。另一家由麻省理工學院畢業生所創立的保養品牌，團隊由癌症研究員、大腦研究員、化學工程師、醫生所組成。該品牌解釋：「首先，我們翻找同行評審的期刊查看驗證過的臨床研究，並與傑出的化學家、皮膚科醫生、整形外科醫師、醫學研究人員合作，制定出配方的完美藍圖。」

值得關注的原因：

科學保養員為了服務越來越多受過優良教育的消費者，因而提升了產品的標準。這些新進品牌以科學級別以皮膚知識和對皮膚的深度了解，滿足顧客對教育的需求，以及他們想深入了解皮膚的求知慾。

NDERMAN　　Above: Atolla skincare
OMPSON　　Right: Noble Panacea skincare

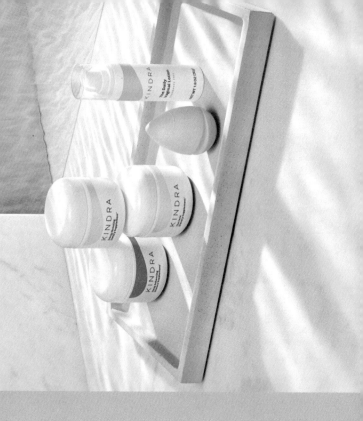

55

更年期美容

美容業正緊抓一批員有強大消費力的客群：經歷更年期的女性。

寶僑集團（Procter & Gamble）旗下的新品牌 Kindra 表示：「歷經幾百萬年之後，我們認為是時候了。」該品牌為更年期的女性提供了美容保健系列商品，但他們只是察覺到這個重大商機的眾多品牌之一。

根據北美更年期協會（North American Menopause Society）的數據顯示：到了 2025 年，全球將有 10 億以上的女性經歷更年期。雖然更年期不是什麼新鮮事，但女性看待這一階段人生的方式正在改變。正如我們的報告「彈性世代：女性選物」（Elastic generation: the female edit）所揭示的，新的世代正在打破規則，重新打造這 50 歲以後的生活。

菲‧芮德（Fay Reid，@9to5menopause）是倫敦欲的部落客，她的目標是要消除更年期的污名。她希望品牌意識到像這樣 40、50 歲的女性仍然喜歡美妝和時尚，就像我們在 30 多歲時一樣，我還是想要過得漂漂亮亮、開開心心。」

NDERMAN OMPSON　Kindra beauty and wellbeing products. Photo by Joel Stans

更年期給女性帶來了許多變化，除了熱潮紅外，還會經歷皮膚乾燥、暗沉、缺水等問題，皮膚變得缺乏彈性，甚至突然變成乾性。

偉門智威智庫的報告指出：「在女性傾向排斥抗老資訊的同時（53至72歲的英國女性中，有68%的人使用美容產品讓自己維持在最佳狀態，而非讓自己看起來更年輕，品牌若能為她們提供專屬、更有效的保養方案，就能需求來商機。」

除了 Kindra 之外，還有其他對更年期一樣友善的品牌於 2019 年進入市場。Pause Well-aging 是一間由蘿鶶爾．魏茨納（Rochelle Weitzner）創立的美國新創公司，魏茨納是一位美容界的資深

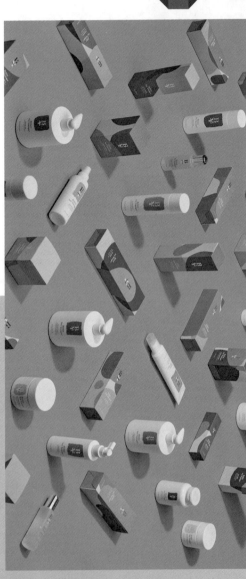

人士。她進入更年期後，意識到市場缺乏合適的保養品。Better Not Younger，一個解決更年期相關髮質問題（如變薄和乾裂）的美國品牌，該品牌同樣由發現市場需求的業界女性創立。除了新創公司外，薇姿（Vichy）這類的大品牌也開始涉此一市場。

值得關注的原因：

這些品牌目前都是針對所得客群推出高價格以及全面性的產品。若能擴大所有婦女的需求，提供更實惠的價格以及全面性的解決方案。滿足所有種族的需求，那麼這一領域還會有更大的商機。布德說：「我敢保證，如果有品牌可以提供全面性的產品，他們的產品絕對會銷售一空。」

56

現實生活濾鏡

數位覆寫技術給帶美妝消費者全新視角，讓他們在實驗造型時能有所參考。

這些美妝濾鏡不僅能激發創意，也能應用到實際生活中。它們重新反映了當代流行趨勢，讓使用者能同時線上和線下生活中體驗樂趣。

2019 年 9 月，全新的保養品牌 Starface 推出了一系列名為 Hydro-Stars 的星形粉刺貼片，將表情符號美學帶進現實世界中。俏皮的痘痘貼與星星符號相似，將青春痘的補救措施展現得更有趣，很適合拿來拍 Instagram 的大頭貼。該品牌的共同創辦人茱莉·蕭特（Julie Schott）告訴《時尚》（Vogue）：「這是一件微妙的配飾——在你和他人對面時，可以觀察的小重點，不超上自上鏡，而且很可愛。」

最近抖音（TikTok）上有一項風潮被《Dazed Beauty》雜誌稱為「身體改造輪盤」。從臨時型的臉部貼紙，到永久型的穿環，抖音上流行的「穿環挑戰」（#piercingchallenge）標籤，在使用者閉眼時，會為其穿環或貼上貼紙再次呈現了昔日於 Snapchat 上蔚為風潮的數位穿環，這項挑戰的重點是，使用者要在隨機數位穿環完成後於

現實世界中也打上同樣的環。直到 2020 年 1 月中旬為止，該標籤的流覽量超過 9800 萬次。有一些使用者確實接受了挑戰，其他使用者則只戴上眼下的穿環。

值得關注的原因

Z 世代和較年輕的千禧世代熱愛數位濾鏡，也願意拓展真的界線。數位濾鏡也因此開始對人體美貌帶來直接和真實的影響。

WUNDERMAN
THOMPSON

Optune by Shiseido

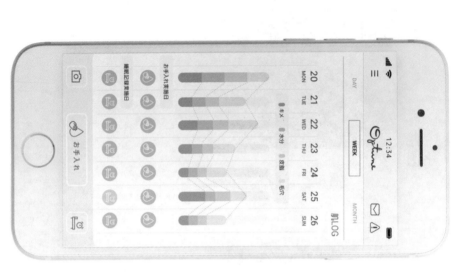

57

肌膚保養 2.0

高度個人化需求成長，
推動產品量身與塗擦方式上的創新

2019 年 7 月，日本專櫃美容品牌資生堂（Shiseido）推出連結物聯網服務的個人化護膚系統 Optune。該系統的應用程式能幫助用戶追蹤皮膚狀況、睡眠時間、荷爾蒙量、環境因子，並配有一組桌面型保養液分裝機，搭配五瓶精華液填充罐。透過 Optune 應用程式每日（甚至每小時）一次的膚況分析，調配出符合使用者當日肌膚需求的客製化精華液，並能及時送到使用者當中。

露得清（Neutrogena）也重新思考了保養品調製及塗擦的方式，以符合高度個人化的需求。該公司研發的「露得清 MaskiD」在 2019 年美國消費電子用品展（CES 2019）上亮相，是一款專門為每個人獨特臉形和肌膚需求所打造的 3D 列印面膜。這款高度個人化、依需求生產的面膜，不僅針對使用者的特殊需求特製活性成分，還能確保這些成分在使用者臉上完全服貼到位。

露得清公司的研究總監暨全球美容技術主管邁克‧索瑟（Michael Southall）向《誘惑》（Allure）雜誌解釋：「透過微型 3D 列印技術，我們可以實際、精準地得知眼睛與鼻子、嘴巴對齊的位置，以及額頭的高度。」

類似魔杖型的裝置，可以數位掃描使用者的皮膚，並使用 LED 燈和內建的數位相機分析膚色，即時偵測斑點並提供專屬的美容保養精華來治療和矯正皮膚狀況。

值得關注的原因：

科技為新型皮膚保養策略鋪路，開創產品創新與應用的全新領域。

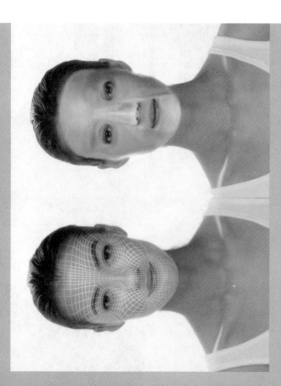

「3D 列印的關鍵在於，我們可以將您想要的活性成分放到面膜上的任何地方，而不是使用單一產品擦遍全臉。」

Opté 也利用 3D 列印重新構思消費者塗抹保養品的方式。Opté 是寶僑集團（Procter & Gamble）所投資的首批品牌之一，由創新部門「寶僑創投公司」（P&G Ventures）所投資提供資金。結合光學、特有的演算法、列印科技，為顧客提供塗擦保養品的全新方式。Opté 於 2019 年美國消費電子用品展上發表，他們的精密皮膚保養系統是一件

NDERMAN
OMPSON

Above: Neutrogena's MaskiD
Right: Opté Precision Skincare System by Procter & Gamble

睫毛綻放

58

眉毛也許是2019年美妝實驗的重點，但2020年似乎將由睫毛取而代之。

美妝大師派特‧麥葛瑞絲 (Pat McGrath) 的創作一向是美妝潮流的先驅。在 2020 年春季的時裝秀上，她展現了許多富有創意的睫毛造型。麥葛瑞絲為時尚品牌 Marc Jacobs 的時裝秀創作了 61 款不同妝容—她稱之為「對現實生活的理想詮釋」—其中包括以誇張的藝術手法呈現 60 年代時尚的蜘蛛狀假睫毛。麥葛瑞絲也為范倫鐵諾 (Valentino) 創作出以以黃金製作而成的睫毛，並命名為「華麗的迷戀」(Opulent Obsession)。然而，這個概念也可能轉往前衛的方向發展。在古馳 (Gucci) 的伸展台上，以左派妝容美學著稱的化妝師湯瑪士‧德‧克魯伊佛 (Thomas de Kluyver) 在眉毛位置和眼睛下方都放置了假睫毛，而另一位以實驗風格著稱的設計師伊薩瑪亞‧弗倫奇 (Isamaya Ffrench) 則為設計師奧利維爾‧泰斯金斯 (Olivier Theyskens) 做出有點扁兄、纏結在一起的睫毛，她稱之為「蜘蛛腿」。

這種對伸展台睫毛造型的關注，是在假睫毛市場的成長背景下應運而生的。根據 Grand View Research 在 2019 年 10 月所做的一份報告指出：「2025 年前，全球假睫毛市場將達到 16 億美元的價值，

年複合成長率為 5.4%。」並補充說:「2018 年美國假睫毛市場價值
超過 4 億美元;到 2025 年前,亞太地區假睫毛市場的年複合成長
率將達到 6.6%。」

值得關注的原因:

睫毛提供了一種突顯眼睛的方式,與近來對眉毛的關注形成對比。「眉
毛似乎退居二線。目前是睫毛取代了一切。」這種對睫毛的關注可
在 2019 年的一次採訪中,麥葛瑞絲告訴《Fashionista》網站:「眉
能會催生出與睫毛膏相關的產品試驗。畢竟近幾年來,睫毛膏的熱
潮已趨於緩和。就像 2019 年時《the Business of Fashion》雜誌所
質疑的:睫毛膏是否「已不再重要?」,睫毛的文藝復興,是否已經悄
悄展開了呢?

NDERMAN
OMPSON

Pat McGrath for Valentino

微生物群系美容

59

美容逐漸朝向生物領域發展：
目前有一系列的美容品牌開始結合生物學與皮膚保養，並將注意力轉向皮膚的微生物群系，也就是保護肌膚的細菌屏障。

Kinship 於 2019 年 11 月成立，是一家致力於解決皮膚微生物群系問題的最新美容品牌。Kinship 的產品是採用 Kinbiome 配製而成，這是一種有註冊商標的植物性益生菌，為勿讓肌膚的天然屏障，使用專利的微生物群系技術開發而成。

同一個月，由美妝品牌 Bite Beauty 創始人蘇珊·朗繆爾（Susanne Langmuir）成立的 SL&Co 公司也推出了一種平衡皮膚微生物群系的產品。這款於 2019 年 11 月發布的青春 1 號粉末（The Powder of Youth No 1）是該品牌產品線中的第一款產品，其潔顏粉、去角質產品、面膜皆由乳酸桿菌發酵製成，可保護肌膚上的好菌。

對於推動這一方面的轉變，獨立品牌並非孤軍奮戰；傳統美容公司也開始投入微生物研究和相關的產品開發工作。

雅詩蘭黛（Estée Lauder）與具有領導地位的微生物群系研究公司

Nizo 合作，於 2019 年 11 月發布成果，說明皮膚老化與皮膚上的微生物群系組成有正向關聯。雅詩蘭黛全球微生物學和發酵研發部門的副總史帝夫·施尼格 (Steve Schnitger) 表示：「雅詩蘭黛一直在研究乳酸桿菌培養工法，並在乳酸桿菌萃取物的局部應用中，發現了幾個正面的益處。」

2019 年 3 月，來雅集團 (L'Oréal) 宣佈與微生物遺傳學公司 uBiome 建立新的合作關係，以推動微生物群系研究發展。來雅科技育成中心 (the L'Oréal Technology Incubator) 全球副總裁吉夫·巴羅奇 (Guive Balooch) 告訴偉門智威智庫，此舉可讓他們「更加了解細菌多樣性與皮膚健康之間的相互作用。」來雅此前還與 Epicore Biosystems 合作，那是一間專門研發微流體平台和穿戴式感測器的新創公司。在 2019 年美國消費電子用品展上，來雅首次公開由理膚寶水公司 (La Roche-Posay) 開發的「我的肌膚酸鹼值追蹤器」(My Skin Track pH)，這是一款穿戴式的感測器，利用與 Epicore Biosystems 合作開發的微流體技術測量皮膚 pH 值。巴羅奇指出，「雖然科學界和醫學界早就知道皮膚 pH 值與常見皮膚問題之間的關聯」，但「我的肌膚酸鹼值追蹤器」更進一步發展此概念，「讓消費者能夠獲得與自身相關的膚況資訊，找出符合個人需求的產品。」

值得關注的原因：

巴羅奇說：「生物學研究可以把肌膚保養帶到一個新的境界。」隨著消費者對使用生物方法，進行保養需求與日俱增，傳統品牌和新創企業都重新將注意力轉向微生物群系美容上。

ᴡᴜɴᴅᴇʀᴍᴀɴ
ᴛʜᴏᴍᴘꜱᴏɴ

60

藍色美容學

美妝品牌轉向海洋，從中找尋最新的天然成分。

天然、永續的保養品越來越受歡迎。據《Global Cosmetic Industry》雜誌報導，由顧問公司 Hamacher Resource Group 於 2019 年 3 月進行的研究顯示，去年有 30% 的保養品消費者（鎖定女性和年輕族群）提高了天然成分產品的購買量，而海洋現在也被認定為含有豐富天然成分的來源地。

One Ocean Beauty 的部分創業使命在於保護海洋，並打造以海洋原料為配方的產品。其創辦人瑪瑟拉・賈西（Marcella Cacci）告訴《Well&Good》雜誌：這個過程包括「從大自然中分離出單個細胞成微微生物，透過生物科技在真實驗室中重新培養，成為永續生產的方式。」該品牌的產品包括由深水魚類水解海洋膠原蛋白所製成的「海洋膠原蛋白膠囊」（Marine Collagen capsules）以及來自日本海的藻類萃取物製成的「深海滋養保濕霜」（Replenishing Deep Sea Moisturizer），宣稱能「緩和發炎症狀，提亮膚色。」

2019 年 8 月，英國保養品牌 Freya & Bailey 於抗污染美妝產品中加入海藻，作為膠原蛋白的替代成份。旗下的「航行吧！海洋眼部

精挑細選的海洋成分不僅功能強大，而且天然、永續。

Company 推出，產品含有來自海洋和植物萃取的天然成分，包括魚子醬萃取物和魷魚墨汁。

值得關注的原因：
保養品中注入精選的海洋成分，不僅能將消費者對天然永續產品的渴望與活性強大的獨特原料結合，而且這些產品的背後，都還有個迷人的故事。

凝膠」(Sail! Marine Eye Gel) 由海藻、水果萃取物、維他命調製而成，可幫助膠原蛋白增生。

以成分層面來說，《CosmeticsDesign USA》網站指出，2019 年北美化妝品展 (In-Cosmetics North America 2019) 上出現了幾種來自海洋的活性成分，其中包括 Seadermium 這款由 LipoTrue 公司所生產的海洋活性成分，源自印度洋的留尼旺島，可讓皮膚豐潤有彈性。另外 Creanatural 系列則由法國品牌 The Innovation

WUNDERMAN THOMPSON

One Ocean Beauty packaging designed by Fabien Baron of Baron & Baron

保
喰

The Attributes

Considered Materials

Considered Processes

61

道德選品

線上精品賣場在規劃系列商品時，道德意識
也隨著美學意識提升。

當今消費者為了價值觀而購物的情形頗甚以往。2018 年秋季，由偉門智威（Wunderman Thompson）發布的報告《新型永續：再生》（The New Sustainability: Regeneration）指出，83%的消費者表示在挑選品牌時，他們會選擇永續表現較佳的品牌，70%的消費者認為如果某項產品或服務能夠保護環境或沒有傷害人權，那麼他們願意為此付出較高的費用。為迎合隨著這股消費意識應運而生的購物風潮，許多零售商正在規畫主打道德意識的系列商品。

布歐（Buho）成立於 2019 年 7 月，是以道德為主要訴求的電商，他們所規畫的品牌選物優先考量環境永續、性別平等、公平交易這三個面向。布歐在販售符合他們意識考量的家居物件和商品的同時，還與致力碳中和的物流夥伴合作，使用能夠完全分解的包材，以可種植的植物種子做吊牌，來販售這些男女性及兒童用品。

2019 年 6 月時，線上精品零售商 Net-a-Porter 發表了「永續時尚計劃」（Net Sustain），是一全新且垂直整合永續品牌的產品線。選出

的 26 個品牌與 500 多樣產品，都至少符合零售商五項永續標準當中的一項。這些標準涵蓋了人類、動物、環境的福祉。

Net-a-Porter 全球採購主任伊莉莎白・馮・德・戈爾茲 (Elizabeth von der Goltz) 表示：「我們的永續選購皆為百提供他們所需的資訊，讓他們可以放心選購，並了解到這些品牌是經過我們仔細的審查，符合我們標準的商品才能納入其中。我們的目標是為這些真正做出正向改變的品牌提供發聲管道，提供平台給他們以彰顯這種優良的作法。」

2019 年 6 月，資深精品設計師德克斯特 (Dexter) 與拜倫・皮雅特 (Byron Peart) 兄弟成立了 Goodee。在這個精品賣場中，他們透過渠道倡導和說故事技巧，來使具有永續價值的零售更加完善。

「我們不僅希望大家購物，也想要培養有目的性的對話。」德克斯特・皮雅特如此告訴億萬智威。「現在大眾想要在生活當中做出更好的選擇，我們則創造出讓大眾能夠參與其中的機會。」

Goodee 的目標在於讓顧客了解永續價值與流行時尚並不互斥。「我們想要改寫有機與永續的故事，讓大家在做出現代的永續觀念，並且用更迷人且容易理解的方式來呈現。」拜倫・皮雅特這麼對億萬智威表示。

「我們想要改寫有機與永續的故事，讓大家在做出現代的永續觀念。」拜倫・皮雅特這麼對億萬智威表示。

這麼對億萬智威表示。

繼續關注的原因：

越來越多消費者會尋找符合自身價值的品牌，零售業者為此量身打造相關產品與平台，展現他們的道德觀並幫助消費者有目的的地購物。

62

對抗過度消費

網紅開始受到質疑，且消費者也意識到
某些事物會對環境造成傷害，於是開始有意識地
退一步思考過度消費的文化。

美妝部落客的存在與成功，過去多半仰賴評論新品的方式來操作，
但現在他們卻主動極端的無限購買新品週圈。有位美妝部落
客採取了非常極端的立場。截至 2020 年 1 月為止，莎曼莎·拉文達
爾（Samantha Ravndahl）共擁有多達 97 萬 6 千名的追隨者，而她
已經請各大品牌不要再送公關組與免費產品來讓她評論了。她對
時尚媒體《The Cut》說道：「每次有新品客來給我的時候，我都會
看著它們，心裡想著：『嗯，產品在這裡，是新品，我不知來評論一
下吧。』但對我來說，如果我前一週已經有人推薦我買某東西了，
這週我一定不希望她再另外推薦一個很類似的新品給我。那樣很
不實際，大家不會這樣購買美妝品，我也一定不會這樣買。」

評論文化不僅不實際、短視近利，甚至還會引發焦慮。美妝消費者
也對由此而生的過度浪費感到日益不安。拉文達爾說：「把他們通
瘋的，其實是實體的垃圾量。我家有八個人，但我一人製造的垃圾，
比其他人加起來還多。」

對於拉文達爾減少美妝品的決定，在美妝社群上收到極大量的正

Depop peer-to-peer second-hand marketplace

面回應，有位讀者留言：「**非常感謝你這麼做。很遺憾美妝界流行越買越多，這實在是很不健康的風氣。**」

網路世界的其他地方也有類似的情形。美妝愛好者紛紛湧入熱門線上社群 Reddit，支持彼此做出減少購買的決定。截至 2020 年 1 月止，擁有 75,000 名成員的「美妝戒斷版」(r/MakeupRehab) 當中，有許多成員原本追蹤的是「美妝上癮版」(r/MakeupAddiction)，他們現在互相替彼此打氣，鼓勵理性消費。

反過度運動也深入時尚產業。全球數據公司 (Global Data) 替二手服裝零售平台 ThredUp 彙整的《ThredUp 2019 轉售報告》(ThredUp 2019 Resale Report) 指出，「二手衣的市場正逐漸步上軌道」，預計在 2022 年前達到 430 億美元的銷售額。這股風潮正在關鍵的千禧世代與 Z 世代當中更為明顯。他們購入二手服裝的速度是其他年齡層的 2.5 倍。二手精品市場的成長速度甚至比一手市場更快。2019 年波士頓諮詢集團 (BCG) 與義大利奢侈品行業協會 (Altagamma) 聯合發布的《全球精品消費者實際報告》(True-Luxury Global Consumer Insight) 估計，至 2021 年，二手精品年度銷售成長率平均為 12%，而相較之下，一手市場的同期成長率卻只有 3%。

品牌與零售商也採取了相應的措施。2019 年 11 月時，英國 Selfridges 百貨成為二手精品衣販售平台 Vestiaire Collective 設立永久專櫃，該百貨也在 2019 年 8 月至 10 月間，替二手交易賣場 Depop 成立快閃店。

英國非營利組織「時尚革命」(Fashion Revolution) 認為，全球供應鏈應該要持公開透明的原則，並負起應盡的企業責任。其共同發起人暨創意總監奧索拉．德．卡斯楚 (Orsola de Castro) 對這門智識說：「我們先前過度消費的情形，可說是瘋狂至極。因此我們的質疑其未來有自。」

值得關注的原因：

典型無法滿足已更具辨別意識的二十世紀的過時遺物。現在的消費者在購物時已成為二十世紀的過時遺物。「千禧世代與 Z 世代擺脫了市場之前的世代的購物時為對社會造成的衝擊。」Vestiaire 如此表示：「新興世代的購物頻率降低了，購物時也更謹慎，為消費主義創造了更好的模範，因此各品牌也必須證實，不應濫無目的地推出產品，否則只會顯得盲目賣弄以及脫離現實。

THE FUTURE 100

63

（擴增實境）零售

擴增實境的發展，將會大幅重塑零售體驗，
並帶來全新發現。

越來越多品牌將資金投入擁有無限可能的擴增實境中，以創造沉浸式的購物版圖。位於紐約的義大利家具店 Natuzzi 跟進直家居（IKEA），設立了新展間，讓顧客能夠戴上微軟的 HoloLens 2 頭戴式裝置，進入自家場景的擴增實境當中。他們可以在這個虛擬場景中放入 Natuzzi 的家具，並能輕易地依照需求調整樣式與顏色。

「這能夠讓他們有空間感，以及有如展示實體家具般的感受，這種體驗有助於讓他們跟自己選擇的物件產生情感連結。」小帕斯奎爾．納圖齊（Pasquale Junior Natuzzi）這樣告訴《Dezeen》。

柯爾百貨（Kohl）最近加入古馳（Gucci）與開特力（Gatorade）等品牌的行列，採用 Snapchat 的擴增實境鏡頭（Portal AR Lens），在 2019 年 11 月的特定時間內，顧客可以造訪零售商的假日虛擬快閃精品店，選購吳季剛（Jason Wu）、王薇薇（Vera Wang）、勞倫．康拉德（Lauren Conrad）等品牌的商品，只要點選這個商品，就能夠直接前往柯爾百貨的網路商店。

接下來是由《時尚》（Vogue）前產品主管內哈．辛格（Neha Singh）開發的動態線上購物平台 Obsess。Obsess 拋棄了多數購物網站

在久遠後的未來，
擴增實境眼鏡與
更新款的隱形眼鏡，
會讓我們的視野
成為螢幕。

Obsess創辦人｜內哈．辛格（Neha Singh）

Natuzzi showroom

WUNDERMAN THOMPSON

零售

採用的平面繪圖。這個網站上使用多重共通閘道介面生的3D虛擬世界，包含了奢華公寓以及天然景色，每個場景中都有不同主題系列產品可供選購。

在中國，亞曼尼公司（Armani）是全球精品品牌中，第一個利用擴增實境技術的品牌。亞曼尼透過合作關係，利用萊雅集團（L'Oréal）的 ModiFace 技術，讓亞曼尼的美妝顧客能夠使用微信載體以家以虛擬的方式上妝，並且能立刻下單購買。阿里巴巴（Alibaba）也為天貓電子商城的美妝客戶重金投資擴增實境，讓像 Tom Ford 和 MAC 這樣的美妝品牌，能透過他們開發的工具，在網路旗艦店上以虛擬的方式幫助線上消費者試用產品。

除了網路商店以外，繼倫敦的處女秀之後，施華洛世奇公司（Swarovski）也在 2019 年春季在成都為中國顧客提供擴增實境

的試戴體驗，顧客進入精品店後，就會看見多個有如鏡子般的互動螢幕，讓他們能夠以虛擬的方式，試戴鑲嵌水晶的首飾，就像美蘭（Sephora）的擴增實境化妝櫃檯一樣。

2019 年 6 月時，深圳的新創科技公司胡羅舶（Coolhobo）展現了未來擴增實境零售可能呈現的樣貌。該公司在合歌舉辦的中國擴增實境零售賽當中勝出，而為他們贏得獎項的概念，主要實現了顧客在沃爾瑪（Walmart）實體超市中，使用擴增實境導航的方式，跟隨指向每樣物品的漂浮箭頭，還有購物清單上的所有物品。一路上顧客會即時看到產品資訊及朋友的推薦款，並透過有趣的沉浸式遊戲與品牌互動。

胡羅舶創辦人暨執行長盧瓦克・科貝斯（Loïc Kobes）問道「智慧眼鏡會帶表示，研發工程師領銜擴增實境進入新境界，也意味著「讓相機有能力了解我們的實體世界，能來新的系統（GPS）一樣，誤差精準到只有幾公分。」他表示，相機和人類一樣，會知道正在看什麼東西，「這點會大幅衝擊零售業，尤其是實體商店。」

值得關注的原因：

現在，大多數的零售業都在一次性的專案當中實驗擴增實境技術，但在 5G 技術推出之後，擴增實境的購物經驗，能來新的深度與意義。辛格對《時尚》表示，她預測「在久遠之後的未來，擴增實境眼鏡與更之後的隱形眼鏡，會讓我們的視野成為新層次的數位資訊與實體物件會變得難以區分，也等於在這個虛擬的擴增實境世界當中被『穿戴上』。」

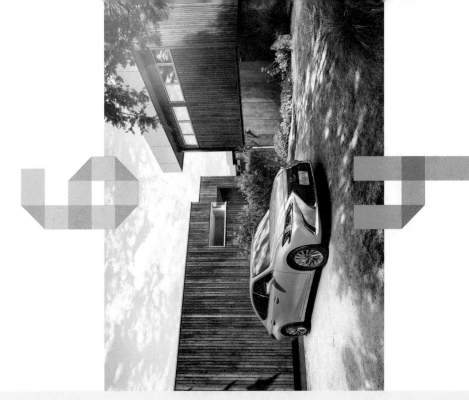

64

訂閱向東行

訂閱制服務不再侷限於新聞與健身房會籍。

說到與日常生活相關的訂閱服務，日本也許是擁有最先進訂閱生態的國家，現在幾乎什麼都能訂閱，包括酒吧飲品、美髮美容服務、汽車、西裝等，甚至連鄉間的美屋也能訂閱使用。

在過去，訂閱意味著事先付款以預訂一定數量的同類產品，不只方便，長時間下來也能省著許多錢。現在出現了更富有想像力的訂閱模式，提供各種不同的套裝組合，甚至模糊了購買與租用間的界線。

在日本，豐田汽車（Toyota）於 2019 年 2 月推出了名為 Kinto 的車輛訂閱服務。最基本的方案 Kinto One 可讓消費者「持有」豐田汽車 3 年之後再歸還，且只需支付一筆費用，並已將保險與維修的費用都涵蓋在內。高價的 Kinto Select 方案則鎖定喜歡變化的年輕駕駛人，讓訂閱者在 3 年的期間內「持有」與「試駕」6 輛凌志（Lexus）汽車。

日本以正式的職場文化著稱，因此出現了名為 Kirudake 的訂閱服務，該服務為企業客戶提供了免除衣裝焦慮的工作服衣櫃，方案從

考量便利與自身的負擔能力，有新一代的用戶已開始擁抱訂閱制服務，連高價物品也不例外。

最低的每月 4800 日元（約台幣 1335 元）起，提供兩套西裝、冬夏季各一套，為符合每個人的身形，還替每位租用者車縫襯衫與領帶。

修改，也能另外選配襯衫與領帶。

訂閱服務增長之迅速，還可從此得知：Kirudake 以及其他 100 項訂閱服務皆被納入大型訂閱服務 Oyo Passport 之下，讓忠實訂閱者能額外省下更多開銷。

最近加入訂閱行列的另一項服務是因應日本嚴重人口老化問題而產生的。世界經濟論壇（World Economic Forum）引用了 2018 年日本政府發布的數據，顯示日本有將近三分之一的人口超過 65 歲，且有 230 萬名高齡 90 歲以上的日本人。

老年人過世後，他們的房子經常無人居住，這種情形在鄉村地區尤為普遍。2019 年 4 月推出的 ADDress 可說是訂閱版的 Airbnb，是解決鄉村地區人口負成長的方案之一。使用者發下為期一年的合約，每月固定支付 4 萬日圓（約台幣 11,000 元），即可入住清單上的

房屋（單月訂閱的費用為 5 萬日圓，約台幣 14,000 元）。這些住宅通常都位於鄉下，並且設有當地「監護人」，他們為用戶傳授當地生活與觀光的祕訣，也維護房屋公共區域的清潔。

ADDress 的社長佐別塗志（Takashi Sabetto）在公司網站上提到，他相信只擁有一個住址「已經是過去式了」，並補充道：「我希望你們能夠攜手合作，創造一個不同的社會，能夠保護與其意義的服務已經引起了知名品牌的注意。全日空最近宣布與其合作，提供低價機票給 ADDress 的會員。

值得關注的原因：
考量便利與自身的負擔能力，新一代的用戶已開始擁抱訂閱制服務、連高價物品也不例外。這種新型訂閱制讓使用者能夠享有他們所追求的彈性與變化。

了該款遊戲的水晶圖案（Plumbob）印花、丹寧服飾，還有與粉紅兔（Freezer Bunny）聯名的唱T，且同時在實體店面與遊戲中販售，讓虛擬角色也能穿上同款造型。

直播體驗也擴展到了全新的領域。蕾哈娜（Rihanna）的自創品牌 Savage X Fenty 宣布與亞馬遜（Amazon）合作，在 Amazon Prime 上直播紐約的時裝周的走秀，讓該影音平台的用戶能直接在平台上購入睡衣系列產品。幾個月後，維多利亞的秘密（Victoria's Secret）也宣布取消其年度時裝秀的現場活動。

值得關注的原因：

全球品牌開始展開非傳統的合作關係。為行動裝置優先與數位原生世代的年輕購物者創造全新零售體驗。無論 Z 世代與千禧世代的用戶在哪，成功的零售商就出現在哪，從虛擬遊戲到新型直播平台都不例外。

65

新型購物世界

從直播頻道到虛擬場景與遊戲、沉浸式零售模式已在下個世代的購物者心中達到新的高度。

電子商務平台開始研發能讓內容吸睛的商品櫥窗如生的創新方式。2019 年 10 月，中國阿里巴巴（Alibaba）的「淘寶人生」針對 Z 世代推出 3D 虛擬購物遊戲，使用者可以用精品街頭風服飾打扮自己的角色，而這些產品也可以直接從平台上購入。這個服務推出不久後，中國偶像童童又霖便在社群媒體上發布了自己和淘寶虛擬角色的照片，兩者穿著同款 MSGM 品牌大學 T 和 Iceberg 品牌便裝。在微博上掀起一股熱潮。

中國社群媒體與行銷專家勞倫・哈洛南（Lauren Hallanan）告訴偉門智威智庫：「市場會持續變得更加年輕，而這些年輕消費者也會被各種品牌訊息給淹沒。」他也表示：「社群遊戲與社群商務會在未來成為一種新的零售管道，因為「遊戲能吸引他們的注意，並且讓他們持續參與其中。」

熱門的電玩遊戲模擬市民（The Sims）讓莫斯奇諾（Moschino）的創意總監傑諾米・史考特（Jeremy Scott）有了新的靈感，他為此打造了一系列的成衣。這個在 2019 年春季發表的成衣系列，包含

NDERMAN
OMPSON

Moschino x The Sims

66

新型美妝遊樂場

在體驗文化於零售業殺出一條血路的此刻，
或許沒有一個產業比美妝業更適合發展這種親身
體驗的零售模式了。

無論產品在網路上看起來有多迷人，都無法取代當代消費者想要親自
試色或是親自感受全新質地的心理。2019 年 4 月，《Business of
Fashion》引用了派傑投資公司（Piper Jaffray）的研究報告，指出
約有 90% 的美國青少年依舊偏好在實體店購買美妝品。雖然電商
的銷售量佔消費者總體消費量的比例日益增加，但「美妝卻是唯一實
體店市佔率仍屹立不搖的類別」，派傑投資公司的主管暨資深分析
師艾倫‧莫菲（Erinn Murphy）表示。

有鑑於此，各大品牌紛紛開始提升店內的美妝體驗，重新將店面塑
造為一座座不折不扣的遊樂場。

2019 年 10 月，哈洛德百貨（Harrods）宣布他們即將推出獨立運作
的 H Beauty 美妝概念店，店面將於 2020 年 4 月開張，座落於英國
埃塞克斯的湖畔購物中心（Intu Lakeside）內。《Retail Gazette》
網站指出：該店占地廣達 2 萬 3 千平方英呎，提供的服務包含從咖
啡到調酒應有盡有的酒吧以及美妝造型與美容服務。店內的品牌
包含香奈兒（Chanel）、迪奧（Dior）、胡達美妝（Huda Beauty）以

UNDERMAN
THOMPSON
After Beauty "beauty playhouse"

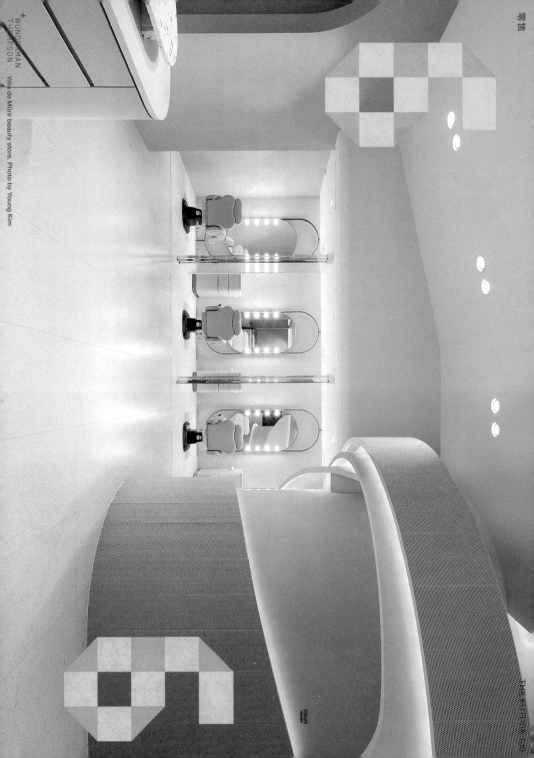

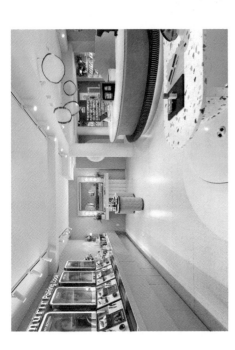

與磨石子面的組合，並陳列著 Villa de Múrir 的自家商品以及其他主流美妝品牌的產品。《Coolhunter》雜誌表示，店內甚至提供了特定的空間，「讓 YouTube 與其他社群平台的創作者能在裡面創作內容。」同時店內還有美容室與咖啡廳。

值得關注的原因：

研究報告指出 Z 世代對實體店的愛好，而美妝零售業顯然接受了他們的建議，2019 年 9 月，顧問公司 AT Kearney 公布的報告指出：14 至 24 歲的受訪者當中，有 81% 的人偏好在實體商店內購物，其中有些人只是要利用這種方式來讓自己脫離社群媒體與數位世界。而有 73% 的人表示他們喜歡在店中探索新產品。這些新的美妝場所被視為是溫暖且好客的地方，吸引顧客進入其中玩耍與體驗。當然也希望他們購買新產品。

反其他新踏入零售集團的品牌。哈洛德居家美妝部的總監安娜黎黛斯·法德（Annalise Fard）說道：「H Beauty 讓我們有機會將理念傳達給更多英國各地的美妝愛好者，我們帶著一份使命，要讓全世界知道今日美妝業能夠做到什麼程度。」哈洛德也宣布會於米爾頓凱恩斯即將開設英國第二家 H Beauty 美妝概念店。

2019 年秋季在倫敦鬧區皮卡迪利圓環附近開幕的 After Beauty 百貨，則將自身定義為「美妝遊樂場」，寬闊的 3 層樓空間當中，共有140 個品牌，包含了 SkinCeuticals、Dermalogica、Holika Holika、Patchology 等等。After Beauty 百貨開設的目的，是想要為美妝界找回樂趣與刺激，耐內拉·林（Zanelle Lim）對《Get the Gloss》網站說道：「我們想要創造一個空間，讓美妝狂能沉浸在各種產品、顏色和創意當中。現在的顧客比過去更了解產品，所以我們希望他們能夠拋開規則並去發現新的事物。」

這股風潮席捲全球，2019 年 10 月，以天然居家用品事業為主力的電子商務平台 Grove Collaborative 在洛杉磯的亞伯特奇尼大道（Abbot Kinney Boulleard）上，開設了潔淨美妝概念店 Roven，作為旗下事業的副牌。《Beauty Independent》網站指出，該店的設計像是「有柔和線條裝飾的粉色書房」，結合了「很好的氣氛」，以及吸睛的色彩與曲線」，Roven 的共同創辦人妮可·法鉑（Nicole Farb）對《Beauty Independent》表示：「若能夠實際接觸並感受一個商品，這個過程所帶來的力量遠遠超過我們的想像。」

在首爾，設計出 Villa de Múrir 概念店的 Collective B 工作室表示，Villa de Múrir 是一個「美妝策展品牌」。這間概念店給人的第一印象是未來風設計，會讓人想要長時間待在裡面，內裝為千禧粉

67

不受中斷的交易

從社群媒體到搜尋引擎，顧客在網路上到處都可購物，且整體過程比過去都還完美順暢。

Instagram 在 2019 年春季推出結帳（Checkout）功能，品牌也開始將其視為一站式購物商城，對於該平台上原生商業活動的熱衷程度也正加速升溫。《Glossy》網站在 2019 年 11 月的報導中指出：Joe's Jeans 與 SoulCycle 等品牌正與 Instagram 上的網紅跟合作夥伴通力合作，透過結帳功能販售服飾，到目前為止成果都相當地優秀。

谷歌（Google）追隨了 Instagram 的腳步，在 2019 年 10 月推出新，讓使用者可以直接透過搜尋引擎來自數千個商家的商品。顧客也可以使用「谷歌購物」（Google Shopping）找出販售商品的鄰近店家，追蹤商品的價格，並且收到個人化的購物推薦。

抖音（TikTok）目前在中國境內已擁有強大的電子商務能力，他們現在也開始在美國試推應用程式內的電子商務服務。在中國境內，品牌可連結到短片內部的商城；且幾乎每兩個中國境內，媒體網站，就有一個網站具備內建的電商平台，例如小紅書或是 Z 世代最愛的嗶哩嗶哩（Bilibili）都有提供。

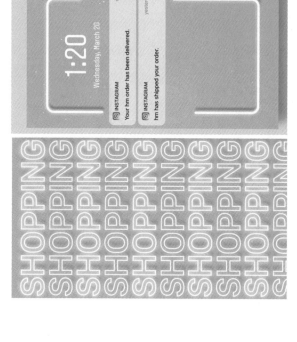

內容當中。對特定族群來說，網路購物已經成為他們逛街找樂子和閒逛的新去處。」

值得關注的原因：

Instagram 提供的資料指出，每月有 1 億 3000 萬名用戶會點擊購物貼文。毫無疑問，顧客會開始使用 Instagram 以及其他線上內容網站來探索產品，品牌也可透過與網紅合作來解決以往購物經驗中的痛點。

中國品牌成長與網紅行銷專家以利亞‧惠利（Elijah Whaley）告訴偉門智威智庫，「這種狀態在中國非常盛行」，並補充說到，顧客把網路購物當作娛樂的心態，會持續推動整合內容與商務完全結合。

他說：「現在十六歲的女孩已經不再去購物中心了，只要坐著滑手機，瀏覽網路商店，或者收看電商直播，甚至會直接進到商務型

Instagram

精品百貨之死

眾多知名百貨公司，因為債台高築與破產而關門大吉，而這也帶出了一個問題：

未來精品零售業的樣貌會是如何？

據《商業內幕》(Business Insider) 統計，美國在 2019 年時，有超過 9000 家零售商店倒閉，這點不怎麼讓人意外。因為各地的實體商店零售收入都大幅下滑。根據美國普查局 (US Census Department) 公布的零售數字，美國的百貨公司從 2007 至 2017 年間的銷售大幅跌了 30%，摩根史坦利公司 (Morgan Stanley) 也預測，到 2022 年前，服飾在百貨公司的銷售量會從 2016 年的 24% 驟降至 8%。

Barneys 百貨在 2019 年 8 月宣布破產，並在同年 11 月宣布正式結束營業。根據美國全國廣播公司商業頻道 (CNBC) 取得的錄音指出，Barneys 百貨當時的執行長丹妮耶拉．維塔雷 (Daniella Vitale) 於同年稍早時候告訴員工：「整個產業都在力求生存，這個商業模式無法奏效。」她還補充：「這個模式對 Neiman Marcus 百貨無效、對 Saks 無效、對我們無效、對 Nordstrom 也無效。」

2019 年 11 月，酩悅．軒尼詩一路易威登集團 (LVMH) 買下擁有名氣

但卻日漸式微的蒂芙尼公司 (Tiffany & Co.)，顯然這間公司的盛名與好萊塢帶給它的名氣，仍無法讓它自行生存。

2019 年 1 月時，百貨公司 Lord & Taylor 在紐約的第五大道旗艦店永久歇業了。這間成立於 1914 年的公司，在歐業的前 18 個月才尺賣 1200 萬美元，因此在 2019 年 11 月時，該百貨的母公司哈得遜灣 (Hudson Bay) 陷入困境，因此將旗下另一間位於第五大道的 Saks 百貨轉手賣給托特來箱公司 (Le Tote)。

這些日漸微薄的利潤反映出零售版圖的巨大轉變。智遊網 (Expedia) 與世代動力學中心 (Center for Generational Kinetics) 的研究指出，有 74% 的美國人重視體驗更甚於產品。Nordstrom 以及 Selfridge 等歷史悠久的零售商是明智的關鍵，他們學辦工作坊發起文化計畫這種立快閃店，而 Snowfields 等新商家則模糊了藝術、商業、體驗的界線，把購物變成沉浸式的多重感官體驗。

Henri Bendel 百貨在營運了 123 年之後，於 2019 年 1 月正式結束營業，Neiman Marcus 也瀕臨破危機，在 2019 年 3 月時才與債權人達成協議，對高達 500 萬美元的債務進行重組。

有理想且有原則的 Z 世代與千禧世代，在購物時會尋找符合自身理念的品牌，貝恩策略顧問公司 (Bain) 的研究指出，這群人讓全球的精品銷售成長了 85%，並在 2025 年之前，會佔精品購物全比 45%。偉門智威獨有的研究工具 SONAR™ 顯示：有 83% 的消費者每一次都會選擇永續貢獻記錄較為優良的品牌，另外 70% 的消費者認

整個產業都在力求生存，這個商業模式無法奏效。對Saks無效，對我們無效，對Nordstrom也無效。

Barneys 前執行長｜丹妮耶菈．維塔雷（Daniella Vitale）

偉門智威智庫說道：「未來的品牌必須立足在目的之上，而精品的定義也有了即時的改變。儘管過去是綜合價格與稀有程度來決定何為精品，但我們認為未來會以品牌背後的動機與目的來決定。」

值得關注的原因

在地位越來越取決於價值與目的而非價格與名聲的氛圍下，精品零售業的版圖開始面臨了重大變動。現代消費者會為「體驗」與「道德價值」買單，過去的精品百貨已無法引起現代消費者的共鳴，正如皮雅特所說：「良好的設計與動機，將成為計算精品價值的標準。」

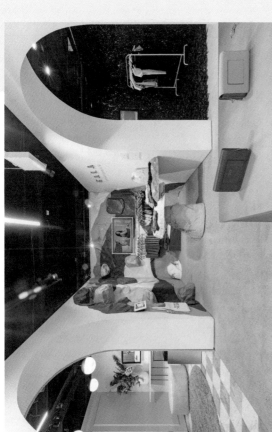

為如果產品與服務對環保有貢獻，或者沒有侵害人權，那麼他們願意付出比較高的費用來購買。

「現在很難有公司不提倡什麼理念了。」《紐約時報》（New York Times）時尚主編暨該報的國際精品會議主持人凡妮沙．費里德曼（Vanessa Friedman）如此表示。「大家買東西不僅是因為好看，更會因為商品代表的價值而購買。」

電子商務平台 Goodee 以及精品配件 Want Les Essentiels 的共同創辦人拜倫．皮雅特（Byron Peart）也回應了這個觀點。皮雅特對

WUNDERMAN
THOMPSON

Lolly-Laputan café, Dalian. Image courtesy of Wutopia Lab. Photo by CreatAR Images

69

新一代零售空間

由於千禧世代有大量時間都用在社群媒體上，因此設計的價值對他們來說相當重要，他們也使用了相同的標準來看待為了他們後代所設計的一切。

夢媒以未的兒童遊戲空間開始在全球主要城市中出現，與過去總是以三原色和光滑表面所組成的遊樂場形成鮮明的對比。

中國蘇州的羅浮游俱樂部，是上海唯想國際建築事務所（X + Living）設計的療癒空間。整個空間充滿了柔和的粉紅與藍色調，圓形燈具散發出愉快而柔美的光線。這裡方有的不只是游泳池，還有一座圖書館，館內有著迷人的拱形曲線座位，附設的奇幻咖啡廳則有裝飾華麗的彎形拱頂，最上方的天花板由鏡子組成，映照著地板上的復古波卡圓點。這裡同時吸引了父母與孩子，也是個以孩子為設計主體的罕見案例。

紐約的 The Wonder 俱樂部為 2019 年在曼哈頓開幕的家庭俱樂部。內部空間的用色非常大膽，使用了大量的紅色、黃色、藍色，並經過精心設計，包含了一間咖啡館供父母使用的共同工作空間，以及遊戲活動區。「我們的終極願景是為新一代的父母發聲。」空間

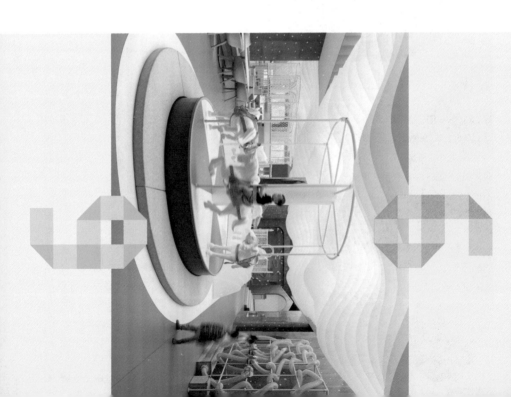

零售

共同創辦人諾麗雅‧摩拉爾斯 (Noria Morales) 對媒體公司 PSFK 如此說到。「父母的觀念都已過時，現在已經變得更多元了。我們用各種不同的方式與孩子互動，陪伴孩子的時間也比過去的父母都還要多。」

兒童餐廳成為了潮店，杜拜的 White and the Bear 就是一間以黑白色調為主的兒童餐廳，內部採用淺色的木頭家具與燈具。Sneha Divias Atelier 工作室向《Dezeen》雜誌表示，這樣才不會「過度刺激感官」，並且補充說明「這樣的配色能夠激發創造力、想像力、學習力」。

《Dezeen》雜誌寫到，在中國大連，非作建築 (Wutopia Labs) 把 Lolly-Laputan 咖啡店打造成「夢幻仙境」，餐廳的設計不采用了奇幻與童趣，但卻同時使用了沈穩、優雅的色調。鋼製滑梯座落在白色球池上，還有座椅白搭配亮金色的旋轉木馬，咖啡座則使用了北歐風的淺色木材。

值得關注的原因：

這些設計感強烈的空間，正好符合千禧世代父母的品味，而他們的孩子則屬於「α 世代」，在 2010 至 2025 年出生的這個崛起世代，是刺激父母消費的動力來源。2018 年 7 月，偉門智威智庫針對 α 世代進行的研究報告指出，美國千禧世代父母當中，有 81% 的人表示，孩子的習慣影響了他們近期的消費，這意味著對實體空間的重視程度不亞於數位空間。Wunderman Thompson Commerce 的思維領導 (EMEA) 暨英國行銷部門主管休‧弗雷契 (Hugh Fletcher) 在 2019 年一份關於 α 世代的研究報告中建議：無論品牌現在開始做什麼，「都必須以 α 世代消費者的期待為根據」。

70

超級便利的超級市場

中國的雜貨巨人變得越來越多元,他們研發了混合型零售模式,來吸引更多不同生活型態的顧客。

中國阿里巴巴的超市「盒馬鮮生」(Hema Fresh) 在 2017 年開幕,鎖定擅長使用智慧型手機的年輕消費者。結合了數位經濟與實體店面進而改變了零售的遊戲規則。到了 2019 年 7 月,這間生鮮食物零售商已在中國各地的 21 座城市中開設了 160 間分店。美國便利商店協會 NACS 指出:這間超市的目標在於深入更多在地場景,並且強化從線上到線下的消費生態,而這項策略的其中一環便是成立副牌,為不同地區的特定消費族群量身打造商品。

到 2019 年底,盒馬鮮生已經開發了 4 個副牌。最初,高科技傾向的盒馬鮮生超市鎖定的是一線城市中追求便利的千禧世代;到了 2019 年 7 月,阿里巴巴設立了副牌「盒馬 Mini」,販售無包裝的生鮮產品,鎖定較年長且對產品價格敏感的郊區消費者,也就是盒馬鮮生最初客群的父母輩與祖父母輩,那些原本只會在附近蔬果市場購物的世代;「盒馬 F2」則針對商業區的上班族,販售可即食的熟食與點心;「盒馬菜市」座落在大型的住宅區附近,每日提供生食類的選擇;而「盒馬小站」則設立在缺乏盒馬實體零售店的地方,僅供取貨。

ANDERMAN
THOMPSON

Hema by Alibaba. Images courtesy of Alibaba.

為了達到真正
無縫的線上線下體驗，
大型連鎖商店開始
在不同地點
針對不同族群
調整其營業模式。

其他連鎖店也開發了類似的模式。2019 年 9 月，家電零售龍頭蘇寧易購（Suning）收購了連鎖超市中國家樂福（Carrefour China）80% 的股份，當月也隨即宣布要將家樂福轉型，使其成為線上與線下連鎖的超市，並根據 200 間超市的地點與顧客屬性，引進該公司的小型家電賣場。連鎖咖啡店瑞幸（Luckin）與喜茶（Heytea）也根據不同的生活型態提供了數種線上線下整合模式，例如外帶專門店或是提供咖啡與茶的高檔店面。

騰訊資助的永輝超市（Yonghui Superstores）在 2017 年創設高端品牌「超級物種（Super species）」，提供現煮現做的服務，不久之後又在 2018 年 6 月開設了廣州超級物種旗艦店，提供用無人機送貨的鮮食。

值得關注的原因：

過去零售業在中國的擴張多半仰賴小城市的崛起，但零售版圖中的數位消費者與供應鏈已出現改變。為了達到真正無縫的線上線下體驗，大型連鎖商店開始在不同地點針對不同族群調整其營業模式。

精品

11

零售業的復古遊戲

精品品牌先分利用千禧世代對於懷舊與冒險的迷戀，並推出經典電動遊戲贏得目光。

路易威登（Louis Vuitton）向來不落於時尚界遊戲產業，他們在 2019 年 7 月推出了一款復古的 16 位元電動遊戲，名為「無盡跑者」（Endless Runner），遊戲設計靈感來自維吉爾‧阿伯拉赫（Virgil Abloh）的 2019 秋冬系列。所有人都可以免費在路易威登的上商城玩這款小遊戲，重溫 1980 年代的低解析度網格美學，這款遊戲並沒有推廣任何商品，也不會重新導向商城。而是操作簡單，像大部分的電動一樣讓人欲罷不能。

古馳（Gucci）稍早於 2019 年 7 月在行動裝置的應用程式上推出了妥後復古遊戲啟發的「古馳遊戲機」（Gucci Arcade）。目前主要有四個遊戲：古馳之唇（Gucci Lips）、古馳之握（Gucci Grip）、古馳王牌（Gucci Ace）、古馳蜜蜂（Gucci Bee）。最後一款遊戲是類似小精靈（Pac-Man）的迷宮遊戲，玩家必須讓蜜蜂（很受歡迎品牌瞭的主題）在不同階層中來回移動，才能收集到代幣並解鎖特殊物件。

而這些品牌之所以推出上述的遊戲，是受到香奈兒（Chanel）的快

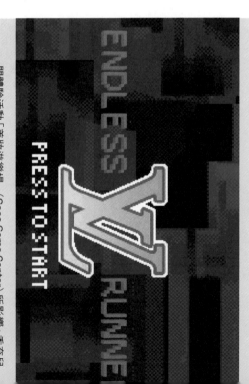

閃體驗活動「美妝遊樂場」（Coco Game Center）所影響，香奈兒將美妝遊樂場打造成 90 年代的電動遊樂場，並結合卡地亞（Cartier）也在 2017 年時，於微信推出小精靈的遊戲，行銷「卡地亞幸運符」（Amulette de Cartier）系列商品。

值得關注的原因：

波士頓顧問集團（Boston Consulting Group）與義大利奢侈品行業協會（Altagamma）合作的研究報告指出：千禧世代的購物者有望在 2025 年前攻佔 50% 的精品消費額。精品品牌為了與年輕的消費者產生連結，紛紛擁抱遊戲文化，改變大眾對遊戲玩家的刻板印象。

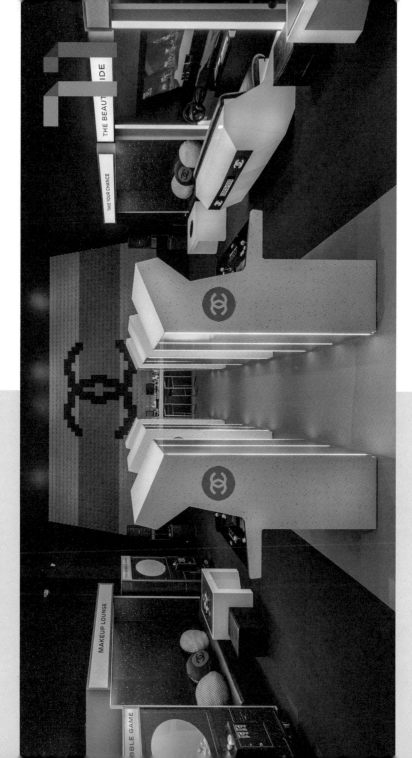

Coco Game Center by Chanel. Image courtesy of Chanel

高級訂製園藝

72

許多設計師、名人、零售業者都以花來賣傳品牌，將花卉提升到精品階層。

2019 年春夏新裝伸展台上，精緻的花朵頭飾主宰秀場，許多品牌與零售商紛紛利用花卉展現高端時尚的華麗。

精品百貨 Selfridges 在 2019 年 9 月使用充滿想像力與浮誇訴求的花藝品牌 Rebel Rebel 的作品。來妝點凱特·哈德遜（Kate Hudson）的「快樂與自然」（HappyxNature）永續服裝系列發表會，以優雅蔓生的花座與花冠來搭配這個系列的產品。這間花藝設計公司也負責生產高級訂製服裝品牌巴迪斯塔·瓦利（Giambattista Valli）製作花朵背板和花藝擺飾，讓這家高訂品牌能在他們與 H&M 服飾合作的 2020 秋冬系列發表會中使用。

零售業者也利用鮮花作為視覺焦點。精品百貨 Neiman Marcus 在 2019 年 3 月開設了第一間位於紐約的零售百貨，店內的「快沒花藝師」（Pop-Up Florist）花店利用半永久型的花車來販售美麗的花束。精品寄售業者 The RealReal 也在曼哈頓精品旗艦店門口擺上一座花台，陳列來自 Fox Fodder Farm 花藝工作室的鮮花。Fox Fodder

WUNDERMAN THOMPSON

Princess Nokia with gypsophila, anthuriums and orchids.
Photo by Petra Collins for Office Magazine. Image courtesy of Phaidon Press

Floral artistry by London-based Bardet Perry Flowers

UNDERMAN
THOMPSON

這些花卉創作共同為花藝世界注入一股新生命，對視覺文化與設計產生了深遠的影響。

《綻花盛開》（Blooms）專文作者，克萊兒·考爾森（Claire Coulson）

Farm 曾被《時尚》（Vogue）與《哈潑時尚》（Harper's Bazaar）評為最佳花藝工作室。

費頓出版社（Phaidon）2019 年出版的《綻花盛開：自然風尚花藝設計新創意》（Bloom: Contemporary Floral Design）更加奠定了花藝的地位。書中稱讚這種技藝橫跨不同領域，從高級訂製服到音樂錄影帶當中都可見到。《綻花盛開》作者之一的克萊兒·考爾森（Claire Coulson）對偉門威智智庫說道：「這些花卉創作共同為花藝世界

注入一股新生命。利用花朵與植物開拓藝術的新視野，對視覺文化與設計產生了深遠的影響。」

值得關注的原因：

因為一群遠見的創意人將前衛又新穎的花藝設計領域，使花藝成為品牌追尋的奢華象徵，花卉本身也從原本的美麗意象躍升為賦有啟發意義的設計風格。

WUNDERMAN THOMPSON

Yellow chrysanthemums and butterfly orchids on a honeycomb-shaped structure for Pandora event at The Calyx, Royal Botanic Garden, Sydney. Image courtesy of Phaidon Press

73

搭機旅遊的寵物

越來越多人把寵物視為家人，帶著他們度過奢華的假期，部分飯店與航空公司也開始為竭盡所能，讓寵物享受竇至如歸的服務。

位於馬爾他群島的私人包機公司 VistaJet 統計，自 2017 年起，動物登機的數量增加了 104%。每 4 位 VistaJet 會員中就有 1 位會固定攜帶寵物同行。這家包機旅遊公司在 2019 年 4 月推出寵物飛行計畫 VistaPet，為四隻閣的旅客提供專屬旅行組、手工睡墊、繩索玩具、生物有機套點。

度假前，容易緊張的寵物可以先參加四週的行前課程，克服飛行恐懼、慢慢習慣汽油味、飛機引擎聲、機艙氣壓與亂流。寵物登機後，空服員會在寵物的飲用水中添加天然花精，進一步幫助寵物放鬆。

抵達目的地後，航空公司也會推薦寵物友善旅館與髮廊、遛狗助手、甚至是攝影師！

北美洲精品連鎖飯店希爾頓嘉悅里酒店（Canopy by Hilton）在 2019 年 11 月時開始與 Bark 合作，這間公司提供每月客製的 BarkBox 訂閱服務，裡面含有主題式的寵物玩具與點心。嘉悅里一

VistaPet service at VistaJet
JNDERMAN
HOMPSON

倫敦梅費爾的Smith & Whistle酒吧提供了一份專屬狗狗的完整飲料清單，裡面提供了Bubbly Bow Bow（適合狗飲用的氣泡酒加藍莓汁）以及Poochie Colada（羽衣甘藍、花椰菜、椰子水）等各式「狗尾酒」（Dogtail）。

向強調質地的體驗，對於狗狗也不例外。除了觸感良好的玩具與全天然的零食之外，還會為「毛小孩」提供附近的狗狗熱門景點指南。

倫敦梅費爾的 Smith & Whistle 酒吧提供了一份專屬狗狗的完整飲料清單，裡面提供了 Bubbly Bow Bow（適合狗飲用的氣泡酒加藍莓汁）以及 Poochie Colada（羽衣甘藍、花椰菜、椰子水）等各式「狗尾酒」（Dogtail）。

這股寵物度假風潮在亞洲也相當盛行。萬豪集團（Marriott）旗下的上海外灘 W 酒店也參與了萬豪集團推出的「寵物友善」（Pets Are Welcome）提供特別的點心、玩具以及遛狗服務。

值得關注的原因：

單身趨勢帶動了寵物精品的風潮。在中國更是如此。單身者往往不選擇生兒育女，而是把大量的可支配收入花費在寵物貓狗身上。美商 Frost & Sullivan 2019 年的報告指出，中國有將近四成的飼主為單身，使得寵物經濟在 2013 至 2018 年間增加了不只三倍，達到將近 250 億美元。

74

健康管家

高端旅宿為了注重健康的旅客
打造量身訂製的健康服務。

四季酒店（Four Seasons）在 2019 年 10 月於夏威夷推出全新的養生會館。這個全包式的度假村特別提供了「今日頂級旅遊者想要的一切—獨享的專屬養生之旅」。四季酒店集團全球營運總裁克里斯汀·克勒克（Christian Clerc）如此表示。

每位旅客都配有一位個人健康教練，負責打造量身訂製的健康課程，當中結合了營養、健身、全方位療法，還包括與健康顧問一對一討論的時間，並透過身體熱感圖等高科技服務進一步了解健康狀況。

2019 年 7 月在紐約開幕的春分酒店（Equinox Hotel），也是以個人健康管家服務為其主要特色。為了讓入住者能夠一夜好眠，旅館提供了隨傳隨到的睡眠教練，分析住客的生理時鐘，同時也在飯店內提供時差調養錠及冷凍療法。

這點是效法本傑明旅館（The Benjamin）的「休息與復原」（Rest & Renew）計畫，該計畫由睡眠專家芮貝卡·羅賓斯（Rebecca

Four Seasons has a fresh focus on wellness

UNDERMAN
THOMPSON

健康管家結合客製服務與專家意見，塑造全球保健旅遊業未來的演進趨勢。

Robbins) 研發。羅賓斯對這門智慧智庫說道：「我們設計了一系列的產品與服務來改善睡眠體驗」，包含不同睡眠型態者能自由選用的枕頭清單，以及與「晨間喚醒服務」相反的「關機服務」，此項服務會有「員工前往你的房間，分享一些好眠的訣竅」。

值得關注的原因：

健康管家結合客製服務與專家意見，塑造了全球保健旅遊業未來的演進趨勢。根據全球健康研究所 (Global Wellness Institute) 的統計數字來看，這個產業的產值超過 $6,390 億美元。

75

健康建築

建築師紛紛設計出更健康的生活環境，
進而帶動健康趨勢的成長。

Delos 建築事務所的亞洲區總裁暨 Well Living Lab 設計團隊成員之一的雪婭（Xue Ya）表示：「有越來越多的室內設計師、室內設計師、工程師和科學家攜手合作，打造健康的室內設計」，她補充說他們的目標是要讓空間「更貼近於人類的自然生活」。

Delos 在 Well Living Lab 當中與 Mayo Clinic 合作，負責檢視室內環境中影響健康的物件。Well Living Lab 於 2019 年開幕的第二座據點位於北京，他們「致力研究出建築物本身及內部的一切是如何影響人類的健康與福祉」。

除了實驗室的健康調查工作之外，Delos 開發的許多計畫也在居家健康方面領先群倫。Delos 在紐約市創造了他們自認為最健康的公寓，結合了抗菌生物表面、添加維他命 C 的過濾淋浴用水、內嵌式全天芮療設備，以及身訂制的生理時鐘照明系統。

在美國 2019 年的消費電子用品展上，Delos 發布了智慧家庭系統「達爾文」（Darwin），用以確保室內環境健康。Delos 創始人兼執

行長夏保羅（Paul Scialla）表示：這個系統為「智慧家庭的版圖再添入一層健康照護機制」。這個系統的特色包含了室內空氣與用水淨化系統，也會在一天當中持續按照時間調控最佳的燈光與溫度，以輔助自然的睡眠循環。

隨著大家待在室內的時間越來越多，創造健康的室內養生所變得更加重要。美國國家環境保護局（US Environmental Protection Agency）發現，美國人有 90% 的時間都待在室內，代表以健康為訴求的室內裝潢確實是潛在獲利相當豐厚的市場。

值得關注的原因：

絲毫未減緩的永續建築風潮極度注重周遭環境的健康，居住者的健康更是納入首要考量。設計師珍妮·莎賓（Jenny Sabin）對偉門智威智庫說：「居住的空間不僅會影響我們，也形塑了我們部分的人格與觀感。」現代生活的每個部分幾乎都加入了健康意識，建築師便把大家關注的焦點融入人建築環境，讓注入健康意識的空間變成最新的奢侈品。

> ## 人的經歷與五感極度相關。現在客戶要找的是專屬於他們的獨有訂製品。
>
> SynerG 創意總監｜艾洛爾・卡貝爾（Errol Capel）

91

感官之旅

在無不誘惑、易於分心的時代裡，奢華旅行利用五感刺激，讓旅人留下難忘經歷。

飯店與航空業者也將調香氛，水療中心也開始提供「鳴鐘銅鑼浴」，大自然變得更受歡迎，不再被拒於千里之外。

對部分品牌而言，這只不過點出了原本就在他們面前的機會，並選定時機加以操作。奢華旅遊公司 Belmond 與徠卡運動光學（Leica Sport Optics）攜手合作推出「第一道曙光」（First Light）漫步大自然之旅，地點包含位在波札那、馬斯卡、開普敦，以及位於阿根廷與巴西交界的伊瓜蘇瀑布等地的貝爾蒙莊園飯店。旅客可帶著徠卡雙筒望遠鏡在破曉時刻出發，探索四周的動植物，柔和日光加上一片寂靜，使客對大自然的美有了深度體會，也讓聚焦於大自然的品牌能以令人難忘的方式打造出與眾不同的旅行。

座落於吉隆坡市中心的 EQ 飯店是國際賓都連鎖酒店（Hotel Equatorial）的全新旗艦飯店。在位於 29 樓的無邊際泳池中，水下喇叭播放著情境音樂；飯店內的勘八日式餐廳（Kampachi）則以帶著香氣的檜木（扁柏屬，以往多製成薰香）壽司檯為一大亮點。EQ 飯店也將香氣用於大廳、宴會廳、酒吧中，以氣味營造出奢華

值得關注的原因：

「活在當下」越來越受到重視。奢華旅行早便將規劃重點放在能夠喚醒回憶的視覺、味覺、觸覺體驗上。現在，也開始將觸角延伸到嗅覺和聽覺。」

感。AllSense 香氛顧問公司和 EQ 飯店共同挑選出名為「黑蘭花」的氣味，這款香氛的前調帶有花香和檸檬香，並以檀香、麝香的木質調為基底。

樟宜機場是 AllSense 香氛顧問公司的另一個客戶，同時也是音效專家 SynerG 的客戶。該座機場透過精心挑選的音樂，來舒緩旅客流量。樟宜機場曾連續七年獲 Skytrax 航空評級機構，選為全球最佳機場。它的四個航廈會播放快節奏的音樂，在離峰時播放放慢節奏的音樂，巧妙地左右了旅客行走的速度。SynerG 的創意總監艾洛爾・卡貝爾 (Errol Capel) 向寶門智威表示：「人的經歷與五感極度相關。現在客戶在尋找的是專屬於他們的獨有訂製品。」

WUNDERMAN
THOMPSON

Above: EQ's sushi counter
Right: EQ's infinity pool

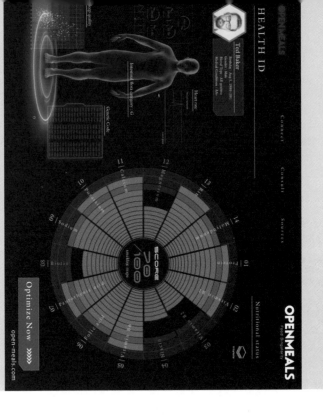

生物數據服務

77

發展迅速、技術成熟的DNA分析技術，正為提升奢華世界早已習以為常的「超個性化」生活體驗鋪路。

Sushi Singularity 預定於 2020 年在東京開幕，這間餐廳將收集客人的生物特徵樣本，用來製作出獨一無二、專為用餐者的營養需求所量身打造的 3D 列印壽司。Passionality Group 創始合夥人丹尼爾·德·歐豪（Daniel del Olmo）將此稱為新時代饕飲。2019 年 11 月，丹尼爾在拉斯維加斯的「饕饕金融與發展會議」（Restaurant Finance & Development Conference）上表示：「我們相信『超個性化』服務將成為未來的常態。」

另一種需要評估客戶 DNA 資訊的壽司用饕體驗，也針對顧客的特定營養需求客製菜單。2019 年 2 月，位於倫敦的 Yo! Sushi 連鎖壽司餐廳，並在寄回唾液樣本的客戶中，選出一小部分人，為其提供免費客製饕飲。

DNA 配對技術也將找尋真愛的過程，轉以科學步驟來進行。位於東京的 Gene Partner Japan 使用 DNA 樣本，來分析原相容的人類白血球抗原。其原理為兩個人的白血球抗原組成差異越大，兩者對彼此的吸引力就越高。他們來自東京的競爭對手 Gene Future，也以較

+WUNDERMAN
THOMPSON

Sushi Singularity. Image courtesy of Open Meals

墨西哥市找到與傳統技藝相關的天然染料工作坊,作為他們文化旅行的一部分」。

值得關注的原因:

雖然基因檢測是否能精確且全面地預測出契合度或文化血統還有待商榷,但可以確定的是,消費型 DNA 服務需求暫時不會有太大變動。隨著測試工具包持續地簡化和進步,其應用層面可能會繼續拓展至其他新領域,並在基本的健康報告和評估之上,增加更多附加價值。

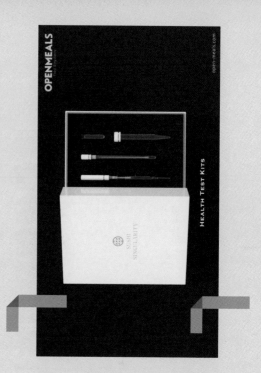

為平易近人的價格,推出相仿的未來伴侶徵尋服務。2019 年 6 月在新加坡成立的基因配對公司 GeneMate,也提供顧客利用生物數據和旗下獨家的演算法,找尋終身伴侶的機會。為與低出生率抗衡,這些在日本和新加坡提供 DNA 配對服務的企業,也受到了當地政府的支持。

在旅遊方面,生物科技則是將獨特的 Airbnb 入住體驗,徹底提升至另一個層次。2019 年春季 Airbnb 公司和 23andMe 基因檢測公司聯手合作,在顧客使用 23andMe 公司的其中一項 DNA 檢測工具後,依照測出來的結果,為其客製與顧客祖先文化遺產相關的活動。Airbnb 公司表示:「舉例來說,具有墨西哥血統的人,就可以在

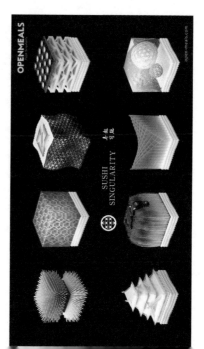

Sushi Singularity. Image courtesy of Open Meals

我們相信超個性化將成為未來常態。

Passionality Group 創始合夥人｜丹尼爾·迪·歐裏（Daniel del Olmo）

70

大麻顧問

隨著大麻文化越來越精緻，專家開始為講究品質的顧客提供鑑賞服務。

大麻二酚（現在普遍稱為 CBD）是大麻製品中有效但沒有亢奮效果的成份，該成分目前已經越來越容易取得，產品類型能也越來越精緻。

2019 年 5 月，CBD 零售商 Standard Dose 從線上商店拓展到實體店面，開設了一家位於紐約市的實體健康基地。店內的「教育人員」會在店中為顧客提供諮詢與導覽，並為他們尋找「符合個人需求的產品。因為 CBD 對每個人的影響大不相同。」Standard Dose 的創立者安東尼·賽內格（Anthony Saniger）對《Coveteur》生活時尚雜誌如此說道。他們提供的指引還包括一系列精心設計的試用體驗，從冥想工作坊到大麻茶飲吧皆包含在內。

若要追求更專屬的服務，居住加州的大麻顧問艾咪·羅伯森（Amy Robertson）可為客人提供超個性化的頂級體驗和推薦，協助他們過濾掉被大肆炒作的商品，找到可以滿足個人需求的工藝級優質大麻製品。當客戶不是為了解決醫療問題而來時，「如果是高端市場，給他們什麼都可以負擔得起的話，那就看着他們想要體驗哪種迷幻的感覺了。」羅伯森向《Vice》雜誌如此表示。有越來越多的奢侈品消費者開始尋找教學和使用指南，希望能在泛的大麻市場和商業倫理參差的品牌大海中找到方向，而各種產品證明和產品本身也會受到更

Standard Dose CBD retailer, New York City

嚴格的檢視。大麻市場分析公司 Arcview Market Research 指出，大麻市場在 2022 年以前，會有超過 230 億美元的商機。

大麻教育公司 Eminent Consulting 的共同創辦人艾瑪·查森（Emma Chasen）向顧門智威廣告表示：「在某種程度上，也是因為食物，也願意花時間找尋有機的當地農產品，那你也絕對要關注你所食用的大麻製品。」

遍來說卻越來越有消費意識了。如果你在意吃進身體的食物，也願意花時間找尋有機的當地農產品，那你也絕對要關注你所食用的大麻製品。」

新興慶典或成沉浸式體驗活動中，往往集結了為著教育、娛樂、社交目的而來的各大品牌、專家。讓飄者和經歷豐富的粉絲。大麻雜誌《Broccoli》在 2019 年 5 月時，於俄勒岡州波特蘭開辦的 In Bloom 節慶便是以展示大麻主題的藝術品、音樂演出、工作坊、座談會、試吃活動為主。幾個月後，洛杉磯的 Weedmaps Museum of Weed 大麻博物館則開書前客踏上一趟文化與政治之旅，破除一般人對大麻製品常有的迷思。

查森表示：「我想大麻教育接下來的目標對象，會是醫療保健專家和醫生。他們如果要用更好的方法來幫助病人，就需要比其他族群更瞭解相關資訊。因此，我預計在不久的將來，會出現更多大學或社區大學開設的大麻學程和認證課程。」

值得關注的原因：

CBD 市場開始湧現無數品牌，他們都是把對大麻製品感到好奇的消費者啟蒙概念的品牌，就能在其中嶄露頭角，而高端消費者在這個領域中要尋找的則是量身訂做的專屬體驗。

79

新世代探險家

在政治、經濟動盪不安的時代裡，許多人藉由旅行獲得喘息的機會，也把旅行視為追尋快樂的管道。

從《Travelzoo》旅遊網站對會員所做的問卷調查可知，有 70% 來自澳洲、加拿大、中國、法國、德國、香港、西班牙、英國、美國的受訪者，計畫將健康活動納入 2019 年的旅遊規劃中；並有 83% 的受訪者表示，渡假時對自己的心理健康有加分效果。

為了回應這股趨勢，《Travelzoo》於 2019 年春季推出「我的五月」（May is for Me）宣傳企劃。在活動專頁上提供聚焦健康的專屬行程以及健康旅行的祕訣。《Travelzoo》將健康渡假定義為改善身心健康的客製假期。「我的五月」網頁上涵蓋了各式各樣的行程，包括在尼泊爾做瑜伽，前往葡萄牙的養生會館，享受英美各地的水療行程等。這些行程都是為了因應逐日增加的健康旅行趨勢而生。

2019 年 10 月，豪華旅遊網站《Black Tomato》舉辦了 Every Cloud 競賽。《Black Tomato》體認到，「有時候，世界就像是陰暗又死寂的地方，舉目所見都是負面消息、不安感、壓力」，但在 Every Cloud 這項競賽，可以「為大家找到一線曙光」。這項競賽的贏家，可以前往

WUNDERMAN
THOMPSON

Black Tomato Every Cloud Inspirational travel program

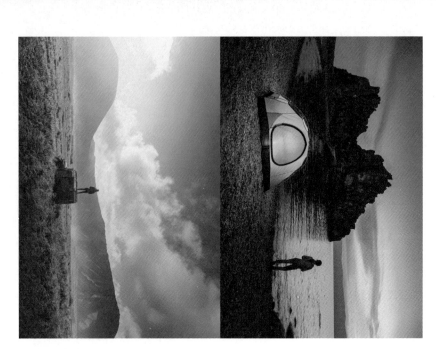

有時候世界就像是隱暗又死寂的地方，舉目所見都
是負面消息、不安感、壓力，但 Every Cloud
這項競賽，帶給大家一線曙光。

Black Tomato

2020 年當中環遊世界整整一年，在這段期間內，除了找尋歡樂美好
的生活體驗，也需要和《Black Tomato》一起創作內容，傳寫大眾
對於旅遊的美好認知，傳達旅遊可以鼓舞人心的概念。

依據《Black Tomato》網站所述，這位成人將會紀錄一段段「與世
上最獨特也最具正能量的人、事、時、地、物相遇的過程」，並將一
整年的體驗與《Black Tomato》網站的讀者分享，把個人旅行變成
啟發大眾的旅程。

值得關注的原因：
隨著消費者嘗試接納更積極的思考模式，旅行同時的目的也從逃避現
實演變為追求樂觀和幸福的體驗，旅行同時也是保持身心健康的
管道。

61

Black Tomato Every Cloud inspirational travel program

80 純素主義飯店

拜睿華飯店開始提供道德與永續生態兼具的服務之賜，高端旅人終於能享受到純素的待遇。

在蘇格蘭高地的維多利亞小鎮內，有一間飯店展示了所謂的「道德奢華」概念。2019 年 6 月開幕的 Saorsa 1875 飯店以由裡到外的全素哲學迎接旅客。從員工制服、盥洗用品、小冰箱內的點心到電力供給，全都顧慮周詳。飯店使用的電力來自擁有純素認證的綠電公司 Ecotricity，飯店內的每一個小細節，從入住到退房也都完全符合純素規範，不但來源符合道德要求也看不見任何與動物有關的副產品。

「我們想向大家展示，純素主義並非只是出於同情或道德所做的選擇，更可以是一種令人開心、充滿活力的生活方式。」Saorsa 1875 飯店的共同創辦人及生活風格主管傑克・麥拉倫史都華（Jack McLaren-Stewart）如此表示。

Saorsa 1875 飯店開幕的時間點正好有越來越多的英國人轉向純素生活。Vegan Society 指出，英國境內的純素人口在 2014 年到 2019 年間成長了四倍。英國市場研究諮詢公司（Mintel）於 2019 年發佈的研究也顯示，截至 2018 年 7 月，有 34% 的英國肉食者在前 6 個月中選擇了彈性素食（flexitarian），並以更積極的方式來降低肉食用量。

從另一個例子也能發現純素市場仍在成長。希爾頓飯店（Hilton）於 2019 年 1 月在倫敦河畔分店推出「全球第一間純素套房」，由 Bompas & Parr 聯合 Vegan Society 共同打造。套房內的纖品完全採用植物纖維製成，包含有機棉地毯、大豆纖維絲質窗簾、蕎麥枕心抱枕。房內的小配件，乃至於住客入住櫃台取得的房卡，也都是利用 Piñatex 這連連從鳳梨葉提取的原料，來製造出類皮革的質感。

「雖然這間套房是為認同永續理念的旅客所設計，但我們還是希望每個人都能享受住在這個套房裡的體驗。這間套房不只提供擁抱純素生活的人入住。」飯店總經理詹姆斯‧克拉克（James B Clarke）向有線電視新聞網（CNN）如此表示。而他也同時透露，這間套房備空關注。接到的許多詢問中甚至「包含知名運動員人士」。

值得關注的原因：

純素主義曾讓人聯想到禁慾和苦行僧的生活方式，但如今這個概念已被道德感強烈的消費者提升至引人嚮往的奢華生活。在食業者集體回應素食市場的同時，奢華品牌也開始將旅行的目的地，轉為不使用任何動物產品的庇護空間，來促使純素生活再進化。

醫療保健

81

心靈療癒節

音樂具有能讓人身歷其境的力量，因此音樂人開始搭上身心療癒的浪潮似乎也不足為奇。

以創造脫俗的情境音樂聞名的冰島樂團 Sigur Rós，舉辦了一系列的「聲音浴」活動，希望樂迷能「和其他人類一起在同一個音樂現場」享受播放清單《Liminal》中的現場人聲。搭配如夢似幻日隨著聲音變化的燈光，讓人欣喜若狂。每個人都臣服於寂靜之中，如果夠投入的話，仿佛還能從各種差異微小的不同角度來觀看一切事物的自感覺。這項活動於 2017 至 2019 年舉辦，場地包括洛杉磯郡的自然歷史博物館（National History Museum）、巴黎的 Days Off、倫敦的 British Summer Time Hyde Park。

Glastonbury 藝術節在 2019 年推出了「養生區」（Humblewell），主辦人描述道：「這個區域涵蓋了『身體、情感、社會面的健康』，整場活動也包含『呼吸節奏計畫』（Breathbeats），融合『呼吸療法與心理原音』，由兩位 DJ－湯姆．彌道頓（Tom Middleton）和瑞奇．波斯塔克（Richie Bostock）共同創作，他們也被稱為 the Breath Guy。」

Newcastle wellness installation at Pharos festival, New Zealand.
Photo by Superimpose

為了呈現節慶中健康當道的趨勢，《衛報》（The Guardian）以結合音樂與跑步的 Love Trails Festival 來做例子。音樂節主辦單位在主舞台上說明這項活動「會在三天內不間斷地播放經典歌曲及新藝人的作品，也有距離長短不一的田徑冒險」。Love Trails Festival 的共同創辦人及活動總監西奧·侖邊斯（Theo Larn-Jones）向《衛報》表示：「音樂節最大的難題是，如何利用渴望來讓生活變得更充實、更健康、更快樂，尤其是年輕人的渴望，也就是那些 20 至 30 歲的人。我自己也屬於這個世代的人。我們還想參加音樂節和派對，但不一定要在過程中喝個爛醉才開心。就像跑步的有受受的愉悅感一樣，跑步產生的腦內啡可以取代在音樂節中狂飲所需來的快樂。」

紐西蘭也於 2018 年在歌手淘氣阿甘（Childish Gambino）的 Pharos 音樂節中，舉辦以健康為主題的多種活動。《Dezeen》雜誌在報導中指出，音樂節中包含了「聲音浴、宇宙嗡鳴、真理連接亭和啟蒙活動」。真名為唐納·葛洛佛（Donald Glover）的歌手向《Dezeen》雜誌表示：「Pharos 音樂節的目的是要成為一種共享空間，一種會演進、會反應文化的空間。我們賣的是貨真價實的親密感。我們要保護這種體驗，讓它成為你能和身邊的人真誠共享的經歷，讓你帶走與眾不同的體驗。」

值得關注的原因：
對千禧世代和 Z 世代的人而言，參加音樂節不一定等於盡情放縱的享樂主義。相反的，他們要找的是透過提升身心靈健康來擴展視野的方式，而思想前衛的音樂人與音樂節的主辦方也妥善運用了這個剛萌芽的潮流。

02

迷幻保健

隨著大麻順利打入主流市場，迷幻藥物也跟著脫穎而出，成為新時代的療法。

科學界的研究指出，賽洛西賓（迷幻蘑菇中可致幻的複合物）可帶領使用者深入自己的意識，進而治療憂鬱症。

2019 年的 9 月，位於佛州的約翰·霍普金斯醫學公司（John Hopkins Medicine）接受 1700 萬美元的私人捐款後，成立了迷幻藥物與意識研究中心（Center for Psychedelic and Consciousness Research）。該實驗室表示，他們將使用迷幻藥物來「研究意識，並藉此找出成癮問題、創傷後壓力症候群、阿茲海默症的治療方法」，這項計畫也包含了對賽洛西賓迷幻蘑菇的研究在內。

倫敦帝國學院亦於 2019 年 4 月開設迷幻藥物研究中心（Centre for Psychedelic Research）來研究迷幻藥物產生的行為，並特別將重點放在憂鬱症的治療研究上。研究中心負責人羅賓·卡哈特哈里斯博士（Dr. Robin Carhart-Harris）指出，開設迷幻藥物研究中心「是迷幻藥學界的分水嶺，象徵它現在已經獲得主流醫學的認可。在不久的將來，迷幻藥將會對照科學和精神病學產生重大影響」。

隨著越來越多的研究指出迷幻藥物的益處，美國國會議員也在為迷幻藥納入主流而鋪路。在丹佛、科羅拉多、奧克蘭，持有賽洛西賓產品皆以除罪化，接下來聖克魯茲也可能會加入它們的行列。

美國食品藥物管理局（FDA）也進一步將鹵素物質列為合法，並於 2018 年 10 月認證 Compass Pathways 生物醫學公司「突破性療法」，近期還有於 2019 年 11 月獲得認定的 Usona Institute。這兩間公司都以臨床實驗證實賽洛西賓可能有助治療重度憂鬱症。美國躁鬱症和憂鬱症學會（Anxiety and Depression Association of America）指出，有 1610 萬的美國人患有重度憂鬱症，如果上列研究結果正確，賽洛西賓可能會成為療法之一。

除了對健康有益，消費者也利用迷幻藥物探索自己的深層意識，使得致幻營（Psychedelic retreats）出現增長的趨勢。英國啟靈學會（Psychedelic Society）在歐洲舉辦賽洛西賓致幻營，並表示他們的「目標對象是身心健康狀況良好，且想要探索現實和心智本質的人」。

Synthesis 是一間位於荷蘭的致幻中心，是提倡「轉化型健康」的先驅。該中心於 2018 年 4 月揭幕，它提供為期三天的活動，要價 1640 英鎊（約台幣 62,870 元），對象為「對迷幻蘑菇感到好奇、想利用中高劑量賽洛西賓蘑菇來催化創新突破、探索意識、找尋意義、改善自信及尋求神秘體驗的人」。

而多虧有了創投公司 Wavepaths，現在不透過藥物來獲得致幻

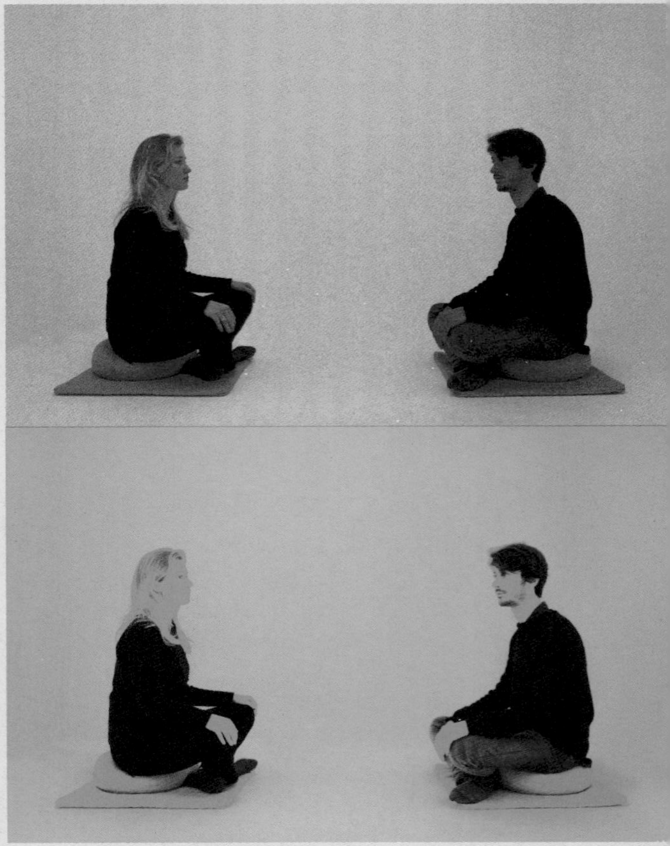

Wavepaths psychedelic experiences without drugs

Synthesis wellness retreat, the Netherlands. Image courtesy of Synthesis

隨著越來越多的
研究指出
迷幻藥物的益處，
美國國會曾議員
也在為
迷幻藥納入主流而鋪路。

體驗已成為可能。這間公司由一群科學家、技術專家、心理治療師、藝術家組成，使命是要「讓大眾都能嘗試心智轉化的體驗」。該公司表示，結合音樂、燈光以及心理治療師的參與，Wavepaths 的沉浸式體驗將引導參與者進入「沈寂與平靜」或「探索內心旅程、連結深層情緒」的狀態。

值得關注的原因：

賽洛西賓有潛力成為新一代的大麻。有越來越多研究迷幻藥物的報告指出，該物質具有治療心理疾病的功效，在緩步推動合法化程序的途中，消費者也轉向致幻幻營，用迷幻藥物開展身心健康的全新體驗。

03 快速療癒空間

寵愛自己的概念也許深植消費者心中，
但是又有多少都市人能夠撥出時間，享受一日水療，
或長時間的療程呢？

快速療癒空間如雨後春筍般出現，這些空間可配合焦慮的都市人
騰出空檔，為他們提供片刻寧靜。

3Den 共同工作空間自述是一間「都會休息室」，這間公司位於紐約
的哈德遜城廣場開發計畫地段。除了工作空間之外，它也提供「安
靜區、午睡艙、噪概供應備品的淋浴間」，讓客戶在城市之中也有
機會替自己充一下電。「我們匯集了咖啡店、飯店大廳、健身房及各
種資源中最棒的元素。」3Den 共同工作空間創辦人及執行長班·史
林佛（Ben Silver）向媒門智威智庫表示：「就消費者行為來看，這
樣做並非多此一舉。雖然這些服務早就有人提供了，但他們則是用完
全不同而且無實際效的方式在執行，而我門是將這些服務匯
整成更優質的消費體驗。」3Den 的入場費用平易近人，使用 30 分
鐘的費用從 6 美元起跳。

Thinx 以生產生理期專用的內衣聞名，他們開設了一間「休息室」
（Rest Room），打造與產品相關的用戶體驗。這是位於紐約蘇活雖然現今的生活步調比以往更快，但消費者也越來越意識到，馬不停蹄的生活習慣會對身心健康造成損害。

南韓的腳步，當地的療癒咖啡廳非常興盛。南韓的連鎖咖啡店提供了多種療癒服務，例如 Shim Story 的「公眾休息室」提供了加熱床位，按摩椅與電玩，而 Mr Healing 按摩椅和眼罩。尤里・費德曼 (Uri Friedman) 向環境中，為客人提供按摩椅和眼罩。尤里・費德曼 (Uri Friedman)「可在已開發國家中工時最長的國家之一，撫慰睡眠嚴重不足的人群」。

《大西洋》（The Atlantic）雜誌表示，這種咖啡店「可在已開發國家中工時最長的國家之一，撫慰睡眠嚴重不足的人群」。

值得關注的原因：

雖然現今的生活步調比以往更快，但消費者也越來越意識到，馬不停蹄的生活習慣會對身心的人量身打造，可以配合飛速運轉的現代世界，讓顧客在忙碌有健康意識的生活之中仍可獲得片刻平靜與喘息的空間。

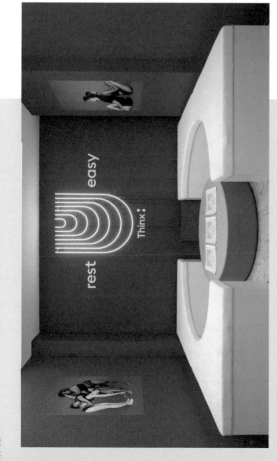

區伊莉莎白街的快閃空間，於 2019 年 10 月 28 日至 2020 年 1 月 1 日期間開放，消費者可在此購買 Thinx 的產品，在快閃沙發區放鬆，也能體驗一系列和婦科相關的活動，包含生育諮詢或 Thinx 產品的使用教學。

療癒空間的概念也攻佔倫敦的市場。Pop & Rest 膠囊旅館在霍爾本和秀爾迪契區附近設有分店，提供午睡和冥想館，使用間 30 分鐘的價格為 8 英鎊（約台幣 300 元）。Inhere 冥想中心目前則是向企業出租並販售時尚木製冥想館，永久店址預計於 2020 年春季開幕。

這些西方公司之所以開始發展功能型如快速療癒空間，其實是追隨著

The Rest Room pop-up by Thinx. Image courtesy of Thinx

04

數位SPA

有許多人會將心理疾病和不良的生活習慣歸咎於社群媒體和科技，但擁有先進思考的應用程式和數位平台已開始巧妙地運用科技，來鼓勵正念並加強身心健康。

在 2019 年 5 月，《Dazed》雜誌成立了《Dazed Beauty Digital Spa》網站，並描述此網站是「為了讓使用者變得更健康、更快樂，遠離日常壓力而設計的沉浸式空間」。這個新網站重塑了傳統的 Spa 概念，定位於線上社群和數位引導的身心健康鍛鍊之間，時長一週的計畫包含現場直播的瑜伽課程，以及一系列發人深省的文章、小測驗、冥想類的播客語音節目，主題從色彩療法到勵志小話等一應俱全。

其他數位平台也開始崛起，為協助使用者放鬆、稍作喘息、找回身心平衡。Headspace 目前正研發全球首見的處方籤級冥想應用程式，以特別的設計來治療與壓力相關的一系列慢性疾病。

甚至連寶可夢公司 (Pokémon Company) 也將注意力轉向身心健康，並製作了 Pokémon Sleep 這款遊戲化應用程式，這款遊戲發表於 2019 年 5 月，並預計於 2020 年在行動裝置上正式發行，

Pokémon Sleep 旨在「獎勵良好睡眠習慣，使其成為健康生活方式的一環」。

Flow 的共同創辦人丹尼爾·曼森 (Daniel Månsson) 向偉門智威指出：「在未來，整合數位健康工具和標準醫學保健程序會是趨勢，比方像治療型的應用程式。」這間瑞典新創公司成立於 2019 年的 6 月初，目前正為憂鬱症創造無須用藥的數位療法。

值得關注的原因：

長期以來，有許多人將不良的心理健康或失眠歸咎於科技產品和智慧型手機，然而，這些新的應用程式和平台正力圖扭轉形象，並準備好要利用科技，為大眾達成理想的健康狀態。

05

無性別生理期

隨著社會逐漸朝開放東容的未來邁進，大眾開始
重新審視性別規範，而一度只對女孩和女人
行銷的生理用品品牌，現在也開始重新
思考他們的目標受眾。

2019 年秋季，好自在衛生棉公司 (Always) 決定停用包裝上的維
納斯符號，力圖讓跨性別或非二元性別的消費者更有認同感。寶
僑集團 (Proctor & Gamble) 說：「過去 35 年來，好自在一直支持
女孩和女人，而我們往後也會一直這樣做，除此之外，我們也會為
多樣性和包容性而努力，並往往後的道路上盡力理解所有消費
者的需求。」

位於紐約的 Thinx 態度更加堅決，不但在 2016 年的品牌宣傳中首
度雇用了跨性別模特兒，還在 2019 年 10 月發表名為「男性經期」
(MENstruation) 的廣告，刻畫出一個男女皆有生理期的世界，並
在廣告結尾加註「如果大家都有生理期，也許我們就會對這件事情
感到更自在。」

過去幾年來以來，許多品牌開始採用對性別包容度更廣的用詞或行
銷方式。如 Lunapads 護墊公司在 2016 年曾「為符合跨性別男消

「女性護理」和「女性衛生」等用詞，將在走向性別包容的未
來社會中成為一種贅字。這個領域的品牌也需要重新評估並措辭和
產品，例如以「經期產品」取代「女性產品」；或是將品牌重新定位
為健康產業，而非女性限定的健康產業。如此一來，就能讓每
位需要經歷生理期的人都能產生認同感。

費者的需求」而設計了四角生理褲；2017 年，內褲品牌 Pyramid
Seven 也創造了這個標語：「內褲是為生理期而設計，不是為女性
別」；衛生棉品牌 Aunt Flow 也積極地使用性別包容更廣的詞彙。

值得關注的原因：

「女性護理」和「女性衛生」等用詞，將在走向性別包容的未來社會中，成為一種贅字。

WUNDERMAN
THOMPSON

Inclusive period brand Thinx

美保健

06

酸鹼平衡一下

酸鹼值有可能成為
了解肌膚和健康問題的新關鍵嗎？

萊雅集團（L'Oréal）旗下的個人護理巨擘理膚寶水（La Roche-Posay），在 2019 年 6 月推出了「我的肌膚酸鹼值追蹤器」（My Skin Track pH）初代樣本。這款微流體感測器可透過微流道網絡，捕捉毛孔滲出的微量汗水，「並於 15 分鐘內測出準確的肌膚酸鹼值」，萊雅集團在 2019 年消費電子用品展（CES 2019）上發佈產品時如此表示。

萊雅集團解釋，肌膚酸鹼值不平衡時會導致發炎反應，進而加速惡化皮膚乾燥、溼疹和異位性皮膚炎等狀況。舉例來說，肌膚的酸鹼度可能會受到壞境因素或個人潛在狀況所影響。

德國明斯特大學（University of Münster）皮膚醫學系主任及湯馬斯·盧格教授（Professor Thomas Luger）在萊雅集團的聲明中表示：「酸鹼值是肌膚健康的首要指標。也是我的病人會提問的領域，如何在診所以外的地方檢測酸鹼值一直是個難題。讓他們願意採取比較健康的肌膚保養習慣，也讓專業醫學人士得以用全新的方式來給予肌膚保養方面的建議」。

NDERMAN
MPSON

酸鹼值是肌膚健康的首要指標，也是我的病人會提問的領域，如何在診所以外的地方檢測酸鹼值，一直是個難題，直到現在終於有了改變。這項工具有潛力啟發消費者，讓他們願意採取比較健康的肌膚保養習慣，也讓專業醫學人士得以用全新的方式來給予肌膚保養方面的建議。

— 德國明斯特大學皮膚醫學系主任｜湯馬斯・盧格教授 (Prof. Thomas Luger)

美國的理膚寶水皮膚科專家正在檢測「我的肌膚酸鹼值追蹤器」，希望其最終能推出消費型產品。

酸鹼值也會影響道健康。因此有些內褲品牌開始推出號稱可平衡酸鹼值的產品。這些品牌之中，內衣褲品牌 Huha 在產品中加入鋅以「預防感染及產生異味的細菌」。Pure 5.5 公司則指出，自家的透氣內褲可藉由平衡陰道酸鹼值來預防感染和異味。然而，婦產科醫生雪莉羅斯博士 (Dr Sherry A Ross) 向《Well & Good》雜誌指出：她並不認為酸鹼平衡內褲「比其他一樣可讓陰道透氣的內褲更安全」，例如棉質內褲。

從禠取自健康資料分析公司 Spins 的數看來，鹼性水 (alkaline water) 也大行其道，《影博雜誌》(Bloomberg) 報導指出：當年截至 2019 年 4 月，在美國瓶裝水產業的大餅之中，即使鹼性水只佔一小部分，也成長了 36% 並來到近 2 億 7 千萬美元的銷售額。鹼性水言有的功效包括「補水效果更好」，瓶裝水市場龍頭 Essentia 則號稱鹼性水可以「超效補水」，讓你有動力做想做的事。同時，葛妮絲・派特洛 (Gwyneth Paltrow) 在她的《Goop》網站中推薦了 Flow 公司的瓶裝水，該品牌也提供「天然鹼性水」，並棄棄塑膠瓶改用紙盒包裝，強調永續環境的品牌精神。

值得關注的原因：

雖然酸鹼值和肌膚健康有關，但鹼性水的功效仍然眾說紛紜。2019 年 8 月，《富比士新聞網》(Forbes.com) 曾發布的「買賣鹼性水等於浪費錢的七大理由」為題的文章。然而，持續攀升的鹼性水市場顯示，消費者對可輕易符合忙碌生活習慣的新一代健康促進產品仍抱有高度興趣。CCD Helmsman 的副總裁凱拉・尼爾森 (Kara Nielsen) 向《影博雜誌》表示：「我們開始提高審視事物的標準——每件事的背後都必須有個代表意義，這就是年輕世代對健康成份的看法。」

陪伴工程學

孤單寂寞不只是社會議題，也與大眾健康有關。

隨著人類的整體壽命持續延長，現今有許多老年族群面臨了獨自老去的問題，目前也開始有幾種新型服務和科技新創品牌正在致力解決此問題。

發表於《華爾街日報》（Wall Street Journal）的研究指出，有 800 萬名 50 歲以上的美國人沒有配偶、沒有伴侶、沒有在世子女，此數據來自美國普查局（US Census）。而發表於《神經學、神經外科及精神病學期刊》（Journal of Neurology, Neurosurgery and Psychiatry）上的「阿姆斯特丹高齡者研究」（Amsterdam Study of the Elderly）則顯示出寂寞的人較有可能罹患憂鬱症、心臟疾病、失智症。

日本研發機器人的新創公司 Groove X 在 2019 年的消費電子用品展（CES 2019）上發表了 Lovot 機器人。外表引人注目的 Lovot 可提供陪伴和關愛，身上安裝的多個感應器使其可與使用者互動，回應擁抱、按壓、敲打等動作。Lovot 由先驅機器人 Pepper 的創造者林要（Kaname Hayashi）所設計，他向《CNET》網站解釋：他的設計並非要取代人與人之間的關係，而是讓人能保留情緒互動的能力。「如果你每天仍愛著一樣東西，那你就能保有愛的能力。」設計師林要如此說道。

同樣在 2019 年度消費電子用品展上發表的還有 ElliQ 機器人，它是一個語音驅動的陪伴型機器人。經過數年的研發，ElliQ 已開放預購，這台多功能的裝置可協助年長者與家人保持聯絡，提供居家陪伴服務，也能對語音、觸摸、凝視等有所反應，甚至還會做做娛樂表演，以及主動提醒同時該喝水、運動、冥想。

值得關注的原因：

美國人口普查局的預測指出，到了 2030 年，美國將出現歷史上第一次 65 歲以上的人口多於 18 歲以下人口的情形。既然老一代人口數將會壓倒性地超過年輕一代，那麼這個成長中的消費族群絕對是不容小覷的。

科技巨頭跨足健康

科技巨頭接下來將瞄準哪片新疆域？
他們也許能讓複雜的美國健保系統獲得解套。

許多間科技巨頭在近幾個月紛紛投入健康市場，而對於科技在基礎建設上逐漸獨占市場，社會也傳出不同聲浪。

蘋果（Apple）於 2019 年 11 月宣布：自家的「研究」（Research）應用程式將參與諸之為具有「里程碑」意義的三項健康研究，包括蘋果的「女性健康研究」（Apple Women's Health Study）、「心臟與活動力」（Apple Heart and Movement）研究、「聽力研究」（Apple Hearing Study）。他們將與諸和研究機構合作：進行多年的縱向研究，如哈佛陳曾熙公共衛生學院（TH Chan School of Public Health）、美國國家衛生研究院的環境健康科學研究所（NIH' s National Institute of Environmental Health Sciences）、布萊根婦女醫院（Brigham and Women' s Hospital）、美國心臟協會（American Heart Association）等，皆參與了此次的「心臟與活動力研究」。蘋果說：「上列機構透過 iPhone 和 Apple Watch 參與研究，為有潛力成為突破性醫療發現之研究人員貢獻一分心力，並協助創造出新一代的醫療產品。」

然而，《紐約時報》（the New York Times）的記者娜塔莎·辛格（Natasha Singer）則認為，蘋果的產品用戶多為高收入消費者，所

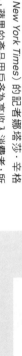

以可能誤導研究結果，除此之外，她也說道：「還有一些其他的疑慮：重塑現代人生活，溝通、娛樂管道的頭條公司，否在找尋另一種影響社會的方式呢？這次是透過健康來進行嗎？」

合歌對於健康市場也摩拳擦掌，2019 年的 11 月，健康穿戴裝置公司 Fitbit 宣佈，他們同意合歌以 21 億美元將其收購，此次收購案預計於 2020 年完成。「合歌是能進一步完成我們使命的最佳夥伴，透過合歌的資源和全球平台，Fitbit 將能加速穿戴裝置的創新與研發，也可以擴大規模使每個人都能更瞭解自己的健康狀態」，Fitbit 的共同創辦人及執行長詹姆斯·朴（James Park）如此表示。

在分析為何合歌會受到 Fitbit 健康穿戴裝置所吸引時，撰稿人派翠克·盧卡斯·奧斯丁（Patrick Lucas Austin）在《時代雜誌》（Time）中寫道：「Fitbit 早就與保險公司、其他企業甚至是新加坡政府合作，他們可能是以相當豐厚的利潤，為消費者、員工、市民提供健身追蹤裝置」，並補充提到「對於合歌來說，將 Fitbit 的醫療穿戴裝置與其早已建立的使用者基數結合，可能正符合他們所需，能為他們與穿戴裝置相關的策略打一劑強心針」。這篇《時代雜誌》的文章同時指出，根據數據統計公司 Statista 預估：「2020 年前，醫療市場可能上看 240 億美元。」

同樣不落人後的還有亞馬遜（Amazon）。亞馬遜發表了亞馬遜醫療照護（Amazon Care），並將其定調為「虛擬和親身照護的最佳產品」。這項產品目前針對亞馬遜公司西雅圖區的員工進行測試，提供了常見的醫療保健服務，如協助判斷感冒、過敏、感染症狀，以及避孕諮詢及性傳染病檢測，並可同時將處方箋用藥送至家門口，同時有人員親自到住所或辦公室採視，也提供遠端諮詢服務。

科技快訊（TechCrunch）科技報導公司也觀察到，雖然蘋果同時替

保健

自家員工提供遠端和內部醫療保健，但「亞馬遜照護」更值得關注的原因在於：「比起矽谷同業提供的服務，它更具有對外開放的特質，加上品牌形象和宣傳方式都更具針對未來潛在的照護市場，不僅僅只考量到自家員工。」報導並指出，亞馬遜在 2019 年 10 月收購了線上病症檢查與分診工具公司 Health Navigator，而美國財經電視頻道（CNBC）寫道：「如果亞馬遜照護在員工測試時順利成功，亞馬遜就有可能在未來的某天，將此服務給已對亞馬遜拍賣商品、娛樂事業、旗下其他產業具有相當依賴程度的上百萬用戶。」

值得關注的原因：

在全面顛覆人類生活方式後，科技巨頭如今將眼光看向醫療保健市場。這些科技大廠的先進技術無疑能創造出無縫接軌的使用介面，並可能對一向難以控管的美國健保系統帶來正面影響。然而與隱私權和消費者個資相關的問題仍是一大隱憂。Fitbit 指出，谷歌收購諧公司，他們也不會售出或將其所有資料分享給該公司的研究計畫。不管矽谷的作為給人什麼要印象，他們想在醫療保健市場佔有一席之地的目標已非常明顯。

蘋果也表示：消費者可以自訂出哪些資料將用於廣告上；同時，

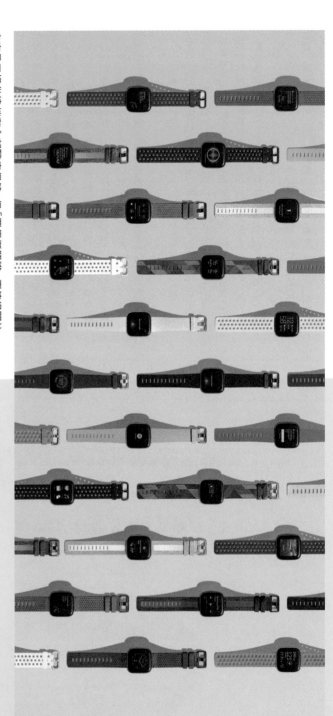

2011年，牛津大學出版社（Oxford University Press）發行的《公共衛生期刊》（Journal of Public Health）提問道：「汽車是新一代於於糖嗎？」並將汽車文化與體能活動不足、肥胖、空氣污染導致的心血管疾病、汽車意外造成的死傷、氣候變遷等現象直接連結在一起。自此之後，全球各地（多數為政府機關）便開始致力於抑制車輛排放的空污，並希望民眾可以用走路或腳踏車代步。

紐約將於2021年把強制措施做到在尖峰時段用車進入市區的交通運輸基費，這是美國首座實施此措施的城市，緊跟在倫敦和新加坡之後。北京則是在新車牌照上採取抽籤制，其中電動車的額度比傳統汽車多，其他們也要求使用汽油的車輛一週需停駛一天，停駛的日期則依據汽車牌照尾數最後一碼來決定。

2019年因為空氣毒害使民眾眼睛刺痛且導致學校關閉後，印度新德里也開始限制車輛的使用，讓汽車需依據牌照號碼輪流上路。新加坡政府則是大量補貼公司設置淋浴間和更衣室，鼓勵民眾多走路、跑步、騎腳踏車通勤，並可於抵達公司後進行盥洗，便能神清氣爽地打卡上班。

值得關注的原因：

幾十年來，都市設計皆以汽車為優先考量，不但為其保留路邊停車位，也雜亂無章地將開發計畫拓展到市郊地區，不過因車輛過多而帶來的負面影響已被更多人所理解，並已到達臨界點。年輕族群越來越傾向不買車，部分原因是因為開銷，另一部分則是因為叫車服務已相當便利，所以這些人寧可將錢花在新體驗或旅遊上，對於庫得薩社區的創立者而言，坦佩大學城的無車社區實驗只是個開端，這間公司最終的目標，是希望能在美國打造出第一座無車城市。

89

無車社區

美國作為汽車量產的領航國家，創造出汽車文化、公路旅遊、得來速餐廳，現在則開始發展專為無車住戶打造的社區。

位於亞利桑那州坦佩市的庫得薩（Culdesac）新社區已於2019年下半年動工，此社區預計在2020年秋季開放1000名同意不買車的租客入住。庫得薩將自己定調為「全球首家為汽車時代的房地產開發商」，並號稱這項1億4千萬美元的計畫將擁有一座狗公園、市集廣場、食品雜貨店、健身房、餐廳。

庫得薩社區旨在推廣環境友善和適宜人居的生活方式，其中設有茂密的林蔭大道鼓勵居民外出散步、玩滑板車、騎自行車，社區內也規劃了可通往坦佩市、亞利桑那州立大學（Arizona State University）以及機場的輕軌電車、且救護車、貨運服務用車、小型共享汽車仍能行進出社區。

這項計畫呼應著全球其他城市的需求，許多城市基於健康考量選擇不再於市中心使用汽車，這當中包括芝加哥、印度的法齊爾卡，以及2019年上半年從市中心移除700個車位以限制用車的奧斯陸。

WUNDERMAN
THOMPSON

醫療保健

Recompose after-death facility. Image courtesy of Olson Kundig

90

新型送行者

有一連串的創新服務，開始以健康、
環保的方式處理與葬儀式。

根據數據統計公司 Statista 統計，2019 年單單美國殯葬業的產值
就高達 170 億美元。百年來少有革新的這項產業，已準備好大刀闊
斧地改變。從新世代葬儀公司到臨終導師，新興行業正在撼動這塊
市場，並重新檢驗生命終點的禁忌和傳統。

新型送行者也稱為死亡助產士，近期開始被視為現代照護產業從業人
員，因此也出現了大量的專業訓練和認證課程。2019 年佛蒙特大
學的醫學院 (University of Vermont's College of Medicine) 成為
首間提供臨終送行專業認證課程的大學學院，加入了國際臨終送
行組織 (International End of Life Doula Association, INELDA)、
臨終藝術機構 (the Art of Dying Institute)、有意識死亡機構 (the
Conscious Dying Institute)、英國臨終送行者 (End of Life Doula
UK) 等國際組織的行列。

Recompose 是一間新型態的喪葬機構，它預定於 2021 年春季在
西雅圖開幕。這間公司將是首間針對傳統葬禮和火化儀式提供永
續選項的機構，他們也提供專用的大體有機堆肥系統。Recom-
pose 的網站上寫到「溫和地將遺體轉化成土壤的一部份，即使死
亡後仍能孕育有新生命」。

「我開始探討我們在這個社會當中，與死亡的關係為何」，Recompose 的執行長卡翠娜‧史派德 (Katrina Spade) 向波士頓公共廣播電台 (WBUR) 如此表示。「我也開始思索：我們是否能在自己的城市中佔有一個位置，在這座城市中，能意識到我們與死亡的關係，並思考我們有限的生命，和我們在循環中的角色。」

Exit Here 禮儀公司在 2019 年 10 月於倫敦開幕，它是一間徹底重新檢視葬禮規劃程序的新型態葬儀社。這家公司由餐廳老闆奧利佛‧佩頓 (Oliver Peyton) 創立。這間公司提供「前所未見的服務、選項、彈性、並且注重細節。」這間公司以對個體的重視為宗旨，並用優雅、有尊嚴、極具現代感的服務項目，提供豐富的全方面體驗。其中還包含獨家設計的棺木、骨灰罈。該禮儀公司於網站上寫道：「從宗教信仰到環境保護，如今我們對於生命有更主觀、更有依據的看法，並提供前所未見的選項。」

值得關注的原因：

大眾對於善終的關注日益增加，使得樂觀臨終的運動也隨之崛起，進一步促成嶄新的臨終服務。如同全球健康研究所 (Global Wellness Institute) 在 2019 趨勢報告中提到的，「「善終」終於成為『完好生命』的其中一環。」

JNDERMAN　Above: Exit Here funeral parlor, London
HOMPSON　Right: Better Place Forests natural alternative to cemeteries, US

5

番外編

100

91

金融新面向

金融科技（Fintech）為死板的金融界注入新活力，不但以新的品牌策略打入流行文化市場，還請來意料之外的形象大使為之代言。

以顛覆性商業模式「先購物，後付款」聞名的瑞典線上支付公司 Klarna，有意為消費者消除金融摩擦，或者套用該品牌的話，他們要「讓購物更暢～快」（沒錯，這個寫法是為了強調程度到底有多順暢）。2019 年 1 月，Klarna 更以跳脫傳統與帶有爭議的舉動來強調自己的主張，宣佈讓饒舌歌手史努比狗狗（Snoop Dogg）成為該品牌的形象大使及小股東。

Klarna 的行銷副總丹尼爾・強頓（Daniel Jontén）表示，史努比狗狗「可說是世界上最暢快的人」，非常符合公司形象，並著著補充說「他讓我們能以嶄新且有創意的方式，來呈現我們的宗旨」。他們共同發想出來的廣告「活得暢快」（Get Smoooth），還為此將史努比狗狗重新包裝為「暢快狗狗」（Smoooth Dogg）。他們將這名饒舌歌手放在有著獨特粉紅絲綢長袍、毛髮柔順的阿富汗獵犬、黃金花生醬的情境中（有時是玩世不恭的古怪風格），藉以強調使用 Klarna 的順暢程度。「Klarna 的順暢付款和史努比的從容不迫，加上古怪的背景與視覺呈現，這些元素都完美地融合在一起。」強頓也表示：

Klarna's "Get Smoooth" campaign featuring Snoop Dogg as Smoooth Dogg

「這是讓 Klarna 跨足流行文化，並成為全球話題的極佳方式。」

「活得暢快」這則廣告發布以後，該公司也於 2019 年 3 月接續推出廣告中出現的產品，包含絲綢床組、喀什米爾圖紙，以及「滑～順長枕」。從行銷語言到付款模式，Klarna 在重視便利、彈性、金融掌控權的千禧年世代和 Z 世代中，人氣節節攀升。

Klarna 於 2005 年成立，並於 2017 年徹底重塑品牌形象，拋開早期的視覺形象和溝通方式。強調指出，此處指的是過往那種「與多數金融業相同的冷靜單調感」，而這項策略顯然奏效了，Klarna

目前是歐洲最大的私人金融科技公司，市值達 55 億美元，並擁有 7,000 萬名購物會員，亦與 17 萬間零售商合作，提供無縫購物體驗。

值得關注的原因：

雖然生活方式與文化不斷演進，但傳統銀行業鮮少做出迎合消費者趨勢的改變。像是 Klarna 這類的金融科技公司，透過改革傳統付款模式以及引用流行文化讓公司成為以消費者為導向的品牌，並因此迎向成功。

92

碳排用額度

**請試著想像一個每筆交易都會影響
個人碳足跡分數的世界。**

隨著新系統開始出現而加強了消費者的意識，並將永續精神轉
化為實際行動，這樣的世界其實已經離我們不遠了。

有許多消費者表示：他們想要以更具永續性且不對地球造成過多
傷害的方式生活。但要實踐這個想法可能有些難度。舉例來說，根
據偉門智威智庫獨有的研究工具 SONAR™ 所進行的「新永續再生」
(New Sustainability: Regeneration) 報告中指出，有 89% 的美國
和英國消費者表示他們會回收家中的資源，但持續進行的人只有
52%；有 85% 的人表示自己會避免使用一次性塑膠，但無時無刻都
能這麼做的人僅有 20%。

2019 年春季，瑞典金融科技公司 Doconomy 推出一種直接了當的
信用卡，可在持卡人達到碳排量上限時阻斷支付行為。他們以碳排
量為標準，而非以傳統的金融額度做限制。這張持卡 Do Black 信用卡
可追蹤每一次購物時的碳足跡，並在持卡人達到每月上限額後停止支
付。碳排限額度是根據聯合國 2030 年的碳排減量目標為計算基準，
而每位使用者的碳排上限，大約相當於已開發國家市民目前人均二
氧化碳排放量的一半。

Doconomy 公司也提供持卡人調額的方式，只要認購開發中國家

所推行之氣候友善計畫，就能調升額度。但網站上也寫道：此選項「不該成為日後過度消費的理由」，這間新創公司將自己定調為「全球第一個為困應日常氣候行動所設計的行動銀行」，此公司也提供 Do White 信用卡，這張信用卡只會追蹤持卡人的碳足跡，但無碳排限額的規定。

各國政府也致力於促進永續發展。以芬蘭赫爾辛基為例，這座城市在 2019 年中推出「永續思考」(Think Sustainably) 平台，供居民、遊客、企業主評估日常行為之用，促使大眾做出更環保的選擇。從名為 Demos Helsinki 的智庫開始，此平台會評價餐廳、藝廊、景點，而溫室氣關的排放量也是其中一項評價準則，該平台也會將廢物管理、保護生態多樣性、無障礙服務、雇備關係及預防疫情等因素納入評價標準。

其他對永續環境也採取大規模行動的城市還包含了丹麥的哥本哈根，這座城市的規劃師預計在 2025 年前讓這座城市達成碳中和的目標。前身為工業重鎮的諾德漢也轉型為「五分鐘城市」，不論要去什麼地方，包括學校或商店，步行時間都不會超過五分鐘。諾德漢希望藉此鼓勵民眾不要開車上路。挪威的奧斯陸也預計將在 2050 年前達成碳中和；瑞典的斯德哥爾摩則計畫在 2040 年前達成完全不用石化燃料的目標。

值得關注的原因：

根據偉門智威智庫獨有的 SONAR™ 研究工具顯示：有 92% 的消費者想要以更環保的方式生活。79% 的人有意識到自己對地球造成的衝擊。然而，要將想法付諸實現，可能還是一項挑戰。不論是信用卡或永續城市的指標，都是將環保想法轉為環保行動的實用新工具。

> **如果你擁有的個資就像資產一樣，你就能用法律保護這項資產。**

資訊透明倡議者｜布特妮・凱瑟（Brittany Kaiser）

凱瑟認為資料使用和獎勵需以財產權框架並加以規範，「如果你擁有的個資就像資產一樣，你就能用法律保護這項資產；若是有任何人想使用你的資產，不論是政府或是私人組織，你都應該弄清楚他們的目的、使用資料的方式，以及他們給你的補償方案」，她表示「財產權屬於基本人權」。

值得關注的原因：

隨著資料複雜度提升，為資料管理和資料維護提供進一步監管措施之需求也隨之增加，這讓品牌與消費者間的傳統資值交換模式產生了重大的改變。

93

個資即為新型貨幣

消費者逐漸體會到個人資料的價值，也開始對無償收集個資的大品牌進行抗爭。

提倡資訊透明的布特妮・凱瑟（Brittany Kaiser）向偉門智威智庫表示，「個資已成為地球上最貴重的資產，但我們這些產出這項資產的個人，目前卻沒有獲得等值的權利」。她曾任劍橋分析（Cambridge Analytica）的業務總監，也是寫書揭發該公司的揭弊者。

長期以來，品牌皆需仰賴數據才能瞭解自己的消費者，而目前為止這些數據仍可無償取得。最近有些消費者開始意識到他們所提供的資料有其價值，並選擇挺身反抗。根據偉門智威智庫於 2019 年 9 月以其獨有的研究工具 SONAR™ 進行的調查顯示：在問及消費者對於品牌取得之資料之預期售價時，美國消費者將人口統計資料定為每個月 87 美元、數位行為每月 105 美元、消費記錄每月 200 美元、位置資訊每月 375 美元，並將與生物測定相關的數據定在每月 550 美元。研究指出：有 91% 的消費者希望企業可以更明確地說明他們使用消費者資料的用途，並有 89% 的人認為企業會刻意以不清楚的方式交代其資料交換條款。

94

生物辨識支付

隨著生物辨識支付的興起,「現金在手」現在似乎多了一層新的含義。

Goode Intelligence 顧問公司於 2018 年做出預測,在 2020 年之前,將有超過 12 億人使用生物辨識支付功能。先進的科技使生物特徵掃描得以拓展至全全球,也讓付款更安全且交易更順暢。

2019 年 4 月,英國國民西敏寺銀行 (NatWest Bank) 為測試新推出的生物辨識簽帳卡,首先對 200 名消費者試行了這項計畫。消費者可以在卡片上註冊自己的指紋,且指紋僅儲存於卡片當中。銀行不會取得消費者的生物辨識資料。這張指紋卡可用於任何使用感應支付的收銀台,即使支付額超過感應支付預設的上限 (30 英鎊) 仍可使用。由於顧客依然使用實體卡片付款,商店也無須更換原有的感應式讀卡機。

為了完全免除對於卡片的需求,丹麥支付平台 Fingopay 於 2019 年 9 月推出採用全新的手指靜脈身份認證支付系統,可於哥本哈根商學院的 Spisestuerne 咖啡廳中使用。Fingopay 耗時一年測試這項新技術,其支付系統可讓學生和教職員在收銀台前以指尖註冊自己的丹麥卡 (Dankort)、Visa 卡或萬事達卡 (Mastercard),接著即能順利付款完成交易。

FINGOPAY

正因靜脈紋路不留痕跡也無法複製，所以它被譽為是最理想的生物辨識方式，最適合用於高安全性身份驗證，如付款或身份證明。

Fingopay 行銷長｜西蒙 · 賓恩 (Simon Binns)

消費者可用臉部辨識進行線上付款，對於可能被信用卡公司視為詐騙的交易，利用這種方式也有助於保障交易安全。

值得關注的原因：

有鑑於越來越多消費者期待在不同場合中都能享受流暢的交易體驗，生物辨識支付將可實現輕鬆和安全兩項要素。

「正因靜脈紋路不留痕跡也無法複製，所以它被譽為是最理想的生物辨識方式，最適合用於高安全性身份驗證，如付款或身份證明」，Fingopay 的行銷長西蒙 · 賓恩 (Simon Binns) 對偉門智威智庫如此表示。

位於舊金山的 Incode 科技公司則是尋求以臉部辨識作為更安全的線上付款方式。透過 2019 年 10 月推出的 Incode Check 結帳功能，

NDERMAN
OMPSON

Left: Fingopay finger-vein payment system
Right: NatWest biometric fingerprint card

56 金融療程

由於大眾對於財務的不安感日益上升，金融療程也開始興起，協助大眾應付財務憂慮帶來的情緒問題。

根據蓋洛普公司 (Gallup) 於 2019 年 4 月發布的民調結果顯示，25% 的美國人「隨時」，或「多數時間」都在擔心家庭收支將會入不敷出，並有 26% 的受訪者表示自己的收支「只是勉強打平」。

2019 年 11 月，英國的金錢與心理健康政策組織 (Money and Mental Health Policy Institute) 發表「2019 年金錢與心理健康宣言」(Money and Mental Health Manifesto 2019)，旨在為 2019 年 12 月的英國大選前呼籲政治人物處理「自殺和財務困難之間的連結」等議題，並建議將與財務相關的諮詢，納入英國國家健保 (British National Health Service) 的心理健康服務之下。

心理研究學家蓋倫·巴克瓦特博士 (Dr Galen Buckwalter) 向《Goop》雜誌提起財務相關的創傷後壓力症候群，他將其定義為「當一個人無法因應突如其來的財務損失，或者長期因為財源不足而造成壓力時，身體、情緒、認知上所出現出的缺陷」。

由於財務不安全感當道，金融療程也隨之崛起，這一現象逐日成長的大餅，能幫助大眾解決潛藏在個人財務決策下的情緒問題。在芝加哥執業的財務治療師妮可·奧賽達 (Nicolle Osequeda) 向《Fast Company》雜誌表示：「金錢和人與金錢之間的關係與許多情緒《傳統上視為禁忌》因此我們必須優先討論這些關係才能讓人有所改變，或讓他們能按照計畫來執行。」

這種以更全面的方式給予理財意見的作法，連帶推動了將情緒問題納入考量的全新金融服務。巴克瓦特博士在《Goop》雜誌中提及 Happy Money (他是投資者之一)。此公司表示，他們「幫助借款人成為存款人」。Happy Money 於 2019 年 9 月獲得 7,000 萬美元的資金後，公司的創辦人暨執行長史考特·桑德思 (Scott Saunders) 向《Cheddar》新聞網說道：他們在自家調查中發現，「千禧世代中約有三分之一的人，在面對財務時，會出現類似創傷後壓力症候群的現象。」

桑德思解釋道，Happy Money 以低利率借出貸款，以便用「更迅速且便宜的方式，幫民眾減輕卡債高利息的債務」，他補充說，Happy Money 和美國國內的信用合作社合作，他們的使命是「讓世上不再有債務。」

值得關注的原因：

情緒和心理健康，一直是美國國內的熱門話題，所以如財務心理健康這類棘手的難題，能獲得較多關注也並不意外。隨著財務治療專家日益增加手的難題，能幫民眾解開財務和情緒問題，諸如此類的 Happy Money 之類的服務也傳達了企業立場的轉變：與其藉由抑制消費者因財務情緒上帶來的不良影響，並幫助客戶從中解脫。

以數位導向的方式教導這些年輕人如何妥善理財。

Greenlight 是一個以美國地區為主的金融卡及應用程式，目的在於教導幼童和青少年如何培養理財觀念。父母可以透過這款應用程式監控孩子的開銷，任需要存錢進去也能限制卡片可用的場所。

「在不久後的未來，我希望這一代的孩子可以學會聰明消費、學到儲蓄的重要性，並對長期投資以建立財富抱有信心。」Greenlight 的執行長及共同創辦人提姆·西漢（Tim Sheehan）如此表示。

其他的金融科技公司也將服務拓展至青少年的市場。根據消息指出，位於英國的 Revolut 金融科技公司將於近期內推出 Revolut 青年卡（Revolut Youth）以及與之相關的應用程式。2018 年，Monzo 公司推出 16-17 歲的青年帳戶，目前也計畫將此方案推廣給更年輕的族群。

值得關注的原因：

隨著金融交易日益轉向數位與虛擬的形式，現今的年輕人即便使不親自碰到到鈔票，也能認識貨幣的價值，培養理財觀念的應用程式可讓 Z 世代和更年輕的世代學會透過工具來增加自身的數位財務管理技能。

96

Z世代金融

透過教學讓數位原住民認識何謂理財。

偉門智威智庫的「進入 Z 世代的未來」（Into Z Future）報告指出，Z 世代當中即使是年紀最小的那一群人，也都具有創業精神。其中有許多是日進斗金。GoHenry 金融卡公司在「青年經濟報告」（Youth Economy Report）中指出：2018 年英國國內介於 6 到 18 歲孩童的收入總共達到 45 億英鎊，他們更擁有超過5 億 5 千萬英鎊的存款。

許多受到大型金融機構資助的新創公司也紛紛踏足此領域，希望

97
單身消費力

長期以來，行銷人員大多只關注傳統的人生階段，從無憂無慮的年輕人，馬上就跳到婚姻與家庭生活中。如今，這些描述已不符合現況。偉門智威近期於報告中指出「單身族群是經濟的發電廠，他們以全新訴求和生活標準重塑市場，是一股不可忽視的力量，於此宣告「單身世代」已然到來。

單身族群傾向買房，在旅遊中花大錢，也可能比已婚人士擁有更高的教育水準。這股趨勢在單身女性中尤其明顯，因為有越來越多女性已達成經濟自足的條件。哈佛大學房產研究聯合中心（Harvard Joint Center for Housing Studies）指出，2015 年的單身女性占單身總人口數的一半以上，同時全國房地產經紀人協會（National Association of Realtors）也表示，在 2017 年時，單身女性買房的比例是單身男性的兩倍。

世界各地的單身現象也越見增加，歐洲統計局（Eurostat）的數據顯示：2016 年在瑞典、丹麥、芬蘭、德國的獨居戶數皆占家庭總戶數的 40% 以上。在中國，由民政部所統計的單身成人百分比也從 1990 年的 6%，暴增到 2017 年的 15%（約 2 億人）。在香港，單身女性購屋之多，幾乎已讓她們成為各地區往單身族生活邁進的主要推力。

值得關注的原因：

現今的單身族群已不吝於展現自己的經濟能力。偉門智威智庫以獨有的研究工具 SONAR™ 對 3000 名橫跨美國、英國、中國受訪者所進行的研究指出，超過 80% 的美國單身族相當享受能夠擁有經濟決策權這件事，並有 85% 的人對「能自行做出財務決策讓他們感到有自主權」表示同意。不論創新服務是以共居、單身用餐或單人旅行為出發點，若企業能理解並迎合這些擁有強大經濟能力的人口，就能往成功之路邁進。

企業終於要著手解決沒有伴侶可以平分帳單的「單身稅」問題了。

商業活動中最醒目的單身慶典應該就屬阿里巴巴集團（Alibaba）推出的「光棍節」了。這個節日於每年的 11 月 11 日舉行，現已成為全球最大的購物盛典，並於 2019 年創下 380 億美元的銷售紀錄。

然而，為了形容無伴侶可平分房租、房貸、健保費等開銷所造成的「單身稅」一詞，仍是目前真實存在的問題。如今，企業也終於要著手解決這個問題了。

許多城市紛紛出現可支持單身生活的應用程式，從食物外送到英國的 Laundrapp 洗衣應用程式，再到 TaskRabbit 零工平台皆是如此。Laundrapp 可到府收件，並將衣物乾洗後送回給客戶；而 TaskRabbit 則讓使用者能將家務外包。

《Refinery29》網站在其中一篇文章中提供了讀者躲避單身族的小秘訣，例如與家人共享 Netflix 影音平台、Spotify 音樂串流平台以及其他平台的帳戶，與朋友一同在假日出遊以便平分住宿費用，以及大批次烹煮食物並將其冷凍保存，以節省食物開銷。

98

全新支付體驗

全新的支付選項讓結帳變得更加順暢。

亞馬遜(Amazon)的工程師正在研發代號為 Orville 的無卡、無手機生物辨識系統,讓全食超市(Whole Foods)的顧客只需揮手即可結帳。Orville 系統目前仍處於測試階段,它使用具有電腦視覺和深度幾何學能力的掃描器來辨識個人手勢,如此一來顧客便無須實際觸碰裝置或使用指紋辨識。

《紐約郵報》(New York Post)於報導中指出,這代表著超迅速的店內購物經驗也讓購物經驗更加愉快。Orville 系統的平均交易時間不超過 0.3 秒,相較之下,使用卡片需要 3 至 4 秒。

《Status Money》的創辦人及執行長馬吉德·馬克塞德(Majd Maksad)向《紐約郵報》表示:「大眾在無須觸摸貨幣這類有形物體的情況下,很容易花更多的錢。金錢的實質效力將變得極為抽象。」

由於目前這種交易方式仍需僱用收銀員,亞馬遜和其他為數不多的

科技公司也爭相設立起無人收銀商店。無人便利商店 Amazon Go 已於全美 21 個地點開設分店,亞馬遜也於 2019 年 11 月宣布:他們計畫設立全新的無人日用品商店,並可能將這項技術授權給其他零售業者使用。

2019 年 9 月,科技新創公司 Trigo 為自家推出的無人結帳計畫募到 2200 萬美元,該服務與 Amazon Go 類似,同樣使用攝影機和感應器追蹤顧客的店內移動路線。Trigo 的技術將會以色列最大連鎖超商 Shufersal 啟用,而使用 Trigo 技術的超商將可實施無人收銀,並收集顧客在店內活動的資料,為顧客設計個人化的購物體驗和常客計畫。

值得關注的原因:

皮夾的風光已不復見。先進支付科技成為零售商的利器,可以解決數位原生世代在店內交易時會有的痛點。企業目前只需要獲得更多消費者和監管機構的技術代選項如手勢支付或成無人商店,或計對消費者更有吸引力。

同時,比臉部辨識更無爭議性的替

99

訂閱式保單

以往改革步調緩慢的保險業，如今竟一腳跨入千禧世代和Z世代早已習慣的訂閱模式中。

從線上影音平台（Netflix）、服裝再到個人照護產品，透過開放性質的訂閱制來取得服務已成為年輕族群的新習慣。根據 MarTech Advisor 顧問公司的資料顯示，有將近 33% 的千禧世代至少是一間零售商的訂閱制會員。

保險業也開始搭上這股潮流，英國的滙豐集團（HSBC）於 2019 年 11 月引進「隨選隨保」（Select and Cover）服務，這項訂閱式保險服務可讓顧客選擇三至七種保單，包含汽車故障、手機、家庭急難險，以及各種小型裝置的保險理賠。訂閱者須擁有滙豐銀行的戶頭，之後可依個人所需，每年更改保險方案。每月保費從 19.5 英鎊（約台幣 760 元）起跳，也可以隨時免費取消。

滙豐集團之所以推出「隨選隨保」服務，是受到 2018 年在英國初登場的 AvivaPlus 保險應用程式啟發。當時英國消費者協會（Consumers' Association）的公正產品評論平台《Which》，將該公司每月的保費與網飛的訂閱模式互相比較。這些每個月支付的費用不收利息，也保證現有客戶在續訂時可享有與新客戶相同或更漂亮的價格，且取消訂閱也不會產生額外費用。

> 保險公司發現
> 千禧世代和Z世代市場
> 相當重要，而且他們
> 會以和過往世代
> 不同的方式
> 經歷各個階段的人生。

英國的 Urban Jungle 保險公司則將焦點放在租房的需求上，為租客提供彈性且「專門為租戶設計」的每月隨收隨付保單，財物險的每月保費從 5 英鎊（約台幣 200 元）起跳。2019 年 5 月，該公司宣布籌得 250 萬英鎊（約台幣 9800 萬元）的種子基金，並表示他們一直與「核保人員密切合作，以消除租戶在購買保險時會被提及的原屋主問題」，讓保單更容易理解，更適合「租屋一族」。Urban Jungle 保險公司也補充說道：「他們希望陪著客戶一起成長，體驗每個新的人生階段，畢竟在他們保單的期間，什麼事都有可能發生，所以該公司日後也會繼續擴大保險產品的範圍。」

值得關注的原因：
保險公司了解千禧世代和 Z 世代市場相當重要，且他們會以和過往世代不同的方式經歷各個階段段的人生。因此，公司為了不願投入長期合約，需求不斷改變的年輕顧客設計出更好理解、且更符合他們需求的新產品。據 2019 年 First Insight 的報告可知，「千禧世代持續維持他們在美國和英國的零售業中的主力地位，他們的購物習慣可能是企業成敗的關鍵」，也是零售模式是否能持續生存的觀察重點。保險品牌也開始轉移重心，開始討好這群重要的年輕世代。

AvivaPlus 保險應用程式提供家或汽車保險三層保障。英傑華集團（Aviva）英國保險品牌執行長安迪·布里格（Andy Briggs）表示：「這項服務與訂閱服務相同，是為了讓顧客能夠隨時根據他們的需求更換保險項目所設計。」更換項目也不會產生額外費用。他補充說：「英傑華集團為了理解保險如何更符合顧客需求，提供消費者現代生活中所需要的彈性服務，目前已經和上千名顧客進行合作。」

位於巴西聖保羅的新創公司 Kakau 也依循相同模式推出了家庭保險訂閱服務。

Marisa Robertson

100

品牌支付

科技巨頭準備改佔金融界，但信任仍是一大問題。

從運輸到娛樂，科技巨頭將手伸向消費主義的每個領域。無處不見的大動作讓人難以忽視。不過，消費者對科技巨頭是否有足夠的信任，使他們願意交出自己的財務資訊呢？

2019 年 10 月，優步（Uber）公布了新成立的部門 Uber Money。這項銀行服務向駕駛提供了金融卡和改良後的支付方案。該公司指出，優步的行動帳戶可讓旗下司機和外送員「透過優步金融帳戶（Uber Debit）即時使用每筆收入」，不需等候每週入帳。此次改革也提供了數位錢包。因此「收費方和付費方現在都能輕易地在同一頁面中，追蹤自己的開支記錄、管理款項、轉帳」並探索優步的全新金融商品」。

2019 年 8 月，蘋果（Apple）推出一張由高盛銀行（Goldman Sachs）發行的「蘋果信用卡」（Apple Card），藉由這張卡片，蘋果企圖在金融產業中達成它在電腦和智慧型手機領域早已實現的目標。以創新、簡化、流暢的銀行卡，透明的銀行卡，『蘋果公司將這張卡片定位為簡單、透明的銀行卡，「用來協助顧客擁有更健康的財務

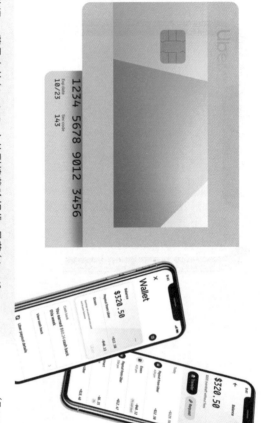

狀況」，蘋果支付（Apple Pay）的副總裁珍妮佛‧貝莉（Jennifer Bailey）如此說道。

雖然這張卡片也引發了性別歧視上的爭議，但蘋果卡的發行仍象徵蘋果跨足金融界的一大步。除了蘋果卡，蘋果支付也持續在金融圈中成長，並於 2019 年第一季經手了 18 億美元的交易額。

科技巨頭在生活品牌上取得成就後，
自然也將矛頭對準了金融界。

（Facebook Libra）也於 2019 年 6 月公開，雖然似乎不太成功，但也著實顯露其他科技龍頭努力擠身進入金融科技領域的意圖。

值得關注的原因：

科技巨頭在生活風格品牌上取得成就後，自然也將矛頭對準了金融界，傳統銀行需多加留意。儘管障礙重重，科技巨頭已準備好切合的行事風格，來挑戰枯燥乏味的銀行業了。

與此同時，社群媒體龍頭臉書推出的加密貨幣「臉書 Libra 幣」

關於偉門智威智庫 (Wunderman Thompson Intelligence)

偉門智威智庫是偉門智威面向未來思考的研究和創新單位，負責
觀察剛興起的現象以及未來的全球趨勢，消費型態變化、創新發
展模式，並在進一步解讀這些趨勢後，將其見解具體提供給品牌參考。

本單位提供一系列諮詢服務，包含客製化研究、簡報、聯名品牌報
告、專題討論，也勇於創新，與品牌合作、在品牌框架下引領未來
趨勢，並執行新產品與概念。本單位由偉門智威智庫的全球總監
Emma Chiu 所帶領。

—

如欲瞭解更多資訊，請造訪：jwtintelligence.com

聯絡人：

Emma Chiu
偉門智威智庫 | 全球總監
emma.chiu@wundermanthompson.com

台灣偉門智威
wt.taipei@wundermanthompson.com

資深趨勢分析師

偉門智威智庫 | Emily Safian-Demers

撰稿人

偉門智威智庫 | MayYee Chen (偉門智威智庫 | Marie Stafford
偉門智威智庫 | Elizabeth Cherian (偉門智威智庫 | Sarah Tilley
偉門智威智庫 | Maeve Prendergast
Nina Jones
Jessica Rapp

副編輯

Hester Lacey
Katie Myers
Harriet O'Brien

藝術總監與設計師

Shazia Chaudhry

圖片研究員

Farrah Zaman

封面圖片：豌豆花與鐵線蓮靜物花藝。圖片來源：費頓出版社 (Phaidon Press)

WUNDERMAN
THOMPSON

The Future

Publisher / Wunderman Thompson Taipei

Address / 13F - 5, No.8, Sec. 7, Civic Boulevard, Nangang District,
Taipei City, 115, Taiwan

Tel / (02) 3766-1000
Fax / (02) 2788-0260

Agent / China Times Publishing Company

Address / No.351, Sec.2, Wanshou Rd., Guisha District,,
Taoyuan City, 333, Taiwan

Tel / (02) 2306-6842

Retail price / NTD 500

ISBN / 978-986-98992-0-8

First published in Taiwan by Wunderman Thompson in April 2020

Copyright © 2020 Wunderman Thompson

All rights reserved.

2020 The Future 100
Writer / Wunderman Thompson Intelligence

Contributors / MayYee Chen, Wunderman Thompson Intelligence
Marie Stafford, Wunderman Thompson Intelligence
Elizabeth Cherian, Wunderman Thompson Intelligence
Sarah Tilley, Wunderman Thompson Intelligence
Maeve Prendergast, Wunderman Thompson Intelligence
Nina Jones
Jessica Rapp

Sub editors / Hester Lacey
Katie Myers
Harriet O'Brien

Art director and designer / Shazia Chaudhry

Picture researcher / Farrah Zaman

Assistant editor / Maggie Lee, Yafan Chang, Irene Chen
Chia Huang, Vik Liu, Yongyan Jiang, Pin Hsu, Tina Chen

Chinese version contributor / Wunderman Thompson Taipei

Translator / Rye Lin Ting-Ru

Introduction

Welcome to "The Future 100," our annual report forecasting what's in store for 2020 in 100 snackable trends.

The turn of this new decade is proving a key marker for positive change as consumers and companies are desperate to look beyond the latter part of the 2010s, which was filled with political, economic and environmental instability. People are now banding together, resulting in increased global action and the untabooing of social norms. The reign of Big Tech is coming to an end and irresponsible companies and figureheads are being held accountable for wider social and environmental issues.

What's in store for 2020? Ethically motivated consumers have created a new value system for brands, one that protects consumers, preserves culture and provides hope (see optimistic futures, p6). They are also inspiring improvements to existing environmental promises, as leading brands go beyond carbon-neutral initiatives and announce climate-positive plans.

Wellbeing and sustainability now go hand in hand, with consumers caring as much about the health of the planet as about their own health. In food and drink, recipes are being cooked up to futureproof our entire ecosystem, while in hospitality, hotels are cementing WELL standards into their environments.

Companies are also noting the positive health implications of human connectivity, addressing the continuing population and lifespan rises with products and services to build meaningful connections. Loneliness is being tackled as a social and public health issue, new neighborhoods in megacities are being envisioned to foster social wellbeing, and even social media is starting to promote meaningful rather than multiple connections.

Data is under the microscope and this is affecting all industries, with the trustworthiness of a brand now tied to the way it uses consumer data and how transparent its terms and conditions are. Rules and regulations are slowly being implemented to protect consumers, and brands are racing to ensure they are using personal data responsibly (see the privacy era, p.47).

Consumers have laid the foundations for change and now forward-thinking brands are working towards building an optimistic and reassuring future for all.

Emma Chiu
Global Director, Wunderman Thompson Intelligen[
JWTintelligence.com

WUNDERMAN
THOMPSON

Introduction

Review the known, master the new, explore the unknown. "The Future 100" was written before the outbreak of COVID-19, and published at the time as it's spreading around the world.

Wishing everyone good health and happiness.

Looking back at 2019, it seems tumultuous with political wrestling, economic depression, and climate change. Since the beginning of 2020, coronavirus has been spreading like wildfire around the world. As the pandemic rages, the hustle and bustle of big cities were replaced by empty streets. Another financial crisis is inevitable. The virus has changed the lives of thousands of people, the impact is difficult to measure. In the unknown future, human beings are facing unprecedented challenges.

Problems caused by climate change are also urgent. Floods, forest fires, droughts, and other extreme climates continue to occur. In the midst of nature's fight against human activities, people have finally started to reflect. Awareness on environmental protection is gradually rising, as well as brands' concern for a more sustainable environment. From IKEA to Gucci, companies have begun to take more responsibility for the environmental impact they've caused; Well-known destinations around the world have come up with new policies to prevent tourists from sabotaging the planet. Luxury travel means more than just material enjoyment. People are recognizing the negative impact of air and car travel. Traveling in a non-polluting and casual way has become the latest trend.

The new generation not only has the concept of environmental protection, health is also on the forefront of their concern. The wave of non-alcoholic beverages has begun to sweep restaurants and bars around the world. The vegan Impossible Burger is not only healthy but also eco-friendlier. Even Burger King, which was known for its unhealthy fast food, joined the trend.

In this turbulent time, people began to have many different reflections. Big crisis has reverse people's beliefs. These new trends are bound to deeply affect everyone in the up-coming decade.

"We are living in a time that requires trust and faith. It is this kind of constancy and confidence that is expressed by PANTONE 19-4052 Classic Blue, a solid and dependable blue hue we can always rely on," said Leatrice Eiseman, Executive Director of the Pantone Color Institute. The Pantone Color Institute announced Pantone's Color of the Year 2020, highlighting the desire for stability and peace of mind in this restless generation.

After the outbreak of coronavirus, what is your desire for the future?

Published by Wunderman Thompson Intelligence, "The Future 100" includes "Culture", "Tech & Innovation", "Travel & Hospitality", "Brands & Marketing", "Food & Drink", "Beauty", "Retail", "Luxury", "Health", and "Finance", which will take you to the future in a simple and digestible way.

Evan Teng
Managing Director,
Wunderman Thompson Taipei

01 11 21 31 41

10 20 30 40 50

culture

01

01

Optimistic futures

Brands are adopting an optimistic outlook for 2020 and beyond.

The past years have left societies across the world adrift in unsettling political, economic and environmental times. Consumers have been feeling more anxious than ever, with Americans among the most stressed in the world, according to a 2018 survey by Gallup. Now brands and consumers, eager to move the conversation on from bleak, dystopic times, are casting a more measured and reassuring lens on the future.

"While many refer to these times as the age of anxiety, I've begun to feel cautiously optimistic," Brenda Milis, creative trends lead at Adobe, tells Wunderman Thompson Intelligence. "A scaling number of creative projects and campaigns now focus on presenting honest emotions, expressiveness and connection. These are the kinds of visuals that have the power to build trust, community and help inspire thoughtful change in the world."

-ego launched a playful campaign in September 2019 with a provocative mission, asking the next generation to take on the challenge to "Rebuild the World." Prada's spring/summer 2020

Top: Scenic view of Aegean Sea with Athos Mountain
By Gencho Petkov/Stocksy/Adobe Stock
Bottom: Portrait of androgynous young man in blue velvet dress
By Alexey Kuzma/Stocksy/Adobe Stock

+WUNDERMAN
THOMPSON

Left: Close up of daisies BY: BORISLAV ZHUKOV/Stocksy/Adobe Stock
Right: View of pink ceiling with surveillance camera BY: Mint Images/Adobe Stock

color palette displays our determined desire for positivity and uplift," says Eiseman. The announcement of Classic Blue as Pantone's Color of the Year 2020 perfectly captures a sense of thoughtful optimism. Pantone describes the color as "evocative of the vast and infinite evening sky," opening up a world of possibilities.

Why it's interesting:

The nihilistic days are over and forward-thinking companies are brightening the gloom by offering a measured and thoughtful outlook, one that is both realistic and optimistic.

men's collection, Optimist Rhythm, captures a "spirit of confidence, of enjoyment, of boundless positivity and possibility." Brands are creatively casting a hopeful future for consumers by addressing change for good with hopeful messaging and energizing visual language.

The Pantone Color Institute has also unveiled a positive forecast in its color palette for spring/summer 2020, leading with the confident and fierce Flame Scarlet red swatch. The overall palette is bright and warm, with colors that are bold but grounded and is described as "a story of colorful expression" by Leatrice Eiseman, the institute's executive director. "Strong and vibrant, this season's

ENDERMAN
OMPSON   "Rebuild the World" campaign by Lego. Images courtesy of Lego

Female sporting revolution

Rising interest in professional female athletes is changing the game for women in sports—they are becoming global influencers, role models for the next generation, and prompting a shift in representation.

Female athletes have had a record-breaking year, drawing unprecedented global media attention. American sprinter Allyson Felix broke Usain Bolt's record for the most gold medals won at the track and field World Championships in September 2019. Kenya's Brigid Kosgei set a new world record at the Chicago Marathon in October 2019, and in the same month, at the Artistic Gymnastics World Championships in Stuttgart, Simone Biles performed two new moves that have subsequently been named after her.

Women's sporting competitions are commanding bigger audiences, and with that, bigger sponsorship deals, as brands hurry to sign up top sportswomen. Visa announced a roster of athlete sponsorships at the 2020 Olympic and Paralympic Games in Tokyo, with leading female names including Biles, soccer star Megan Rapinoe and swimmer Katie Ledecky on the list. Barclays is investing £10 million in the Women's Super League in the UK as part of a three-year sponsorship that the Football Association has called "the biggest ever investment in UK women's sport by a brand." And Adidas has

If they think your dreams are crazy, show them what crazy dreams can do.

Just do it.

launched an initiative to "break down barriers faced by women and girls in sport," kicking off a series of short *She Breaks Barriers* films.

As women's sport moves into the limelight, high-profile instances of gender bias in pay and treatment are coming into the public eye. In March 2019, the women's national US soccer team sued the United States Soccer Federation for "purposeful gender discrimination" in pay. Nike also came under the spotlight when runner Mary Cain detailed the toxic culture she endured at Nike Oregon Project, where she was body shamed. The company's "Dream Crazier" campaign showed the grit and strength of women, but actions within the company did not align with the ad. Female athletes also called out the brand for cutting their pay during pregnancy, and female employees have filed a lawsuit against it for violating equal pay laws.

Beyond excelling at their profession, female athletes represent a bigger shift not only in sports, but also in attitudes to gender equality and female strength, and set an admirable example.

Why it's interesting:

Women in sports are creating a new paradigm for female strength. Physicality, passion, agency, sweat and grit are the new hallmarks of femininity. But credibility in this space means 360-degree behavior and transparency. Like every brand or company that seeks to champion its female-friendly ethos, brands seeking to tap into the women's sports revolution need to think carefully about their practices on every level.

NDERMAN
OMPSON   "She Breaks Barriers" campaign by Adidas

03

The new neighborhood

Emerging social enterprises are reinventing conventional living models, creating new community structures built around core pillars of digital infrastructure, regenerative resources and social wellbeing.

In the next evolution of coliving, residents share more than just a dwelling. The newest urban living concepts turn the metropolitan community of the future into self-sufficient energy syndicates, communal ownership cooperatives, cross-generational social hubs and farming collectives.

In June 2019, Ikea's Space10 introduced "a new way of living together" with its Urban Village Project. The project rethinks how the home of the future will be designed, financed and shared. The concept is designed for life-long, cross-generational living, with shared facilities and services such as communal dinners, joint daycare, urban gardening, public fitness facilities and shared transportation. For self-sufficient sustainability, the community will be responsible for its own water harvesting, clean energy generation and local food production.

The project also establishes a new financial model for homeownership. A unique legal framework would allow residents to access ownership progressively by offering the option to buy sha

of the property each month or sell shares back to the cooperative. Eventually, the property would be fully owned by members of the community, creating a radically new form of democratic housing cooperative.

A mobile app serves as the connective tissue of the community, creating a space where residents can make rent payments, monitor equity investments, schedule laundry services, reserve a bike or car, book a workspace, manage food delivery subscriptions, track energy usage, sign up for community dinners and chat with neighbors.

This follows Space10's March 2019 SolarVille prototype of a neighborhood powered by solar energy. The community would share the energy through a microgrid. The neighbor-to-neighbor trading scheme enlists blockchain technology and solar panels, creating a circular clean energy system that would allow residents to make and share their own affordable, renewable energy.

NDERMAN   The Urban Village Project by Space10 and Effekt Architects. Images cour-
OMPSON   tesy of Space10

> We can create new realities that promote a sense of wellbeing and turn the spaces we inhabit into healthier and happier places, all while being more affordable and efficient for those that live there.
>
> Jamiee Williams, architectural lead, Space10

In August 2019, TC Plus unveiled G-Lab, a house design that blurs the line between private residence and community hub. It is both a family home and a space that can be shared by the neighborhood. In place of a traditional front door, the home's entry is marked by an eight-meter-wide curtain that can be drawn for privacy. Inside the house, spaces range from public to private, with movable dividers and beds behind folding wooden panels.

Why it's interesting:

Urban dwellers are ready for a new style of living that is kinder to residents and the planet alike. "It is clear that unless we rethink our built environment, our cities will become increasingly unsustainable, unaffordable and socially unequal," comments Jamiee Williams, architectural lead at Space10. These projects start the conversation of future coliving and of how, as Williams says, "we can create new realities that promote a sense of wellbeing and turn the spaces we inhabit into healthier and happier places, all while being more affordable and efficient for those that live there."

04

Data creatives

A new class of AI artists is leading a modern creative renaissance.

New artistic projects are inviting machines to be part of a creative dialogue that recasts data as the raw creative material of the future. By endowing technology with creative agency, these creatives are throwing into relief what it means to be human in the digital age.

In November 2019, Jean-Michel Jarre—a musician who has been dubbed the godfather of electronic music—unveiled an "infinite album." The project, called Eon, uses seven hours of Jarre's music to create an evolving, dynamic musical experience during which no two listening experiences will be the same. The result is a "never ending, never repetitive, organic art-piece that will live and grow forever in everyone's own singular space-time continuum," Jarre explains on his website.

"The emergence of AI is a revolution," he told the BBC. "For the first time, we're combining the creative process itself with a machine. In 10 or 15 years, robots will have a sense of nostalgia and will be able to cry. I think that's quite cool, quite exciting. It will mean a new approach to the creative process entirely."

NDERMAN
OMPSON   AI: More Than Human exhibition at the Barbican, London

WUNDERMAN
THOMPSON

AI: More Than Human exhibition at the Barbican, London

> ## What makes data so exciting for me is that it's not just data, it's kind of a memory. It's a memory for a moment in life.
>
> **Refik Anadol, artist**

Refik Anadol is another artist fascinated by machines' emotional and psychological faculties. His projects visualize the memories and dreams of machines, exploring the definition of consciousness at a time when machines hold so much of our shared cultural memories. "What makes data so exciting for me is that it's not just data, it's kind of a memory. It's a memory for a moment in life," Anadol tells Wunderman Thompson Intelligence.

His most recent project, Machine Hallucinations, explores New York through the mind of a machine. The project opened in September 2019 as the inaugural installation at Artechouse New York, a new gallery dedicated to digital art in Manhattan's Chelsea Market. To create the exhibit, Anadol mined hundreds of millions of images of New York City's iconic architecture and urban landscapes, then deployed machine learning, artificial intelligence (AI) and bespoke algorithms trained on the images to "visualize a consciousness of New York" from a machine's perspective.

The images are projected onto the walls, ceiling and floor for an immersive viewing experience. Anadol calls this format "latent cinema," which he describes as "a new way of exploring narrative

NDERMAN
OMPSON   Machine Hallucination by Refik Anadol

WUNDERMAN
THOMPSON
Mapping Hallucination by Refik Anadol

By giving tech and machines creative freedom, artists are fueling a new era of AI creativity into one that is more than human.

conceived from the mind of a machine, one that has the ability to create its own reality."

In Melting Memories, he integrated AI with output from an electroencephalogram that measures brain wave activity, to create "ethereal abstract data sculptures visualizing the moment of remembering," he tells Wunderman Thompson Intelligence.

The Barbican in London is also exploring the concepts of humanity and creativity in a digitally steeped world. The arts center's 2019 exhibition AI: More than Human questioned "what it means to be human in a time when technology is changing everything."

Why it's interesting:
By giving tech and machines creative freedom, artists are fueling a new era of AI creativity into one that is more than human.

05

Reframing time

The age of non-linear sequencing is upon us, as people increasingly opt for a flexible and open approach to how they engage with narratives and entertainment.

The popularity of streaming content has shifted the way consumers engage with entertainment, fueling freeform viewing habits not restricted to a predefined timetable or sequential path. According to Nielsen, 56% of US adults stream non-linear content to their televisions, while research by Hulu shows there are twice as many non-linear TV views among consumers under the age of 35. The flexibility of non-linear TV allows people to approach time in a personalized fashion—viewing when it suits them, rather than according to a network's schedule.

Perhaps as a result of this, the cultural perception of time is shifting towards the unpredictable. This may be why the Metropolitan Museum of Art Costume Institute decided to focus on this broad subject matter for its spring 2020 exhibition. However, the press announcement in November 2019 posed problems for a number of publications, as journalists attempted to explain the theme. *Vogue's* headline ran "24 hours later, the internet is still working out this year's Met Gala theme." "The Met Gala 2020 theme is confusing a lot of people," wrote *Marie Claire*.

INDERMAN   Surreal by David Bailey. Image courtesy of The Metropolitan Museum of Art.
OMPSON   Photo © David Bailey

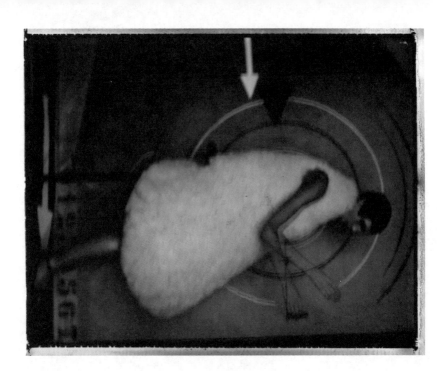

What exactly does the Met's About Time: Fashion and Duration theme mean? According to the official release, the theme is inspired by Virginia Woolf's time-oriented novels and French philosopher Henri Bergson's concept of la durée, "time that flows, accumulates and is indivisible." Yes, a bit of a head-scratcher. But perhaps not, as, for consumers rooted in an age of non-linear formats and speed-controlled consumption (see speed-control entertainment, p.44), the way time is distributed is no longer constrained by the clock and is instead a far more liberating concept.

The show will open to the public in May 2020 and will take a "nuanced and open-ended" approach to time, according to Andrew Bolton, Wendy Yu Curator in Charge of the Costume Institute at the Met. "It's a reimagining of fashion history that's fragmented, discontinuous, and heterogeneous," he told Vogue.

Why it's interesting:

The way time is being broached is evolving, as consumers increasingly adopt on-demand habits and distribute their time more freely. For innovative brands up to the challenge, there's space to help redefine the quotidian and restructure modern life for the 2020 consumer.

06

Next-gen superheroes

The entertainment industry is evolving the definition of "superhman."

A superhero, according to the Merriam-Webster dictionary, is "a fictional hero having extraordinary or superhuman powers" or "an exceptionally skillful or successful person." Superheroes symbolize cultural exemplars in strength, bravery and altruism, and are often looked up to as role models by fans. With an introduction of LGBTQ superhero characters, the next generation is presenting a broader picture of what it means to be heroic.

LGBTQ representation in television has hit an all-time high. As of November 2019, the percentage of returning LGBTQ characters on broadcast cable networks had reached 10.2%, up from 8.8% in 2018, according to media monitor GLAAD. Showtime's *Billions* and Netflix's *13 Reasons Why* cast nonbinary actors, while NBC's *Good Girls*, Netflix's *Chilling Adventures of Sabrina* and ABC's *Grey's Anatomy* all feature transmasculine characters played by trans actors.

Notably, a number of these characters are action and superheroes—shedding outdated gender tropes and redefining superhuman strength. In July 2019, it was confirmed that Valkyrie

INDERMAN
OMPSON   Batwoman. Image courtesy of CW TV

will become the first LGBTQ superhero of the Marvel Cinematic Universe franchise when *Thor: Love and Thunder* hits theaters in November 2021. "Our entire success is based on people that are incredibly different," Marvel's production chief Victoria Alonso told *Variety*. "If we don't put pedal to the metal on the diversity and the inclusivity, we will not have continued success. Our determination is to have that for all of the people out there watching our movies."

The CW television network represents a vanguard of nonbinary and LGBTQ superheroes. In October 2019, Batwoman, portrayed by gender-fluid actor Ruby Rose, became the first gay superhero in a TV series. And when the new season of *Supergirl* aired in January 2019, it included Dreamer, the first transgender action hero in an American television series, played by transgender activist Nicole Maines. This follows the network's *Arrow*, which features several openly gay and bisexual superheroes like vigilante Mr Terrific, White Canary, and assassin Nyssa al Ghul.

WUNDERMAN
THOMPSON

Above: Valkyrie in Marvel's Avengers Endgame. Image courtesy of Disney
Right: Supergirl. Image courtesy of CW TV

Why it's interesting:

With generation Z and millennial consumers eschewing outdated and sexist biases in everything from dress codes to dialogue, restrictive superhero archetypes are being re-examined. The next generation of cultural heroes reflects a broader perspective on what it means to be human, rejecting the unfounded notion that the ideal human is informed by gender identity or sexual orientation.

07

Untabooing in the East

Slowly but surely, some long-established taboos are falling away in Asia.

Attitudes to mental health, sexual health and gender are catching up with the region's rapid economic development, helped along by technology.

In Thailand, a mental health tech startup called Ooca offers video sessions with therapists through a website and a smartphone app. Users can select what's troubling them—whether it's work stress or relationship blues—and check out doctor bios before making an appointment. In pursuit of happier workers and better productivity, large employers are signing on, marking a shift in societal attitudes. Part of the appeal is that the app's software can analyze anonymized data and spot budding problems, such as overwork or other stress.

"It's like a silent heat map within the company," Ooca founder Kanpassorn "Eix" Suriyasangpetch, who has personal experience with depression, tells Wunderman Thompson Intelligence.

Sexual health is also starting to be taken seriously as an important part of general health. In China, a platform called Yummy provides

ooca
It's okay

The Tele-mental Health
Platform for Southeast Asia.

ooca
It's Okay.

an environment where women are free to discuss sexual matters, from intimacy to orgasm, and health issues such as breast cancer prevention, in a country where most online sexual health resources are directed at men. User numbers have reportedly topped two million.

Discussions around gender discrimination are also coming to the fore. In Japan, a bastion of tradition, the #KuToo movement campaigns against gender inequality—its name nods to the #MeToo movement in the West. It was founded by freelance writer and actor Yumi Ishikawa after she was forced to wear high heels for her job at a funeral parlor.

Ishikawa combined the Japanese word for shoe, kutsu, with the word for agony, kutsuu, to coin #KuToo and denounced Japan's high-heel requirement for women as a form of gender discrimination that results in real harm—bunions, blistering and bleeding. An online petition she started in 2019 urged the government to make it illegal for employers to force workers to wear high heels. It has garnered more than 31,000 signatures but hasn't managed to change the law yet. In October 2019, Ishikawa appeared on the BBC list of 100 inspiring and influential women from around the world. She has also launched her own brand of flat shoes called KuToo Follower, styled like men's lace-ups, in smaller sizes for women.

Japanese women are also chafing against prescribed hairstyles at work. In 2018, shampoo brand Pantene built a campaign around deconstructing the neat ponytail female Japanese job seekers are expected to sport, encouraging women to let down their hair. The "More Freedom in Job-Hunting Hair" campaign was followed in 2019 by Pantene's "Hair We Go: My Hair Moves Me Forward"

campaign, aimed at both job seekers and HR professionals and urging an end to forced conformity.

Why it's interesting:

Asian survey data and anecdotal evidence show a shift in openness about traditional taboos and gender straitjackets. Mental health is a big concern across all generations, according to a survey of 2,500 consumers in five countries (China, Japan, Indonesia, Thailand and Australia) by Wunderman Thompson Intelligence. Of the survey respondents, 38% associate sexual health with overall health, with men more likely to say this than women. A new generation is entering the workforce, with new expectations. In a nine-country survey of 4,500 consumers for Wunderman Thompson Intelligence's "Generation Z Asia" report, eight out of 10 respondents say gender doesn't define a person as much as it used to. These changes are coming from the ground up.

Attitudes to mental health, sexual health and gender are catching up with Asia's rapid economic development, helped along by technology.

Breakup coaches

New services are hitting the market to help modern daters heal after heartbreak.

According to data from SONAR™, Wunderman Thompson's proprietary research tool, 86% of American singles say being single means they have more freedom, 83% say being single means they have more time for things they enjoy, and 77% say being single is their choice. But there are still hurdles to be cleared before reaching that point of contentment. As more and more people opt to stay single, driving a rising appreciation for singlehood, new services are shifting the cultural focus away from finding a match to smoothing the way for those coming out of relationships—and helping them enjoy the transition to life uncoupled.

Soft-launched in November 2019, Breakup Tours is a new travel service aimed at those coming out of relationships. The service personalizes itineraries based on individual circumstances and preferences, and offers curated "heart-healing and soul-cleansing" experiences, a Circle of Travelers feature to foster friendships, and bespoke "first-aid kits" tailored to each traveler, containing items such as therapeutic writing exercises.

"Breakup is hard as changes are hard," cofounder Stephen Chung told *CNN Travel*. "When you stick to your routine, you become very aware of the things missing in your routine. Traveling allows you to

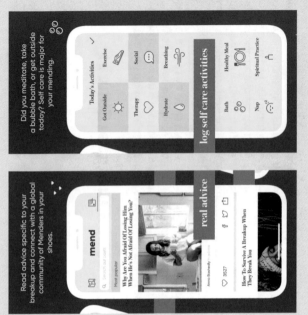

Did you meditate, take a bubble bath, or get outside today? Self care is major for your mending.

log self care activities

Read advice specific to your breakup and connect with a global community of Menders in your shoes.

real advice

(mental, financial, legal and physical health) for clients. Onward matches members with a concierge who prepares a "personalized Road Map to solve immediate pain points and manage next steps," Meck explains.

Why it's interesting:

These services are reframing the transition from coupled to single for a growing faction of consumers reveling in singledom, "creating a new conversation around a traditionally stigmatized narrative," says Meck.

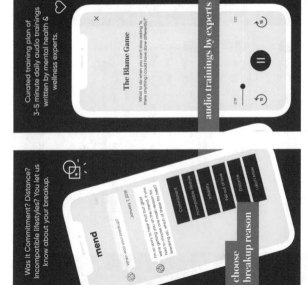

Was it Commitment? Distance? Incompatible lifestyles? You let us know about your breakup.

choose breakup reason

Curated training plan of 3–5 minute daily audio trainings written by mental health & wellness experts.

audio trainings by experts

break away. It gives you new perspectives."

What if your breakup was not a breakdown, but actually a breakthrough—a chance to lead a better life?" asks Lindsay Meck, CEO and cofounder of Onward. Launched in February 2019, Onward is a breakup concierge service that helps those exiting long-term relationships "physically relocate and emotionally relaunch their lives," Meck tells Wunderman Thompson Intelligence.

The service tackles both logistics (moving, housing search, address/utility changes, furnishing setups) and holistic challenges

The Mend app is designed to help users navigate a breakup

09

Taming tech's influence

In the run up to the 2020 US presidential election, politicians and tech companies alike are exploring ways to manage how political discourse plays out online, amid the Wild West atmosphere of social media.

In October 2019, Twitter CEO Jack Dorsey announced in a series of tweets that the company had "made the decision to stop all political advertising on Twitter globally," as "we believe political message reach should be earned, not bought." He added: "We're well aware we're a small part of a much larger political advertising ecosystem. Some might argue our actions today could favor incumbents. But we have witnessed many social movements reach massive scale without any political advertising. I trust this will only grow."

Twitter's actions could have "an unintended consequence or two" for users, as highlighted by the Associated Press. The article also stated that "among those potentially affected could be public-interest nonprofits eager to reach an audience larger than their official followers, challengers to incumbent officeholders, and—obviously—political consultants who make a living placing ad buys for their candidates."

There was outcry in the United Kingdom in November 2019 when

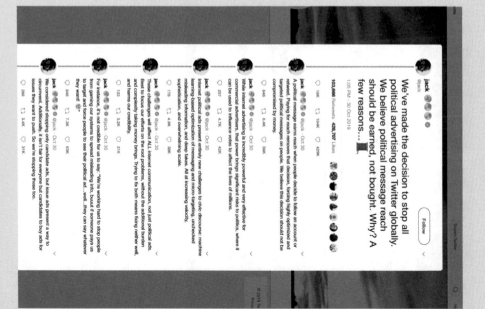

the Conservative party rebranded one of its official verified Twitter accounts as "factcheckUK" during a debate between party leaders, in the run-up to the general election in December 2019. Following the move, Twitter said in a statement that "any further attempts to mislead people by editing verified profile information—in a manner seen during the UK election debate—will result in decisive corrective action."

In late November 2019, Google said that it would limit the targeting of election advertising in the United States to general categories such as age, gender, and postal code-level location. In the past, political advertisers could target US Google ads based on public voter records and general political affiliations, such as left-leaning or right-leaning (Google had already prevented this practice in the EU and the United Kingdom). Scott Spencer, the VP of product management for Google Ads, published a blog post in November 2019 that referred to the changes. "Given recent concerns and debates about political advertising, and the importance of shared trust in the democratic process, we want to improve voters' confidence in the political ads they may see on our ad platform," he wrote. "Regardless of the cost or impact to spending on our platforms, we believe these changes will help promote confidence in digital political advertising and trust in electoral processes worldwide."

He also outlined how the internet giant's policies prohibit "ads or destinations making demonstrably false claims that could significantly undermine participation or trust in an electoral or democratic process."

Spotify is the latest company to take a stand on political ads by announcing in Decemeber 2019 to suspend them on the music

We believe political message reach should be earned, not bought.

Jack Dorsey, CEO, Twitter

streaming platform from 2020.

On a macro level, Democratic candidate Elizabeth Warren has already made breaking up Big Tech's monopoly one of the central tenets of her campaign. Her plan, *Bloomberg* explains, involves "unwinding old acquisitions," such as Facebook's purchases of Instagram and WhatsApp, and ensuring "that the tech giants—those with more than $25 billion in revenue—that operate an online marketplace or exchange, shouldn't be allowed to offer services that compete with the participants on those platforms." Amazon, therefore, wouldn't be allowed to sell both its own-brand products and third-party brands on Amazon.com. "Amazon crushes small companies by copying the goods they sell on the Amazon Marketplace and then selling its own branded version," Warren wrote in a March 2019 *Medium* article that set out the plan.

By rolling out its trial of hiding "likes" on a global scale, Instagram is addressing negative perceptions of some elements of the platform. "Our interest in hiding likes really is just to depressurize Instagram for young people," company head Adam Mosseri tweeted in November 2019. "It'll likely affect how much some people engage on Instagram, probably liking a bit less and posting a bit more, but the main thing we're trying to learn is how this affects how people feel."

Why it's interesting:

The wildfire speed of social media has taken political and social discourse to a new level in terms of pace, content, and veracity. Now, politicians—and tech companies themselves—are recognizing this, and aiming to turn the tide on the more malign aspects of its influence. Between the push of regulation and the pull of free speech, 2020 will see a new focus on how information, particularly the political, is disseminated through these channels.

10

Into the multiverse

Inspired by dystopic projections that nod to the end of the world, artists, designers and experimentalists are creating infinite alternative realities where time, space, energy and matter collide.

For Burning Man in August 2020, the event's temporary city will be themed around the multiverse, inspired by the theory that there are other universes beyond our own. As well as referencing paradoxical worlds, surrealism and pataphysics as inspiration, it will also explore "the quantum kaleidoscope of possibility," the organizer states, and offers attendees the chance to encounter their "alternate selves." With many provocative questions that probe quantum entanglement and the Many-Worlds theory, Burning Man 2020 will be a multidimensional creative testing ground where attendees can disconnect from the stress of today's anxious times and propel themselves into a limitless universe.

In June 2020, the Victoria & Albert Museum will invite visitors to "experience a mind-bending journey into Wonderland" with its in-depth exploration of Lewis Carroll's book *Alice's Adventures in Wonderland*. The exhibition, titled Alice: Curiouser and Curiouser, looks at the origins, adaptions and reinventions of the 155-year-old story, showing that the world of Wonderland and its characters not only stand the test of time, but also continue to inspire.

ZeroSpace. Image courtesy of ZeroSpace. Photo by Matan Tzitsmon.

WUNDERMAN
THOMPSON

Otherworld

Immersive installations are also propelling audiences into another time, space and dimension. ZeroSpace in New York City, opened in summer 2019, transports visitors into a "multiverse where art, technology and humanity converge," with its "immersive art playground" of large-scale installations from the world's leading new-media artists. Otherworld in London leverages virtual reality to encourage people to leave reality behind and enter "a parallel universe of infinite possibilities."

Why it's interesting:

While reality of late has pointed towards a dystopian future and hopeless outlook when it comes to the planet, artists are creating alternative worlds that inspire infinite possibilities. Consumers tired of today's mundanity are seeking portals that offer escapism, adventure, and a glimpse of what life could be like elsewhere.

11

Tech & Innovation

20

Protective tech

In a world rampant with worry, brands are creating new products to soothe, reassure and offer security.

Confronted with unnerving environmental, political and economic instability, people are more anxious than ever. A survey by the American Psychological Association (APA) undertaken in April 2019 found that 32% of Americans felt more anxious than they had the previous year. A previous APA survey found that millennials are the most anxious generation to date. With this uptick in worry and unease, consumers are looking for products and services that offer comfort and protection from the world around them.

At Consumer Electronics Show (CES) 2019, the annual tech extravaganza, a host of products promising protection was showcased. Lishtot is a portable, keyring-shaped device that allows users to check the quality and safety of their water in an instant. Mitte, a smart water filter, promises to filter out modern aggressors such as microplastics, hormones and chemicals. Larq received an innovation award for its self-purifying water bottle, which is designed to remove "99.9999% of bacteria and viruses" from drinking water using UV-C LED technology.

In a 2019 study, researchers at the Massachusetts Institute of Technology (MIT) found a direct correlation between happiness and

NDERMAN
OMPSON   Larq self-purifying water bottle

Besides enabling people to breathe better air at home, we hope that Gunrid will increase people's awareness of indoor air pollution, inspiring behavioral changes that contribute to a world of clean air.

Lena Pripp-Kovac, head of sustainability, Inter Ikea Group

air quality, showing that higher levels of pollution are associated with a decrease in people's happiness levels. With pollution reaching record-breaking highs—in New Delhi due to overwhelming smog—brands are designing products that offer personal protection.

With its new product Bot Air, Samsung tapped into consumers' fear of harmful environmental factors that are invisible to the naked eye. Introduced at CES 2019, Bot Air is a self-operating air purifier that patrols the home and monitors air quality. Ikea plans to debut the Gunrid air purifying curtain in 2020; unique technology woven into the fabric breaks down air pollutants when light shines through it. "Besides enabling people to breathe better air at home, we hope that Gunrid will increase people's awareness of indoor air pollution, inspiring behavioral changes that contribute to a world of clean air," says Lena Pripp-Kovac, head of sustainability at Inter Ikea Group.

Why it's interesting:

Growing concerns about pollution and the negative impacts of the today's environment are behind a new wave of products and services created to mitigate unease about the world around us.

WUNDERMAN
THOMPSON

Gunrid air purifying curtain by Ikea. Image courtesy of Ikea

Captured from PS4 Pro

Captured from PS4 Pro

12

Anti-bullying gaming

Game designers are working to reverse the toxic behaviors that have plagued the gaming community.

In October 2019, Microsoft added a new Xbox Live feature that allows players to set filters on in-game messaging. The update gives each individual the power to decide "what's acceptable and what isn't in the text-based messages you receive across Xbox Live," explains Microsoft.

Dave McCarthy, head of Microsoft's Xbox operations, said in an interview with the *Verge* technology and media platform that there are stories of "female gamers in competitive environments being called all sorts of names and feeling harassed in the outside world, or members of our LGBTQ community feeling like they can't speak with their voice on Xbox Live for fear that they'll be called out. If we really are to realize our potential as an industry and have this wonderful medium come to everybody, there's just no place for that."

In November 2019, Samsung Brazil launched a local initiative in partnership with online game *Fortnite* to fight a specific type of cyberbullying. Players in the popular game can acquire "skins," a graphic asset that changes a character's appearance, but the

skins—which can cost around $50—have become a status symbol among players, and those who can't afford the accessory are often mocked and ridiculed. To counteract this, the campaign created a new skin, called Aura Glow, that players can gift to other players to foster camaraderie and inclusivity.

Other games are also nurturing more constructive behaviors. Google's new gaming platform, Google Stadia, launched in November 2019 with an original exclusive game centered on an anti-bullying message. It takes players on "a journey where you face your worst fears and are confronted with the emotional impact of your actions," the creator, Tequila Works, explains.

Released in October 2019, *Concrete Genie* is bringing a new perspective to gaming by encouraging players to turn to art as an antidote to bullying. Created by Sony's in-house studio Pixelopus, the game is designed to inspire players to counter negativity with creativity, offering a new framework of positivity in the gaming community. The goal, explains Pixelopus designer Jing Li, is to help the player feel "like they're the light of the world, and they're the magician of the world. And we want them to feel like they're filling the world with art and creativity and positive energy."

Why it's interesting:

The gaming community, which has been often been blamed for rewarding violence and normalizing toxic behavior, is banding together to build a more positive, safe and welcoming space.

13

New digital communities

Social media is having a private moment, as a new generation of users eschews the endless friends list in favor of more intimate connections with a select few.

Fueled by a growing desire for privacy, authenticity and wellbeing, young consumers are seeking ways to digitally engage with only their closest companions, whether through bite-sized direct messaging communities, such as the new Threads app from Instagram, or niche interest-based groups on Discord. In our article on social media safe havens we reported on a survey of 1,500 generation Zers and millennials by the Royal Society for Public Health in the United Kingdom. Many respondents said that platforms such as Instagram put too much pressure on users to display perfect versions of themselves online, and many users are wising up to the influencer culture's effect on their mental health.

Threads launched in October 2019 with a mission to help users more seamlessly communicate to their true confidantes the personal information they don't want to share with their hundreds of followers. Friends on Threads can easily keep in touch throughout the day even if they can't talk thanks to a feature called Auto Status, which, when turned on, communicates whether a user is on the move or out to eat.

INDERMAN
HOMPSON   Instagram Close Friends feature. Images courtesy of Facebook

As consumers shift into smaller, tight-knit, like-minded groups, brands will have new opportunities to make more deliberate and genuine connections in these online spaces.

In July 2019, Snapchat leveraged its first global campaign to show how its platform helps family members and pairs of friends from around the world stay close and connected. Snap Inc's chief marketing officer Kenny Mitchell told *Adweek* that the Real Friends campaign demonstrates that Snapchat is "really a response to some of the challenges of social media. It became a bit of an escape from social media, where people can really be themselves."

Earlier in 2019, Snap launched Bitmoji Party, a multiplayer mobile game played with users' virtual avatars, which offers an alternative terrain for interacting with best pals.

Even Tumblr, a platform known for cultivating niche communities for creative expression, is exploring ways to make public chat groups a staple of its repertoire. In November 2019, it began testing the messaging feature on its mobile platform, giving thought leaders the chance to form discussions based around extremely specific hobbies and passions, from self-care to K-pop.

Why it's interesting:

"It takes a new business mindset, but this is the future of marketing," Mark Schaefer, author of *Marketing Rebellion*, tells Wunderman Thompson Intelligence. As consumers shift into smaller, tight-knit, like-minded groups, brands will have new opportunities to make more deliberate and genuine connections in these online spaces. "To accomplish this, you have to be invited into these groups," he says. "You have to treat people like friends, not prospects."

Korean car manufacturer Kia is aiming to incorporate emotion-reading tech into the daily lives of its drivers. At the CES 2019 tech show, the company unveiled its Real-time Emotion Adaptive Driving (Read) system, which monitors a driver's emotions using bio-signal recognition. The system analyses facial expressions, heart rate and electrodermal activity to decipher the driver's emotional state and adjusts the car accordingly, for example by altering the lighting or the music to reintroduce a sense of calm.

Why it's interesting:

Technology has long faced scrutiny for its effects on our mental health. Now it's providing new ways to help enhance our wellbeing.

Sentient tech

Brands are using new technologies to recognize and respond to human emotions, with the aim of relieving stress and anxiety.

In March 2019, Clear Channel in Sweden launched the Emotional Art Gallery, a series of 250 digital billboards in Stockholm's metro stations that used digital artworks to reduce commuter stress. Harnessing data available from Google searches, social media, news articles and traffic information, the system selected an art piece to display on each screen, responding in real time to the mood of the city. The works all aimed to instill positive emotions in travelers, enhancing feelings of comfort, calmness, happiness and energy.

In October 2019, Microsoft's research artist in residence Jenny Sabin unveiled Ada, an emotionally responsive AI sculpture, at Microsoft's Redmond campus. Ada is a large, skeletal-like structure that is able to translate people's emotions into a colorful display. When a person in the building interacts with a camera or microphone, Ada reads their facial expressions and tone of voice, and responds in real time by changing color. The more people engage with the sculpture, the more alive it seems, colorfully fluctuating between a range of emotions.

15

Speed-control entertainment

As attention spans grow ever shorter, tech solutions are being developed that speed up cultural experiences—but at what creative cost?

Directors and actors were aghast in fall 2019 when Netflix tested a function that could speed up or slow down its content on Android devices. Filmmaker and actor Judd Apatow called the move "ridiculous and insulting," while director Brad Bird tweeted that the feature was "another spectacularly bad idea, and another cut to the already bleeding-out cinema experience." Why, he questioned, "support and finance filmmakers' visions on one hand and then work to destroy the presentation of those films on the other?"

Perhaps one factor that drove Netflix's move is the oft-cited figure that the attention span of generation Zers is a mere eight seconds, compared to millennials' attention span of 12 seconds. The speeding up and shortening of media content comes amid the rise of social platforms such as TikTok, whose 15-second videos have been an enormous hit with gen Z.

Among the roster of streaming services flooding on to the market is Quibi, a platform that will offer "snackable" eight-minute video content when it launches in April 2020. The platform has been founded by veteran producer Jeffrey Katzenberg, while Meg

Whitman, who previously headed Hewlett Packard, is its CEO.

"What we say internally is we'd like to be the quality of HBO and offer customers the convenience of Spotify," Whitman told the *Los Angeles Times*. "We're not Instagram TV. We're not YouTube. We're Quibi, and it's not denigrating those platforms at all... but we're staking out a premium position relative to those."

The service will cost about $5 a month with ads and $8 a month without ads, and according to the *LA Times*, it will offer "premium films shot by award-winning directors like Steven Spielberg and Catherine Hardwicke and present them in short episodic chapters."

Why it's interesting:

As attention spans shrink, entertainment companies are striving to find new ways to create the bite-sized content that they believe will appeal to younger consumers. But at the same time creators are pushing back against this, aiming to preserve the immersive, absorbing nature of a cultural experience. As tech allows for an ever more customizable cultural experience, time will tell which stance wins out.

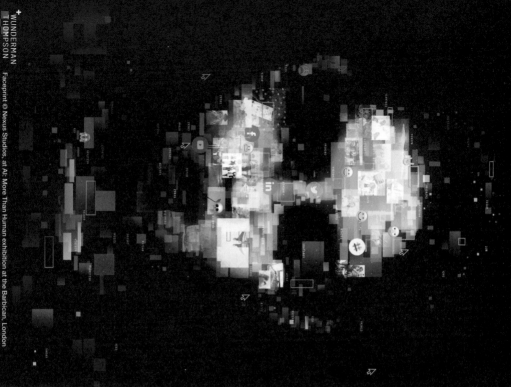

The new rules for facial recognition

Privacy concerns are increasingly trumping convenience in the world of facial recognition.

Brands employing the tech can survive public backlash and tightening regulations, but only if they change their tactics.

In November 2019, Chaayos provoked a storm of outrage on Twitter after the Indian cafe chain forced customers to pay for their drinks using facial recognition technology, with no clear way to opt out. Countless US companies have faced similar discontent over the technology, including Ticketmaster's parent company Live Nation Entertainment (LNE). Protesters claimed LNE's efforts to develop facial recognition at concerts in a bid to replace traditional ticketing could harm at-risk communities (see our report on facial recognition tech for more).

As brands increasingly begin to recognize facial recognition's potential, it seems consumers aren't quite ready for a mass roll-out. Approximately 60% of US consumers think that brands and companies storing images of their faces is creepy, according to a report from SONAR™, Wunderman Thompson's proprietary research tool.

RESEARCH & INNOVATION

A marked shift in how regulators think about facial recognition technology is expected in 2020, especially when it comes to protecting people's data and privacy. Brands will see more rules denoting how and when data can be used. Brittany Kaiser, a data transparency advocate and former business development director for Cambridge Analytica, tells Wunderman Thompson Intelligence that data garnered from the likes of facial recognition tech has the potential to be treated in the same way as property rights.

"The idea is, in the future, that we'd have a lot more access and transparency into who wants what type of data," Kaiser says. "Then we would have the choice to produce or share that data with all of those organizations, be it for profit or non-profit, or governmental, or anyone interested in using those data sets."

There's one exception to all this: China. "At the end of the day, the privacy concerns around biometrics in China are very different from the United States," John Artman, editor in chief of *TechNode*, tells us. "In the United States, facial recognition is seen as kind of something Orwellian—*1984*-ish, Big Brother is watching you—whereas in China, it's just like 'Hey, I can use my face—alright, why not?'"

> **At the end of the day, the privacy concerns around biometrics in China are very different from the United States.**
>
> **John Artman, editor in chief, TechNode**

Why it's interesting:

Facial recognition provides countless opportunities for brands to collect data on customers to improve and hyperpersonalize their shopping experience, and also offers unprecedented convenience. However, companies will need to be transparent about how they plan to use the data in order to retain the trust of customers and lawmakers. "If people don't want to be bothered then they'll tell you that and you can stop wasting your advertising spend on them," Kaiser says. "In the end, it's actually an improvement of the business model because you're cutting out people who don't want to be advertised to and you're going to get real, updated information in order to target a better experience to the customers who do want to interact with you."

WUNDERMAN
THOMPSON

Affectiva Driving Game, © Affectiva, at AI: More Than Human exhibition at the Barbican, London

Privacy. That's iPhone.

The privacy era

The day of reckoning arrives for data privacy.

Data use was originally intended to help make consumers' lives easier by connecting them with personally relevant information, products and services, with minimal effort. But this intent was quickly forgotten as brands fell prey to the siren call of data mining. Today, brands' use of data is generally perceived as underhanded and unethical: 89% of consumers feel that the way companies collect and use data is "sneaky," according to SONAR™, Wunderman Thompson's proprietary research tool. With consumers nearing a breaking point amid increasingly frequent and severe data breaches—from the seminal Cambridge Analytica scandal to the massive Equifax credit breach to the September 2019 Ecuador data leak—brands are starting to course-correct, shedding light on their policies and practices.

"Brands are getting more aware that developing loyalty means transparency," Brittany Kaiser, data transparency advocate and former business development director for Cambridge Analytica, tells Wunderman Thompson Intelligence. "It doesn't mean constantly trying to grab your consumers' attention. It means developing a conversation and a trusting relationship."

concerns, alerting them if their passwords are vulnerable or have been compromised in a third-party breach.

In May 2019, Google opened a privacy engineering hub in Europe. The new Google Safety Engineering Center (GSEC) is founded on the belief that "privacy and safety must be equally available to everyone in the world" and will work on "building privacy and security into the core of our products," explains GSEC CEO Sundar Pichai.

Why it's interesting:
While these initiatives mark the first step in repairing the damage already inflicted in the data privacy battle, there is still a way to go. "This idea that we can control our own data and our digital identity is not a figment of our imagination or a wild hope for the future, it's actually possible," says Kaiser—and brands that are able to reliably and ethically bring this future to fruition will find success among consumers.

The future is private.

**This idea that we can control our own data and our digital identity is not a figment of our imagination or a wild hope for the future, it's actually possible.
Brittany Kaiser, data transparency advocate**

Big Tech companies—arguably some of the worst offenders—are tripping over each other in their rush to release new privacy initiatives in a bid to regain consumers' trust.

Apple is leaning heavily into privacy with its 2019 campaign, which featured slogans such as "Privacy. That's iPhone." and "What happens on your iPhone, stays on your iPhone." In November 2019, Apple updated its privacy website to read like its product pages, communicating its privacy policies in a simple, intuitive and easily digestible format. This addresses the 68% of consumers who find companies' terms and conditions and privacy policies difficult to read, resulting in only 28% reading them often, according to findings from SONAR™, Wunderman Thompson's proprietary research tool. This follows Apple's September 2019 rollout of the iOS 13, an updated operating system that puts data privacy front and center. One of its features blocks voice over internet protocol (VoIP) apps from running in the background when not in use, preventing these apps from collecting data from unwitting users.

In October 2019, Google announced a new Password Checkup function that automatically checks users' passwords for security

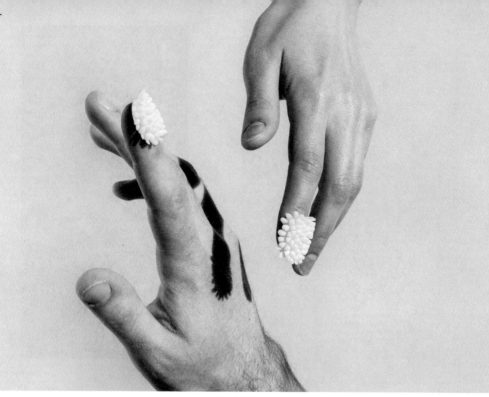

Haptic tech

Haptic technology is set to gain significant traction in 2020, empowering companies to offer a tactile experience for virtual environments.

Haptics refers to any technology that produces the sensation of touch and motion. It works in tandem with AR (augmented reality) and VR (virtual reality), simulating physical interaction in an otherwise audiovisual landscape. A raft of haptic products that made a splash at the CES 2019 tech show will hit the market in 2020, just as 5G rolls out in most major markets around the world, offering the necessary processing power to seamlessly run the tech. Everyone from Alibaba to Disney is racing to explore how the technology can augment their current offerings.

Retail has been quick to adopt this innovation. Alibaba in China, the largest marketplace in the world, has launched its Refinity haptic technology solution, which brings a multisensory experience to online shopping. Gone are the days when potential buyers had to imagine how a product might feel. "The ability to simulate texture and fabric on smartphones and tablets is a breakthrough for online shopping, connecting the physical and digital worlds," explains Dominique Essig, chief experience officer at Bonobos, a US online retailer that has collaborated with haptic technology firm Tanvas.

TECH & INNOVATION

Education is another area already innovating with haptics, as the tech empowers people to test their skills and make mistakes without harming others or themselves. For example, UK-based medical training software company Generic Robotics uses haptic technology and VR to train health professionals in real-world simulations, without the need to practice on actual patients.

Brands have also been quick to realize the opportunities afforded by haptics to the $150 billion gaming industry. Facebook's Research Lab is working on a sensory wristband called Tasbi, while Disney has produced a protype for its haptic Force Jacket. Both are designed to produce physical sensations for VR environments.

In addition to making a digital experience more realistic, haptics can also activate something far more fundamental. As the Fulu website of London-based designer Ryo Tada states, "Touch is important for creating trust and empathy, such as when babies first create a connection with their mother by a simple touch." Fulu is a fingernail-mounted haptic interface, much like EPFL's artificial skin, developed by Tada at the Royal College of Art.

There are clear benefits for brands that elicit an emotional response from consumers, so haptics are being employed across a range of industries, from gaming to advertising and beyond. The 2017 "Ads You Can Feel" study by IPG and Immersion found that ads with haptics outperformed traditional versions on a number of indicators. Perhaps most significantly, ads with haptics outperformed standard ones by a wide margin among potential new

Fulu haptic interface

Why it's interesting:

Haptic technology is set to revolutionize everything from entertainment to education. It elevates 3D digital environments to something far more interactive and emotional. As haptic-enhanced products improve, demand will grow and R&D will see further investment. Now's the time for brands to assess how haptics can enhance their product innovation strategy.

customers.

WUNDERMAN
THOMPSON   Tanvas haptic technology

Touch is important for creating trust and empathy, such as when babies first create a connection with their mother by a simple touch.

Ryo Tada, designer, Fulu

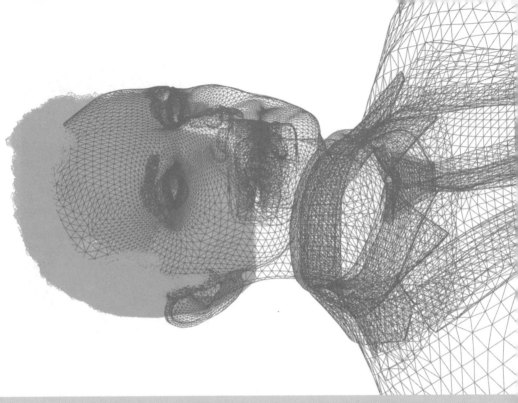

Navigating the AI workplace

AI in the workplace is evolving from simple automated chatbots towards more cognitive functions.

Companies around the world are adopting avatars and AI software for recruitment purposes. While offering savings in terms of time and cost, this technology is rife with potential hazards and public concern is high. Data from the UK's Royal Society of Arts revealed that 60% of consumers were opposed to the use of automated decision-making in recruitment, and some law firms are already preparing to act in AI-related lawsuits.

With over 700 clients, including Unilever, Hilton, JP Morgan Chase, Delta Air Lines, Vodafone, Ikea and Goldman Sachs, HireVue offers software for video interviews and pre-hire assessments that scans candidates' language—from active or passive phrasing to tone of voice to speed of delivery—and also analyses facial expressions, such as furrowed brows, smiles and eye-widening.

This part of the recruitment process has become so common that some universities are even beginning to offer students training for AI-driven interviews.

NDERMAN
MPSON   Digital avatar of Daniel Kalt, chief economist at UBS, created by FaceMe

Oben virtual identities

While some applaud the use of AI in removing human bias, there are widespread concerns about the effectiveness of the platform. In her October 2019 book *Artificial Intelligence: A Guide for Thinking Humans*, author and Portland State University computer science professor Melanie Mitchell notes that there are a number of flaws in the systems currently at play. AI can be easily tricked and is vulnerable to hackers, and facial recognition technology is significantly more likely to produce errors when applied to people of color.

The global law firm Paul Hastings launched an AI practice group in March 2019 to help clients using AI services and products. The aim is to assist clients to defend against class-action lawsuits and give legal advice in areas such as compliance with laws and regulations, data privacy issues, AI governance and ethics. "AI tools are going to drive decisions like who ought to be promoted and who should be fired," Bradford Newman, a member of the law firm's AI practice group, told the Society for Human Resource Management. "When you have algorithms making decisions that impact humans in one of

their most essential life functions—which is their work—there are going to be issues of fairness and transparency, and legal challenges, and I think we are going to see those legal challenges start very soon."

Cognitive AI that's less oriented to decision-making is, however, proving more palatable. Already gaining in popularity in China—where California-based tech company Oben is at the forefront—AI avatars will likely encounter fewer hurdles.

In January 2019, China Central Television, the country's largest broadcast network, aired its Lunar New Year special, which was viewed some 1.8 billion times. Four life-sized "personal artificial intelligences" (PAIs)—three-dimensional holographic replicas of the show's presenters—moved, spoke, and even sang. Oben, which produced the PAIs, is banking on eventually developing the technology for mass consumption, potentially as celebrity stand-ins or in the workplace for remote meetings.

China's Xinhua News Agency began using avatars on air at the end of 2018. The avatars were created in collaboration with the search engine Sogou and allow for "tireless" 24-hour news broadcasts.

Why it's interesting:
In her book, Mitchell questioned which problems in AI were still unsolved. Her ultimate answer was, simply, all of them. AI as a decision-maker is already posing uncomfortable questions in the workplace and there are concerns among a majority of people. With questions of bias and ethics at play, deeper regulations are not far behind—so brands will have to tread carefully.

20

Menotech

New digital-forward resources and tech-enhanced products are reinvigorating life during menopause for an increasingly tech-savvy consumer base.

By 2025, women experiencing menopause will make up 12% of the entire global population, according to the United Nations. While the market for advances in this area remains largely untapped due to residual stigma, pioneering brands are working to change this.

Apple hopes to advance knowledge of women's health and contribute to "the next generation of innovative health products." In November 2019, Apple launched a new health app with an opt-in women's health study to help consumers and doctors better understand menopausal transition, among other gynecological events and conditions. This is crucial because, currently, "there is no 'what to expect when you're expecting' for menopause," Jill Angelo, CEO of digital health platform Gennev, tells Wunderman Thompson Intelligence. "Technology gives us the means to start to build that data."

Gennev is also leveraging data and technology to help improve the experience for women going through menopause. "We're using technology to start to build the world's largest database of menopausal health data that, over time, will allow us to recommend

Rory menopause health vertical

Three ways to start feeling better.

Get your personalized plan

Tackle your symptoms with 6-week programs and on-demand health coaches. From hot flashes to fatigue to weight management, you now have access to an action plan.

Get your plan

Speak with a doctor

Amazing menopause-trained practitioners including nutritionists and OB/GYNs are now just a click away. It's simple and convenient to get the care you need.

Book an appointment

Shop solutions for relief

Designed specifically around common menopausal symptoms, our growing product line was created to help you feel better. From hot flashes and vaginal dryness to insomnia.

Shop menopause relief!

and create a roadmap for women in menopause where none exists now," Angelo reveals. The platform puts technology at the core of its offering to help empower women and demystify menopause.

In March 2019, men's health startup Ro launched Rory, a new vertical for women in perimenopause, menopause and postmenopause. Rory merges telemedicine with the direct-to-consumer model to bring digital health to this generation of women. Through Rory, women are able to connect direct with health providers, treatments, information and community.

"I hope that, collectively, this focus on menotech will start to normalize menopause so that it's not this thing that's brushed under the rug," says Angelo. "Technology is an enabler. I've seen what it

does to transform how we think about education, or banking, or personal finance, or healthcare; menotech is just another slice of that. And we're just beginning."

Why it's interesting:

Women in their 50s, 60s and 70s have been largely overlooked by brands and marketers. But as this vibrant cohort is increasingly upending the status quo, defying expectations and ditching tired stereotypes, the market is ripe with opportunity for tech brands to innovate menopausal and perimenopausal lifestyles.

I hope that, collectively, this focus on menotech will start to normalize menopause so that it's not this thing that's brushed under the rug.

Jill Angelo, CEO, Genney

Genney menopause-centered digital health platform

Travel & Hospitality

21

30

Biocontributive travel

The travel industry is cleaning up its act with a wave of pioneering initiatives that move beyond doing no harm to actively contributing to a carbon-positive future.

Norway broke ground on the world's first energy-positive airport city in late 2019. Oslo Airport City will be powered entirely by renewable energy and will also function as a local source for clean power; it will have the capacity to sell all surplus energy it generates to neighboring buildings and communities, extending sustainable contributions beyond city limits. The city will also serve as a testing ground for urban initiatives to reduce carbon emissions, piloting innovative green technologies including driverless electric cars, automatic lighting for streets and buildings, and smart-tech solutions for waste and security management.

"This is a unique opportunity to design a new city from scratch," Tomas Stokke, director at Haptic Architects, told *Dezeen*. "With the latest developments in technology, we will be able to create a green, sustainable city of the future."

The development, which is backed by the Norwegian government, is an extension of Norway's nationwide initiative to transition from oil to green energy. Oslo Airport, which is owned by the Norwegian government, plans to run a fleet of electric-only vehicles by 2025,

and by 2040 all short-haul flights in and out of Norway will be run on electric aircrafts.

In Trondheim, 300 miles north of Oslo, Snøhetta unveiled the world's northernmost energy-positive building in September 2019. The Norwegian city is situated 63 degrees above the equator and here sunlight varies drastically between seasons, presenting what the architecture and design firm describes as "a unique opportunity to explore how to harvest and store solar energy under challenging conditions." Called Powerhouse Brattørkaia, the building produces more than twice as much electricity as it uses daily. Unused resources will supply renewable energy to neighboring buildings, electric buses, cars and boats through a local micro grid.

Snøhetta describes the project as "aiming to set a new standard for the construction of the buildings of tomorrow: one that produces more energy than it consumes over its lifespan, including construction and demolition. This also includes the embodied energy in the materials used to construct the building."

Snøhetta is also espousing this standard with Svart hotel, which will become the world's first energy-positive hotel when it opens in 2021, generating more solar energy than it uses—including enough energy to power its own construction.

Why it's interesting:

Doing no environmental harm is no longer enough. As these projects prove, the future of travel, tourism and hospitality will be rooted in conscious contributions to a carbon-positive future.

DERMAN
MPSON   Oslo Airport City renders

22

Gated tourism

As popular sightseeing destinations become overrun with tourists, new regulations are limiting entry— and laying the groundwork for a future iteration of luxury travel.

With over-trafficking putting culturally significant sites in danger of destruction, gatekeepers are enforcing stricter measures for those who wish to visit—or closing them to the public altogether.

Uluru is a sacred site for Australia's aboriginal Anangu people. For decades the remote rock in the Northern Territory has annually attracted hundreds of thousands of tourists intent on scaling the summit—in spite of the many signs imploring visitors to stay off the rock, both out of respect for the Anangu people and for their own safety. "It is an extremely important place, not a playground or theme park like Disneyland," Anangu community member Sammy Wilson, former chair of the Uluru-Kata Tjuta National Park board, told the BBC.

In October 2019, the site permanently closed to climbers in deference to the Anangu people. Yet in the face of impending closure tourist numbers significantly increased: Parks Australia reported that the site received 70,000 more visitors in 2018 than in 2017, when the ban was announced.

⁺WUNDERMAN THOMPSON

Uluru. Image courtesy of Parks Australia

In March 2019, the *Washington Post* reported that Lake Elsinore, a small city in southern California, declared a public safety crisis after "Disneyland-size crowds" descended to witness a rare "super bloom" of wildflowers.

In order to protect such landmarks—not to mention the safety, livelihood and religion of local inhabitants—many sites are instituting new requirements for entry. In December 2018 the renowned I Amsterdam sign in front of the city's Rijksmuseum was removed in an effort to staunch overtourism and since then the Dutch capital has been developing an initiative that targets and attracts luxury travelers. "Focusing on this group will get locals excited about welcoming travelers, as opposed to being concerned about the number of tourists," says Antonia Koedijk, North America director of the Netherlands Board of Tourism and Conventions.

Other heritage sites are implementing high-end hurdles for entry. In October 2019 Indonesia announced a new membership system to limit the number of visitors to famed Komodo National Park; premium memberships will go for $1,000 and grant full access to the entire park—including Komodo Island—while non-premium memberships will give access to specified areas only. At Machu Picchu a stricter ticketing policy was instituted in January 2019. In April 2019 the Philippines' Boracay Island introduced a ban on cruise ships during peak season. In May 2019 Iceland announced that the popular Fjaðrárgljúfur canyon will be open to visitors for only five weeks each year.

Why It's Interesting:
To preserve iconic sites and ecological marvels, stanchions are being put in place to restrict overcrowding at heavily trafficked landmarks. The ensuing costly entrance fees and restrictive access are turning these sites into exclusive destinations for luxury travelers.

I Amsterdam. Photo Jan-Kees Steenman, SeeItYourself.com

Overcrowding is occurring worldwide. In April 2019, during the Netherlands' famous tulip festival, barriers were erected in an attempt to prevent tourists from destroying the fields of flowers in their pursuit of the perfect picture. In an interview that appeared in the *Guardian*, translated from Dutch paper *Algemeen Dagblad*, Simon Pennings, a grower near the town of Noordwijkerhout in the bulb region of south-west Netherlands, remarked that the visitors "are so careless." He said that while the large groups of people visiting can be fun, they flatten everything. "It is a shame and we suffer damage as a result. Last year, I had a plot with €10,000 ($11,000) in damage. Everything was trampled… They want to take that selfie anyway."

In addition to the tulip fields being fenced off, the Dutch tourism board released a dos and don'ts guide to photographing the flowers. The local tourist office also organized a group of ambassadors to teach visitors about the history of the fields and the work that goes into maintaining them.

Scientific expeditions

Modern explorers are going to the ends of the earth in pursuit of once-in-a-lifetime experiences—and the opportunity to contribute new findings to the scientific community.

In December 2019, Airbnb hosted Antarctic Sabbatical, a month-long research expedition for five intrepid travelers. Run in partnership with Ocean Conservancy and led by environmental scientist Kirstie Jones-Williams, the program's mission was to better understand the impact of microplastics on the Antarctic ecosystem. Participants, who were not required to have any scientific background or experience, received a crash course in glaciology, field sampling and research protocols before arriving in Antarctica.

Ahead of the trip, Jones-Williams let participants know that this was a vacation with a difference: "This expedition will be hard work, with scientific rigor required during unforgiving wintry conditions. We are looking for passionate individuals with a sense of global citizenship, who are excited to be a part of the team and to return home and share our findings with the world."

Travel company Luxury Action is also catering to citizen scientists with an excursion to the North Pole in April 2020. "We provide all of the equipment," Luxury Action founder Janne Honkanen told CNN,

TRAVEL & HOSPITALITY

VANDERMAN
THOMPSON

Airbnb Antarctic Sabbatical. Image courtesy of Airbnb. Photo by Christopher Michel

"but you definitely need to have the spirit of an explorer or scientist."

It is billed as the world's northernmost hotel, and those who can afford the $100,000+ price will stay in heated igloos, accompanied by arctic wilderness guides and private security teams.

"We're not just providing the experience, we want to spread the word on what's happening," Honkanen said. "How the climate crisis affects local culture, local food and the Arctic animals—we see the effects first-hand."

In March 2020, Polar Latitudes will run its second expedition to study humpback whales, in partnership with the Woods Hole Oceanographic Institution. Alongside marine biologists, environmental scientists, geologists and historians, citizen scientists tag whales and study their behavior.

Why it's interesting:
The mark of luxury travel is shifting away from material and creature comforts. Scientific pursuits are becoming the ultimate status symbol for an emerging echelon of elite adventurers prioritizing purpose-driven travel.

We're not just providing the experience, we want to spread the word on what's happening.

Janne Honkanen, founder, Luxury Action

24

Slow travel

A wave of mindful travel sees travelers luxuriating in the journey rather than rushing to their destination.

Echoing modern mental-health mantras, travelers are embracing a longer journey as an opportunity to savor the moment. The journey, once simply a means to an end, is being relished as much as the final destination. And with growing awareness of the negative environmental impact of air and auto travel, train travel is experiencing a sweeping resurgence.

Climate activist Greta Thunberg famously renounces air travel, instead commuting around Europe exclusively by train. Now, as the flight-shaming movement gains momentum, global tastemakers are piping up in support of the romanticized train trip.

Supermodel Edie Campbell opted for a 12-hour train trip from London to Milan for fashion week in fall 2019 instead of flying. In an October 2019 article she wrote for *Elle* addressing the fashion industry's carbon footprint, Campbell described her trip as "heaven.… I was gently rocked in my comfortable seat, while gliding past glittering lakes and mountain passes, and catching glimpses of Italian nonnas hanging out their bloomers."

In October and November 2019, model and activist Adwoa Aboah took to Instagram to extoll the virtues of rail travel, captioning one

WUNDERMAN
THOMPSON

Above: Chanel Resort 2020. Image courtesy of Chanel
Right: The Outnet FW19 holiday campaign. Image courtesy of the Outnet

carousel post of images taken on board the Belmond British Pullman. "To be chic on a train with my Mumma dearest is already my favorite thing."

Iconic fashion house Chanel emphasizes the luxury of train travel in its Resort 2020 collection. Rather than sending models down a traditional runway, the collection debuted against a recreated beaux arts-style train station. The marketing campaign that followed brought to life the elegance of the modern train journey, evoking "the promise of an adventure," the brand explains.

"Luxury travel, so we are told, is life in the fast lane; private jets and champagne at 40,000 feet," Campbell wrote. But this definition of luxury is outdated, she argued, instead declaring that "luxury is taking your time, and moving more slowly."

Why it's interesting:

Train travel, which harks back to a slower pace of life, is redefining modern luxury travel as consumers hunger for opportunities to step back from the stressors of daily life and engage more deeply with the world around them.

25

Farm-to-plane dining

Airlines are bringing a crop of garden-fresh ingredients to in-flight menus.

Planes, with their limited storage and postage stamp-sized prep areas, are not conducive to gourmet meals. But as health and wellness remains a top priority for consumers, airlines are making major strides towards offering meals that cater to wellness-obsessed and sustainably minded passengers. The latest feat? Runway-adjacent gardens to fuel flyers with hyper-fresh produce—grown and picked planeside.

As part of its wellness cuisine initiative, Singapore Airlines has launched a menu in collaboration with hydroponic farm company AeroFarms. From October 2019, arugula, baby bok choi and mixed greens grown in AeroFarm's Newark vertical gardening facility have been served as part of the "farm-to-plane" menu on flights from New Jersey's Newark Liberty International Airport to Singapore's Changi Airport.

"Imagine boarding a plane and enjoying a salad harvested as close to departure as possible—literally the world's freshest airline food," says Antony McNeil, global food and beverage director for

Imagine boarding a plane and enjoying a salad harvested as close to departure as possible— literally the world's freshest airline food.

Antony McNeil, global food and beverage director, Singapore Airlines

Singapore Airlines. "The only way to get fresher greens is to pick them from your own garden."

Silicon Valley food startup Crop One is bringing fresh produce to flyers on a mass scale. The hydroponic farming company partnered with Emirates Flight Catering to construct the world's largest vertical farm in Dubai. From December 2019, produce harvested from the facility began making its way onto in-flight menus out of Dubai, which ranked as the world's busiest airport for international passengers in 2017 and 2018 (the most recent numbers available at the time of writing).

Chicago's O'Hare International Airport has been a pioneer in hydroponic produce since 2011, when a vertical garden was planted in one of the airport's terminals. Vegetables from the garden are sourced directly to restaurants and cafes in the terminal, offering diners fresh produce year-round for pre-flight meals.

Why It's Interesting:

These new initiatives are taking freshly picked produce to the skies, enabling travelers to eat just as well in the air as they would on the ground.

因为我们每做出来一个产品都是独一无二的
Everything we make is one of a kind

最重要的是我们不知道接下来体验的东西会呈现出来什么样的
But most importantly we can't predict exactly how it will turn out

26

Legacy preservation

Travelers and companies are becoming far more conscious of how tourism can threaten the future of heritage landmarks and cultural traditions.

Overtourism has become a buzzword—the *Oxford English Dictionary* made the term one of its words of the year in 2018. Now destinations and companies are fighting back, both in terms of mitigating current overtourism levels and offering tours and activities that positively impact landmarks and local communities.

Alongside moves such as Venice introducing a €10 ($11) fee to enter the city for short stays and Amsterdam removing the I Amsterdam sign that attracted hordes of Instagrammers (see gated tourism, page 57), steps are being taken that aim to include tourists in a destination's preservation. Mark Tanzer, chief executive of the Association of British Travel Agents, says that "tourism brings with it considerable benefits that the industry should rightly be proud of. Economies and people depend on tourism, it protects and promotes cultural exchange and can support the preservation of natural environments and cultural heritage."

In tune with the move to conserve, in October 2019 Airbnb in China launched a campaign called Lost & Found. An article on *Marketing Interactive* explained that this aims to "preserve China's heritage

sites as masters hailing from traditional industries face an increasing loss of awareness and recognition for their craft." Airbnb's Chinese platform offers travelers the chance to learn Chinese crafts and traditions from 40 masters, as part of its traveling experiences. Mia Chen, head of marketing at Airbnb China, told the publication "we want to inspire a combination of travel and participation in cultural heritage experiences," adding that the platform seeks to encourage the younger generation to explore, care for and value the treasures of China's traditions.

In another initiative, Airbnb sponsored a project called the Italian Sabbatical, in which selected visitors became temporary members of the southern Italian village of Grottole. The aim, the company states, was to "revitalize a village that is at risk of disappearing" as its population ages and younger people move away. Out of 280,000 applicants, five were selected to live in the village for three months, where they volunteered with Wonder Grottole, which was rehabilitating Grottole's historic center. Wonder Grottole's site says that the project, experimented "with a new tourism model." The traveler, it explains, doesn't visit passively, or just enjoy the experiences offered by locals, but becomes a participant in change.

Illustrating the strength of sentiment behind preserving cultural landmarks, there has been heated debate in France over the restoration of Notre Dame cathedral after it was extensively damaged in a fire in 2019. According to data from Odoxa-Dentsu published in Le Figaro in May 2019, 55% of French citizens believe its landmark spire should be rebuilt identically. French president Emmanuel Macron, however, is pushing for a "contemporary architectural gesture" to replace it and the French government has invited architects to submit proposals for the roofline. This, the Guardian reported, resulted in a Twitter hashtag

#TouchePasANotreDame (don't touch Notre Dame). General Jean-Louis Georgelin, the army general overseeing the Notre Dame restoration, has said that a final decision on the spire's design will be reached in 2021.

Why it's interesting:

Travelers and brands can no longer ignore the cultural and environmental impact that traveling has on heritage destinations and local culture—and the importance of this heritage to locals and travelers alike. These initiatives are taking proactive steps to preserve heritage and aim to bring a sense of altruism to the tourism trail, and some experiences dovetail with young consumers' desire to do good while seeing more of the world. Expect more travel experiences that take a 360-degree view of how they impact a destination.

21

Social stays

Solo travel is on the rise — and hotels are investing in providing ready-made entertainment for lone guests.

More and more travelers are choosing to go it alone; a survey by the Association of British Travel Agents found that 15% chose to vacation by themselves in 2018, up 12% compared to the previous year. Hotels are catering to these solo visitors by transforming themselves into social and cultural hubs.

Among the venues experimenting in this sphere is the Stratford, a hotel and loft apartment development that opened in spring 2019 in east London. Its Happenings program is intended to bring "lifestyle, fashion, wellness, art, culture and entertainment to Stratford," the hotel says. Among its events in 2019 were life drawing classes with artist Alexandria Coe, cocktail masterclasses and doga—yoga for dogs and their owners.

In January 2019, *Skift* published an article on luxury hotels' desire to "make you feel culturally relevant." Among those it cited were Heckfield Place in Hampshire, England, which opened in late 2018. This restored Georgian house's Assembly Events program has spanned tours of its art collection with a curator, a talk on recovery by Russell Brand, and a "mud and guts" outdoor experience for children. "The inspiration behind the Assembly really came from our

Life House. Images courtesy of Life House

TRAVEL & HOSPITALITY

owner," Olivia Richli, general manager of Heckfield Place, told *Skift*. "He's an academic and very keen that you take away more than a luxury hotel experience, that you leave with something you learned."

This follows on from Moxy Hotels' established social programs, which have included knitting classes in its Times Square hotel and a collaboration in 2018 with networking and dating app Bumble—as part of this, Moxy's hotels were verified as "inclusive environments to meet your Bumble connections, across dating, friendship and professional networking."

Moxy San Diego, downtown/Gaslamp quarter. Images courtesy of Moxy Hotels, Marriott International

The Life House hotel chain has an app that allows guests to connect with each other during their stay. "The travel industry has a unique opportunity to match new people with other people," Rami Zeidan, CEO and cofounder of Life House, tells Wunderman Thompson Intelligence. "Everyone is traveling and doesn't necessarily have a home base or safety network of friends in a given location. Hotels have a particularly unique opportunity to connect people."

Why it's interesting:

In the face of competition from the likes of Airbnb, hotels are pitching themselves as more than merely a place to stay. Expect to see more hotels launching social and cultural events to engage travelers and locals alike, to cement their status as a powerful hub for visitors and the community.

Jewel Changi Airport, Singapore. Image courtesy of Jewel Changi Airport Devt

28

Elevated airports

Airports are getting an experiential upgrade, becoming exciting cultural destinations in their own right.

ong lines, bad food and grim terminals are horrors of the past hen it comes to new airports. Cities are opening up mega airport paces which deliver seamless, interactive and even enchanting xperiences.

ingapore's Jewel Changi Airport opened in April 2019. The space osts the tallest indoor waterfall in the world, at 40 meters high, hich is fed by rainwater collected on the terminal's huge donut-haped roof. The atrium is made of glass panels, allowing natural ght to shine on visitors as well as on the multistory garden that is ome to more than 2,000 trees and 100,000 shrubs. Travelers can ake a guided tour to explore the garden as well as shop, eat and rink at the 280-plus outlets in the airport. According to Safdie rchitects, the practice that designed the airport, the space was uilt for travelers and non-travelers alike and devised to be more nan a transit hub. The designers intend Jewel Changi Airport to stablish "a new model for airports as discrete destinations for hopping, entertainment and social activity."

eijing's newest airport opened on September 25, 2019. Designed

DERMAN
MPSON

Cities are opening up mega airport spaces which deliver seamless, interactive and even enchanting experiences.

in a starfish pattern that utilizes the principles of movement, Beijing Daxing International Airport also features the latest technology to speed up the airport process—which will be necessary for the 72 million passengers it aims to service by 2025. The airport, designed by the late Zaha Hadid, is sure to become a landmark worth a visit whether or not you plan to fly.

Saanen Airport in Gstaad, Switzerland, is the location of Tarmak 22 gallery, which in 2019 hosted an exhibition by German artist Andreas Gursky and a selection from the collection of Mexico-born artist Alex Hank. The gallery is open to the public as well as travelers and was created as a space where visitors and locals can view contemporary art shows and enjoy cultural talks and performances. It is a permanent addition to the luxury ski resort's airport. Antonia Crespí Bennàssar, the gallery's cofounder, tells Wunderman Thompson Intelligence, "with Tarmak 22, we hope to contribute to a cultural dialogue and make Gstaad an inspiring destination for curious travelers and locals alike."

Why it's interesting:

By providing new experiences like these, where visitors can be inspired or entertained, airports are going beyond merely facilitating travel. In expanding their offerings, they are attracting new audiences and becoming unique cultural destinations in their own right.

Disaster-proof destinations

Forward-thinking architects are designing homes to withstand apocalyptic weather conditions.

With freak weather events becoming the norm, from category five hurricanes to raging wildfires, architects are designing more resilient buildings to withstand an increasingly volatile climate.

Lebron Lackey's home on the coast of Florida gained renown in October 2018 as one of few homes to emerge unscathed amid the devastation wreaked by Hurricane Michael. Lackey reportedly spent twice the normal construction cost to protect his dwelling against 250-mile-an-hour winds and flooding. "We wanted to build it for the big one," Lackey told the *New York Times*. "We just never knew we'd find the big one so fast."

Architects are turning to maritime construction techniques that stand up to heavy rain, flooding and coastal storms. Completed in 2018, Raad Studio's Beach House in New Jersey is designed to counteract the seaside home's vulnerability to storms and flooding. We created a set of hydrodynamic dunes with penetrations that allow water to sluice through the land, while simultaneously elevating the house well above the historic high-water mark," the firm explains. A trough-like path bracketed by concrete retaining

ANDERMAN   Raad Studio Beach House. Image courtesy of Raad Studio.
THOMPSON   sPhoto by Eric M Townsend

walls runs underneath the home and serves as a storm drain during heavy rainfall, creating a building that James Ramsey, designer and director of Raad Studio, describes as "in sync with the land and water in a way that allows it to survive."

An oceanside home constructed by Specht Architects on Long Beach Island, New Jersey, which was hit hard by Hurricane Sandy in 2012, takes its cue from nautical construction with the highest grade hurricane-proof windows, stainless steel components and a fiberglass roof to withstand heavy weather.

Bruce Beinfield of Beinfield Architecture has constructed a fortress on the coast of Connecticut. The house features several components that were specifically engineered to protect it from

extreme weather conditions. Salvaged wood sidings and roll-down steel shutters create an "exoskeleton of lateral-bracing shield storm shutters that protect the large operable glazed surfaces from storms," the firm explains. The house is raised on concrete pillars 15 feet above sea level—two feet higher than the Federal Emergenc Management Agency's flood regulations require. The ground-level garage is constructed on a base of reinforced concrete, with vents where flood water can enter and equalize water pressure.

Why it's interesting:

As climate concerns mount, the next generation of luxury homes is being built to provide heightened protection from extreme conditions.

31

WELL hospitality

The next generation of hotels is taking healthy hospitality to new heights, building health-enhancing elements into their very structures.

According to the most recent data from the Global Wellness Institute, in 2017 wellness tourism accounted for $639 billion of the global wellness economy. Pioneering hotels are working to capture share of the market by constructing environments specifically formulated to optimize wellbeing.

In July 2019, the Inn at Moonlight Beach in Encinitas, California, became the world's first hotel to earn a WELL building certification. Introduced in 2014, the International WELL Building Institute exists "to improve human health and wellbeing in buildings and communities," and "enhance people's health and wellness through the buildings where we live, work, and play." There are some 3,880 projects applying WELL standards across 58 countries, the majority of which are workplaces.

To meet the certification's standards, the Inn at Moonlight Beach reviewed its buildings and offerings to align with standards from WELL's seven categories—air, water, nourishment, light, fitness, comfort and mind. The inn's features include a biodynamic farm,

a meditation garden and a top-of-the-line air filtration system.

While the Inn at Moonlight Beach is the first hotel to be WELL certified, several others are also pursuing the certification, including the Keihan Kyoto hotel in Japan, the Zem Wellness Retreat in Alicante, Spain, and California's Stanly Ranch.

Why it's interesting:
Wellness-obsessed vacationers are seeking out new ways to supercharge their rest and relaxation—and are starting to look beyond activities alone to achieve this, choosing carefully considered environments built on a foundation of health and wellness.

DERMAN   Inn at Moonlight Beach, Encinitas, California
MPSON

Brands & Marketing

31

Gamefluencers

GlobalData predicts that the gaming industry will be worth $300 billion by 2025, and brands want a slice of that multibillion cake.

pple Arcade launched in September 2019, upping standards and ccessibility for mobile gaming, and Google is also attempting to hange the way games are accessed with the launch of Stadia in ovember 2019.

s the gaming universe diversifies and the uptick in users ontinues, brands are turning to gaming influencers to engage with nis growing audience. In August 2019, *Fortnite* megastar Tyler Blevins, better known as Ninja, entered a multiyear partnership with adidas. Earlier in 2019 in China, Nike signed a deal to become the fficial and exclusive apparel and footwear partner for *League of egends Pro League* (*LPL*) players, and the company even tapped PL player Uzi (real name Jian Zhao) to appear in one of its ampaigns. In 2018, K-Swiss sponsored footwear for the esports eam Immortals.

Beauty brands are collaborating with female gamers. In March 2019, *Fortnite* and *League of Legends* streamer Pokimane (real

DERMAN
MPSON   Nike's League of Legends Pro League team kits 2019. Image courtesy of Nike

name Imane Anys) released an eyeshadow palette in collaboration with makeup brand Winky Lux. In February 2019, Mac Cosmetics partnered with Tencent mobile game *Honor of Kings* in China to launch a limited edition of lipsticks, which reportedly sold out within 24 hours.

Louis Vuitton has also been spotting in-game brand opportunities. The luxury brand partnered with Riot Games in September 2019 and is offering two unique "prestige skins" for *League of Legends* champions. These are designed by Nicolas Ghesquière, artistic director of Louis Vuitton's women's collections. The Qiyana skin dropped in November 2019 and the Senna skin's release is expected in early 2020.

+ WUNDERMAN THOMPSON

Above: League of Legends prestige skin by Louis Vuitton. Image courtesy of Louis Vuitton
Right: Ninja partners with Adidas. Image courtesy of Adidas
Far right: Pokimane collection for Winky Lux

Why it's interesting:

Gaming is shaping up to become the next frontier for brand activations—and esport stars are becoming the newest class of celebrities. "Brands have historically been cautious when approaching gaming as it's somewhat unknown. However, the scale at which talent is building audience—particularly mobile gamers—simply can't be ignored now," says Charlie Baillie, cofounder of esports media company Ampverse.

32

Sonic branding

From finance to fashion, companies across industries are creating bespoke sounds to reinforce their brand identities and forge multidimensional connections with today's consumers.

s noted in the sound empires trend report in "The Future 100: 019," ears have become a key gateway to audiences, thanks to the se of audio entertainment and an abundance of sound systems— nd brands are starting to take note.

n September 2019, Coach published a series of Instagram posts equesting that viewers put the sound on, and highlighted noises ssociated with Coach, from the "always satisfying sound" of its urnlock bag fastenings to the clink of its metal buttons and the whirr of a sewing machine stitching one of the brand's pieces. In the same month, Bao Bao Issey Miyake invited London Design Festival attendees to visit Bao Bao Voice, an "interactive, multisensory vent" that included more than 100 sounds attached to its enowned geometric bags.

n the auto world, audio innovation is unsilencing electric cars, which have raised safety concerns for being too quiet. The European Union (EU) is already rolling out rules to equip electric

Bao Bao Voice by Bao Bao Issey Miyake

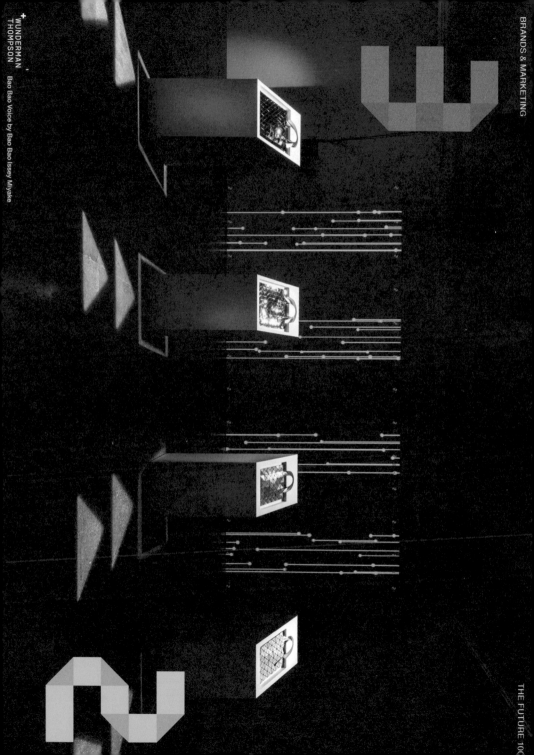

+ WUNDERMAN THOMPSON

Bao Bao Voice by Bao Bao Issey Miyake

NDS & MARKETING

cars with sound for new models, and from July 2021 all cars in the EU must have an acoustic vehicle alert system. BMW has decided to up its game by rejecting the traditional sound of a car engine and tapping composer Hans Zimmer and sound engineer Renzo Vitale to create audio cues for its BMW Vision M Next electric car. The partnership was announced in June 2019 and Zimmer and Vitale have developed the BMW IconicSounds Electric series of sounds. The brand says that its aim is to address the "gap in the emotionality of the driving experience" when driving a nearly inaudible electric car.

In early 2019, both HSBC and Mastercard unveiled new sound identities. HSBC worked with composer Jean-Michel Jarre to create "a bespoke piece of music that will help people instantly recognize the bank." Mastercard devised a sonic logo and ensured the originality of the melody by hiring musicologists to compare it with a database of music.

In June 2019, US music platform *Pandora* launched an audio consultancy called Studio Resonate, which, according to *Businesswire*, will help "propel brands into the new era of audio." In the same month iHeartMedia and WPP announced Project Listen, a new content and research service providing sonic branding.

Audio branding services are being ramped up as a result of the reinvigorated need for bespoke sounds. "Consumers are listening more than ever and we already know the power of music, voice and sound to create engaging and emotional human connections," says Mark Read, CEO of WPP. "As consumers' behavior evolves, from the media they enjoy to how they relate to brands and make purchase decisions, it's essential to have a modern approach to creative and strategy for all media, including audio."

NDERMAN
MPSON

Hans Zimmer composing BMW IconicSounds Electric

Why it's interesting:

Companies are tapping into the science of sound to strengthen brand identities and better resonate with consumers. Sound, after all, is our fastest sense; according to auditory neuroscientist Seth Horowitz it takes our brains at least one quarter of a second to process visual recognition but only 0.05 seconds when it comes to sound. Brands seeking to leave a long-lasting, emotional impression on consumers should look to trademarked audio identities.

Singles lexicon

Call them self-partnered, or consciously uncoupled, or sologamists—but don't call them single.

A new vocabulary is emerging to describe the myriad, multifaceted ways to live without a partner, reframing tired stereotypes and stigmas.

Gwyneth Paltrow and Chris Martin made headlines for their "conscious uncoupling" in 2014. The neologism opened the door for a new way of talking and thinking about life without a partner, and now culture is starting to catch up.

In an interview with British *Vogue* for its December 2019 issue, actor Emma Watson described her lifestyle as "self-partnered." The term, like that of Paltrow and Martin, set off a media maelstrom. Amidst the frenzy, one thing was made abundantly clear: traditional vocabulary about single lifestyles no longer applies.

"When Emma Watson and Gwyneth Paltrow come out and use phrases like 'self-partnered' and 'conscious uncoupling,' it challenges the psychological implications and narratives behind the phrases being 'single' and 'getting a divorce'," therapist Travis McNulty told NBC News.

These high-profile women join the ranks of a growing, empowered group embracing singlehood for the fulfillment and freedom it provides. Author Glynnis MacNicol, who in 2018 published *No One Tells You This*, a memoir on singledom, tells Wunderman Thompson Intelligence that she sought to "add some new language to the story around women's lives."

She says that "we don't really have a way of talking about women's lives outside of marriage or babies." But, as she expands, "that's what's happening now: we're creating a new language around women's lives. It's happening in fits and starts. Sometimes it looks good and sometimes it's: wow, they did a really bad job with this. It's messy, it's hard and it's new."

In our report "The Single Age," interviewee Joe Staton tells Wunderman Thompson Intelligence that if brands were to address him as a single person "they would be immediately off my

> **Culture of late is experiencing a push to reframe single people as they really are: confident, fulfilled and empowered.**

consideration list. I would find it quite patronizing, I think. I don't think it would resonate with me. Although I am very happy being single, my typology is not singledom."

As this discourse widens, traditional tropes of singlehood in the media are changing, shedding the portrait of immature, pitiable desperation and trading it for one of independent freedom.

According to findings from a survey of 3,000 respondents across the United States, the United Kingdom and China commissioned by SONAR™, Wunderman Thompson's proprietary research tool, 82% of American singles think that it's becoming more acceptable to be single in today's society and 77% think society places too much emphasis on being in a relationship. The majority of respondents—regardless of age, gender or nationality—say that they love being single, with upwards of 70% saying single is their choice. Across generations, more than 50% of Americans prefer being single to being in a relationship.

Why it's interesting:

Culture of late is experiencing a push to reframe single people as they really are: confident, fulfilled and empowered. The evolving dialogue reflects a fundamental and seismic paradigm shift to adulthood uncoupled. Armed with a more nuanced and accurate arsenal of terminology, society is able to meet this growing cohort as they are.

The new super-creatives

Digital tools are enhancing the creative habits of the next generation of consumers—and giving them a powerful voice.

Generation Z, the cohort aged 13 to 22, is the first generation that will grow up surrounded by tech. The group's digital capabilities and hyper-connectivity have equipped its members with an unmatched fluidity in creative expression. This super-creativity is being used for the greater good; in "Into Z Future," a report from the Innovation Group in partnership with Snapchat, when asked to offer a slogan for their generation, gen Zers first say "be yourself," followed quickly by "save the planet."

In November 2019, the women behind the Gen Z Girl Gang community—cofounded by outspoken advocate for women's reproductive rights Deja Foxx, now 19—partnered with Samsung to present the "College Access for All" campaign as part of Samsung's Galaxy Innovator Sessions. They used their platform to discuss inclusivity in education and a new mentorship opportunity, and collaborated with tween-focused wellness brand Blume for a self-care workshop.

Other prominent gen Z creatives include indigenous rights activist and poet Kinsale Hueston, who recently worked with *Refinery29* and Target on a campaign called "Future Seekers"; Matt Bernstein,

Into Z Future

Understanding Generation Z: the Next Generation of Super-Creative

who uses makeup as a storytelling device to speak out on LGBTQ rights; and 19-year-old Em Odesser, who was listed in *Teen Vogue*'s 21 under 21 in 2019 for the way she uses her creative talents to break down stigma around mental and sexual health for young people.

"I don't know if I want to be a journalist, a dildo slinger, a novelist, a magazine editor, a comedian, a stylist, or what," she told *Teen Vogue*. "But I hope I'm still expressing myself in a way that feels authentic."

Why it's interesting:

Teens are charting new territory for digital and artistic expression. Many are doing so with an activist streak at various scales, and brands looking to reach this generation need to communicate on their level. "You have to completely remove any sense of binaries or rules—there are no contradictions for gen Z, it's just all raw material," Molly Logan, cofounder of gen-Z run think tank Irregular Labs, tells Wunderman Thompson Intelligence in the "Into Z Future" report. The companies that succeed with these young consumers will be those that align their activities with what gen Zers care about, from authenticity and inclusivity to the environment.

NDERMAN   Above: "Into Z Future" report
OMPSON   Right: Future Seekers, Refinery29 x Target. Photo by Heather Hazzan for Refinery29

You have to completely remove any sense of binaries or rules — there are no contradictions for gen Z, it's just all raw material.

Molly Logan, founder, Irregular Labs

35

Analog renaissance

Cultural creators are turning to analog formats to cut through the digital noise.

A growing number of artists are reviving analog formats that had seemed consigned to the media dustbin.

In June 2019, Radiohead frontman Thom Yorke teased the launch of his album *Anima Technologies* with a series of mysterious ads placed on London Underground trains, in Italian phone booths and in the classified section of the *Dallas Observer*.

The ads also offered a telephone number which, when dialled, played the cryptic message *"Anima Technologies* has been ordered by the authorities to cease and desist from undertaking its advertised business."

Coldplay also chose the analog route for their eighth studio album release, promoting the launch with a series of small ads placed in the classified section of a selection of newspapers. In the *North Wales Daily Post*, the advert for *Everyday Life* reportedly appeared alongside sales notices for hay bales and a fridge freezer.

The band also took the opportunity to revive a much-loved tradition,

sending seemingly personally typed postcards to selected fans via snail mail.

Completing the analog-fest, the album has been released on humble cassette, too, which is itself seeing a nascent revival as a format. Cassette Store Day, an annual event dedicated to the format, originated in the United Kingdom in 2013 but is now thriving across the world in China, Indonesia, the United States and Canada among others.

In the United Kingdom, sales of cassette tapes are at their highest since 2004; according to a November 2019 Guardian article, the number of tapes bought that year were predicted to reach 100,000.

In the digital age, analog formats offer novelty with a helping of nostalgia, and even anemoia—nostalgia for a time you have never known.

In the United States, sales were up 23% in 2018, amounting to 219,000 tapes sold. Artists such as the 1975, Madonna, and Catfish and the Bottlemen are all driving this surge with their own cassette launches.

Teen singer Billie Eilish, who was not even born when cassettes were in their heyday, released her debut album *When We All Fall Asleep, Where Do We Go?* on a limited-edition lime green cassette, including a UV glow-in-the-dark version.

The latter perhaps nods to collectability and Instagrammability rather than any serious dedication to the format. But nostalgia plays a role in cassette sales as many music fans hark back to the distinctive sounds of their youth.

Gennaro Castaldo of the BPI British recorded music trade association attributes the shift to the "element of nostalgia." He adds that the *"Guardians of the Galaxy* film franchise, which features the cassette as part of its storyline, has also helped to reawaken interest in the format over the past few years."

Why it's interesting:

In the digital age, analog formats offer novelty with a helping of nostalgia, and even anemoia—nostalgia for a time you have never known.

Unbiased interfaces

The ever-present issue of gender bias has infiltrated everything from the media to algorithms in recent years.

A prime example is the furor in fall 2019 over the Apple credit card, which customers reported was offering women lower credit limits than men. While card issuer Goldman Sachs said its algorithm "doesn't even use gender as an input," *Wired* pointed out that "a gender-blind algorithm could end up biased against women as long as it's drawing on any input or inputs that happen to correlate with gender," adding that studies had shown "creditworthiness can be predicted by something as simple as whether you use a Mac or a PC. But other variables, such as home address, can serve as a proxy for race. Similarly, where a person shops might conceivably overlap with information about their gender."

With this in mind, companies are thinking up inventive ways to weave gender neutrality into their interfaces.

In May 2019, Vice Media's creative agency Virtue launched Q, the first genderless voice assistant. Virtue says that Q "is an example of what we hope the future holds; a future of ideas, inclusion, positions, and diverse representation in technology." It points out

German's can now choose third gender option on legal records.

Colorado becomes fifth state to allow third gender on licenses.

Q, the first genderless voice assistant, by Virtue. Images courtesy of Vice Media

that "technology companies often choose to gender technology believing it will make people more comfortable adopting it. Unfortunately, this reinforces a binary perception of gender, and perpetuates stereotypes that many have fought hard to progress."

Virtue has asked people to share the innovation, so that Apple, Amazon, Google, and Microsoft implement it in their voice assistant products.

Ben Fisher, the founder and CEO of MagicCo, a company that deploys brands onto connected home interfaces, including voice assistants, tells Wunderman Thompson Intelligence he believes that "in the future consumers will be able to select a variety of voice options on these assistants, and genderless voice assistants will be one of many options. I think having a genderless option will impact a company's sales, especially if consumers make their preference for this option known."

Fisher adds: "I think it is unfortunate that the first home voice assistants defaulted to female-sounding voices. I imagine this is because so many decision-makers in tech are men. But I think, in the long term, there will be options for different people. The voice assistants are merely platforms for software that can be configured, and they will be."

Fisher notes, however, that there is a degree of uncertainty over what exactly a genderless voice sounds like. He says it is "hard to truly get right and it may take time to figure that out." With the service currently offering voices that can be altered and configured, Fisher says that this "will make the technology feel accepted and trusted by the user."

People would not assume gender based on voices anymore in the future.

The concept of redressing gender balance is coming to search engines too. In April 2019, Procter & Gamble brand Pantene launched SHE (Search, Human, Equalizer) to "shine a light on bias in search." The search tool, P&G states, "operates on the search back end by filtering results to produce less biased and more balanced results, ultimately giving the women behind some of the world's greatest accomplishments and transformations the visibility they deserve." The launch chimed with Pantene's "Power to Transform" campaign, which saw the haircare brand spotlight how women are "transforming the world." It also marked the launch of a $1 million Pantene partnership with women's member's club The Wing, to help fund female entrepreneurs and women-led businesses through a pitch investment competition.

Why it's interesting:

Rather than simply paying lip service to gender inequality and bias, brands are trying to innovate with products that actively strive to address these issues. From taking on a gender-neutral identity to actively promoting women's achievements, these innovations could be a signal of change for tech's reputation for gender bias.

31

Original content economy

As the streaming wars heat up, brands are increasingly investing in original content.

Viewing habits are shifting. According to an August 2019 report from YPulse, "millennial parents are raising their kids without cable. Their kids are more likely to watch streaming services than anything else—shaping a future where cable is seen as a rare exception." The report found that only 33% of US 13-18-year-olds surveyed watched content on a TV set weekly, while 73% said they watched video content on their smartphones, and a mere 18% watched cable weekly or more.

In this climate of on-demand viewership, entertainment brands are under pressure to deliver unique offerings—and are turning to original content to differentiate themselves from competitors.

Apple TV+ debuted in November 2019 with a slate of exclusive shows, movies and documentaries, including an Emily Dickinson biopic starring Hailee Steinfeld and a mental health docuseries collaboration between Oprah and Prince Harry.

Disney+ hit screens 12 days later with a roster of new launches including *The Mandalorian*, a new show set in the Star Wars

universe, and a lineup of scripted and docuseries expanding the Marvel franchise. Further highlighting the growing importance of original content, Disney announced a newly created VP of international content role at the end of November 2019, which is dedicated to the development and production of global original content.

NBC Universal's streaming service Peacock will launch in April 2020. The company said in September 2019 that it offers "a world-class slate of originals" alongside favorites from the NBC vaults. And WarnerMedia's HBO Max, launching in May 2020, has signed movie production deals with Reese Witherspoon and Greg Berlanti.

Brands outside the entertainment industry are also looking to capture consumers' attention with original content. In September 2019, Procter & Gamble premiered Activate, a six-part documentary series created in partnership with *National Geographic* and focused on inspiring global activism. "It's not product placement. It's not sponsored content. It's prestige television," wrote *Fast Company*.

In October 2019, dating app Tinder released the original interactive video series "Swipe Night," offering a new way to connect on the app. In June 2019, email marketing platform Mailchimp unveiled Mailchimp Presents, a new entertainment division creating original series, films and podcasts for entrepreneurs and owners of small businesses.

OTT video revenue in the United States will grow at a rate of 10.3 percent to reach $23.7 billion in 2023.

◢◢ PwC ◢◢

BRANDS & MARKETING

In April 2019, home rental platform Airbnb announced its plans to develop original shows and content that would promote Airbnb hosts, guests and travel destinations. And in January 2019, e-commerce platform Shopify expanded into TV and film production with Shopify Studios, which will develop docuseries and feature-length documentaries geared towards entrepreneurs.

A PwC report has forecasted that OTT video revenue in the United States will grow at a rate of 10.3% to reach $23.7 billion in 2023, and the importance of original content shows no indication of lessening. PwC noted that "exclusive and original commissions have proven to be the crucial determinant in the battle to attract subscribers to streaming services. The level of content spend being poured into the market by both new and existing players is prodigious and shows no signs of lessening any time soon."

Why it's interesting:

Branded original content is becoming a key pillar in a fracturing entertainment industry—as well as a novel way for brands to capture the attention of consumers who are looking beyond linear television formats for entertainment.

Climate-positive brands

Pioneering brands are yoking sustainability to their business models, putting their money where their mouths are.

According to Wunderman Thompson Intelligence's SONAR™ research, 90% of consumers believe that companies and brands have a responsibility to take care of the planet and its people. As climate concerns reach fever pitch, brands are assuming greater responsibility for environmental impact.

"More and more, we're seeing brands and retailers really focus on sustainability as a business priority," Lizzie Willett, retail consultant at BJSS, tells Wunderman Thompson Intelligence. Brands need to move beyond "clever advertising campaigns," Willet says.

"Consumers can see through it. It's not just about marketing and advertising, it's about your whole company ethos and how you really bring that through in your products."

In November 2019, Dame became the first climate-positive period brand. Its new carbon offsetting initiative dovetails with the brand's founding ethos to cut down on single-use plastic with its reusable tampon applicators. Dame's new initiative—which will remove twice as much carbon from the atmosphere as it has generated since it launched in 2018—earned it the UK's first Carbon Neutral Plus Productcertification from Carbon Footprint.

"As a business, we have a huge responsibility to do everything we can to help tackle our climate emergency and give consumers better options," Dame cofounder Celia Pool told the *Evening Standard*. "To us, becoming climate positive wasn't a choice, but an absolute necessity."

Mass market brands are also responding to this necessity. Since 2017, H&M has been working towards its aim of becoming carbon neutral by 2040, while Unilever has pledged to be carbon positive by 2030, eliminating all fossil fuels from its production processes and supporting its supply partners in doing the same.

In September 2019, Ikea announced plans to generate an excess of renewable energy for its stores. The homeware company also plans to make solar panels available for sale in all of its markets by 2025, helping consumers achieve carbon neutrality on their own.

"Being climate smart is not an added cost," Jesper Brodin, chief executive of Ikea's holding company Ingka, told Reuters. "It's actually smart business and what the business model of the future will look like."

Why it's interesting:

Carbon-positive practices are becoming more than just a trust-building exercise to earn consumer loyalty—they are evolving into a modern business imperative. "We are entering a new decade of corporate accountability," Gucci CEO Marco Bizzarri wrote in a November 2019 open letter that invited CEOs to join his Carbon Neutral Challenge. "As businesses, we all have a responsibility to meet the reality of our global climate and biodiversity crises head on." But patience is key: given that sustainability planning requires a timeline of 20 to 30 years to fully implement and scale, brands, consumers and stakeholders alike will need to adopt a long-term view.

We are entering a new decade of corporate accountability. As businesses, we all have a responsibility to meet the reality of our global climate and biodiversity crises head on.

Marco Bizzarri, CEO, Gucci

Unconventional brand actions

Can the most counterintuitive brand activations be the most impactful?

Brands that are serious about sustainability are making some unexpected moves to underline their commitment to the cause.

Taking a stance against the excessive consumption of Black Friday, brands including REI and Deciem opted to close their stores on what's become a major US shopping day. Deciem announced that it would shut both its website and retail stores for Black Friday 2019, and states that it "no longer feels comfortable being involved in a single day so heavily centered around hyper-consumerism." Deciem instead opted to offer a 23% discount off all its products throughout November 2019. "We strongly believe that skincare decisions should be based on education rather than impulse and we want to give our audience the time for research, reflection, and consideration," the brand says.

In 2019, outdoor clothing brand REI closed its doors for the fifth consecutive year on Black Friday, alongside launching a "cleanup" mission across the United States in the run-up to Thanksgiving, with customers invited to take part in organized cleanups in their neighborhoods. It also launched the Opt to Act Plan, arming

consumers with a checklist of actions for all 52 weeks of the year to help the environment. "As a single company, our impact is limited, but as a community, we can drive change that powers meaningful action beyond our walls," Eric Artz, CEO of REI, wrote in a memo to members of the brand's co-op scheme. "As a co-op, we know that many people taking many small steps together can add up to big changes. Collective intention will drive collective impact."

Patagonia, Lush, Ben & Jerry's, and Seventh Generation all joined the global climate strikes in 2019 and closed their stores on September 20 that year in solidarity with the climate activists.

"These businesses are rejecting some revenue to bolster a larger cause—climate change—and that's a potentially radical move," an article in Vox stated, while AdWeek wrote that "the closed door represents to consumers that a brand is willing to put their money where their mouth is."

Harriet Vocking, chief brand officer at London-based sustainability consultancy Eco-Age tells Wunderman Thompson Intelligence that these unconventional activations are "less about sacrificing sales and more about putting purpose at the heart of the brand. It is about building a business that will last 20 years and not five." Vocking adds that one of Eco-Age's clients, jewelry house Chopard, has chosen to use Fairmined gold after working with the consultancy. Chopard now works with the Alliance for Responsible Mining in Colombia to directly support four gold mines. Vocking explains: "As it is, Fairmined gold has a premium attached, but Chopard absorbs this as a company so that it is not passed onto the consumer."

Declem closed stores on Black Friday 2019. Image courtesy of Declem

As a single company, our impact is limited, but as a community, we can drive change that powers meaningful action beyond our walls.

Eric Artz, CEO, REI

"Customers want to know that they are buying from a brand that they can trust and one that has committed to being better," she adds. "This is not about being perfect—it is about brands beginning to look at their supply chains and production processes, and starting to change the system."

In another unconventional move, Travalyst launched in September 2019. Led by Prince Harry, the initiative was founded by competing companies Booking.com, Visa, Ctrip, TripAdvisor, and Skyscanner, with the aim of being "the driving force that paves a new way to travel, helping everyone explore our world in a way that protects both people and places, and secures a positive future for destinations and local communities for generations to come."

George Wallace, chief executive of retail consultancy MHE Retail, notes that "in the last 12 months, sustainability's gone from being a bit fringe to being really very, very mainstream. Everybody has to have a position on it." But he also believes that "some of the moves don't really have much meaning or impact. Closing stores during climate demonstrations in reality doesn't contribute anything other than 'we're on your side.'"

Wallace says that it's broader actions by mass retailers that will end up having a wider impact, such as UK supermarket chain Tesco's pledge in November 2019 to remove a billion pieces of plastic from its products by the end of 2020. "That's heavyweight stuff. That's what really has a proper impact. I think customers respond well to that. It's not just a gimmick," he says. "The smaller gestures are still valuable; the exciting thing about this now is that big businesses are doing something about sustainability."

Why it's interesting:

Consumers care about sustainability and now, thanks to the wealth of information available online, they can be forensic in examining the transparency behind companies' sustainable and environmental claims. Brands going against the capitalist grain, to stand up for sustainability and against climate change, demonstrate that they're truly aligned with these causes—and their actions are moving larger businesses to make sustainability a priority, too.

40

Asia's generation Z

Asia's generation Z is coming of age in the world's fastest-growing region, amid trade battles and territorial disputes. They are shaped by the maturing of China's great market experiment, the opening up of Vietnam to the world and Japan's long economic stagnation.

Yet despite this turbulence all around them, gen Zers in Asia are working towards a future they see as largely positive, and in many cases using the technological tools now at their disposal.

Overall, they are more socially progressive. They think race matters less than it used to and seven out of 10 are willing to date outside their race, according to a survey of 4,500 gen Z respondents across nine countries in the new "Generation Z: APAC Edition" report by Wunderman Thompson Intelligence. Brands are likewise starting to emphasize inclusivity. Beauty brand Sunnies Face in the Philippines, for example, features warm colors suitable for all skin tones, without a whitening product in sight. Likewise with China's cult beauty brand Hedone, featuring men sporting their makeup range.

Gen Zers move easily between online and offline worlds, with 76% saying they are as comfortable shopping online as offline, although

Sunnies Face beauty brand

To remain relevant to this rising consumer group, brands need to understand and cater to gen Z's drive to make the world better—environmentally, socially and politically.

62% say they still like buying in a physical store. In Thailand, JD. com-backed fast-fashion platform Pomelo seamlessly merges online with offline retail. After placing an order on the brand's mobile app, consumers pick up their purchases at local checkpoints—in cafes, coworking spaces and gyms—where they can try on their clothes and instantly return items they don't want.

Like their global counterparts, gen Zers in Asia worry about climate change and environmental pollution, and are willing to stand up for political and social change. In Hong Kong, schoolchildren are balancing homework with protesting for greater freedoms, while young LGBTQ activists are showing up in force at Viet Pride, Singapore's Pink Dot SG and Taiwan Pride events.

Seven out of 10 overall think being LGBTQ isn't a big deal anymore, although young Indonesians are most likely to think it still is. In Taiwan, an ad for Kimlan soy sauce showed a household with two mothers in the kitchen, with the voiceover, "Different families have different flavors."

And yes, family still matters. Gen Zers in Indonesia, the Philippines, Thailand, Singapore and Vietnam are most likely to pick family members as personal heroes, mostly followed by teachers. Those in China, Hong Kong and Taiwan are most likely to pick celebrities as

personal heroes; and young people in China also hold scientists, entrepreneurs and politicians in higher esteem.

Why it's interesting:

Gen Zers are entering adulthood saddled with huge challenges, including climate change, political upheaval and shifting gender and sexual identities—with a modern set of values to match. That means everyone's an activist in some way. "They are really questioning the norms and don't want to be straitjacketed," Gerda Binder, UNICEF's Bangkok-based regional gender advisor for East Asia and the Pacific, tells Wunderman Thompson Intelligence in the new "Generation Z: APAC Edition" report. To remain relevant to this rising consumer group, brands need to understand and cater to gen Z's drive to make the world better—environmentally, socially and politically.

41

Food & Drink

50

41

Futureproof recipes

As pressure to reduce food waste continues to mount, climate-conscious consumers are opening up to new recipes that are not only healthy for themselves, but for the planet too.

Future Food Today is a cookbook that aims to overhaul nonsustainable foods in today's fridges and pantries, and offer wholesome, environmentally friendly options. Released in May 2019 by Ikea's research lab Space10 in collaboration with creative agency Barkas, the recipes introduce ingredients tailored for the future palate. From bug burgers containing mealworms to algae chips to microgreen popsicles, the future of food is served in a familiar form and made from unusual—but potentially planet-saving—ingredients. "The aim is to inspire people to explore new delicious flavors and sustainable and healthy ingredients," Simon Caspersen, cofounder of Space10, tells Wunderman Thompson Intelligence, "and to be a bit more curious and open-minded about food diversity."

The research lab recognizes that dramatic changes need to be made to the way we consume and produce food. "In the next 35 years, our demand for food will increase by 70%, and we simply do not have the resources to achieve this demand on today's diet," says the lab.

Innovative food brands are utilizing technology, science and food to tackle food's impact on the environment, and consumers are readily embracing these options. Take Impossible Foods' Impossible Burger, the plant-based burger that "bleeds," which is now widely available for sale at supermarkets and even on the menu at Burger King and White Castle.

Dairy Farmers of America reported that sales dropped by over $1 billion in 2018 compared to the previous year, while sales of dairy alternatives continue to grow. It appears that mainstream consumers are open to substituting unsustainable food and drinks with comparable or superior sustainable choices.

Why It's Interesting:
Consumers are pivoting towards a "climate diet," consuming less meat and dairy, and seeking environmentally friendly alternatives. Food brands will need to start producing healthy and sustainable foods that not only feed consumers but also nourish the planet.

NDERMAN
OMPSON   Future Food Today, by Space10 and Barkas. Image courtesy of Space10

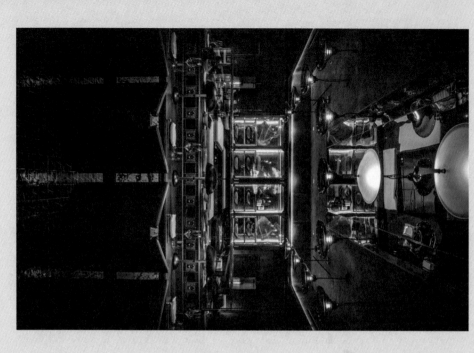

42

Anti-Instagram interiors

The newest restaurants are turning away from the monotonously predictable design vernacular fetishized by social media.

Lucky Cat restaurant in London, opened in June 2019, consciously avoids the color-saturated, eye-catching aesthetic popularized on Instagram. In contrast to the vivid palettes, bold wallpapers and punchy light fixtures found in the countless trendy eateries just begging to be photographed, Lucky Cat's deep colors and dim lighting create a shadowy atmosphere that isn't meant to translate well on screen.

Design studio AfroditiKrassa "deliberately went dark" to discourage people from sharing images on Instagram. "We tried to work with materials and colors that are subtle and classic, not too shouty," the studio's founder, Afroditi Krassa, told *Dezeen*. "How many times do you visit a place because it looks great in a picture but disappoints in real life?"

Lucky Cat's distinctive environment prioritizes the tactile over the visual, creating depth through texture rather than relying on attention-grabbing graphics. "There is relatively little contrast between colors, pattern and finish, yet a lot of richness in texture

DRINK

RMAN
SON

Lucky Cat. Photo by AfroditiKrassa

Going forward, consumers will respond to spaces that encourage them to live in the moment, rather than through the lens of their phone.

and tactility—Lucky Cat is a layered design that reveals more every time you visit," Krassa explained.

The dark and sensual design at Marcus, the restaurant and bar at Montreal's new Four Seasons hotel that opened in May 2019, similarly encourages in-situ enjoyment. The design is "deeply rooted in intimate interactions, singular moments, and glamor," Atelier Zébulon Perron, the design studio behind the space, told Dezeen.

In spring 2019, architect Bernard Khoury redesigned Beirut's B018, a nightclub in an underground bunker that has become an institution since it opened in 1998. Khoury has doused the interior in a monochromatic deep gray, with macabre design elements adding to the somber aesthetic.

Why it's interesting:

These designs signal the end of a flashy "look at me" era that canonized experiences and spaces crafted expressly for sharing on social media. Going forward, consumers will respond to spaces that encourage them to live in the moment, rather than experiencing the world through the lens of their phone.

43

Solving the surplus

Companies are designing sophisticated solutions to tackle food packaging waste.

Evolving efforts are trying to resolve the waste issue around food packaging and make it easier for consumers to make waste-free choices. New contenders are offering waste-free alternatives to everyday products and name brand favorites, so consumers don't have to change their daily habits.

In September 2019, Swedish food-waste app Karma expanded its partnership with household goods brand Electrolux, piloting the Karma smart refrigerator in Stockholm's central underground station. Consumers can purchase discounted food on the Karma app and collect their items from the fridge, making it easier to pick up food on the journey home. The pilot follows the 2018 launch of the smart fridge in Stockholm's ICA Kvantum Liljeholmen supermarket, where shoppers can purchase surplus food items at a reduced price in store. Charlie Humphries, Karma's UK marketing manager, tells Wunderman Thompson Intelligence that it's changing the "small patterns in our behavior that can make the difference."

Loop, which launched in the United States in May 2019, allows consumers to purchase everyday grocery, personal care and household products in durable, refillable packages. Shoppers pay a

NDERMAN
DMPSON

Karma food-waste app

You love a saving, don't choux?

Gander

refundable one-time deposit to join the scheme, and Loop delivers the products to their door in a durable Loop Tote box. As products run out, users put the packages back in the Loop Tote. They then schedule a pickup and the packages go back to Loop to be cleaned and reused. An auto-refill option automatically adds favorite products to the next shopping list.

In Northern Ireland, the new Gander app recently partnered with Henderson Group, the parent company of a number of popular supermarkets, to help minimize waste in food stores. The app notifies local shoppers as soon as a food item's price is reduced, giving them a heads-up to get to the store. The SpareEat app combats food waste in Israel by connecting users to restaurants, supermarkets and cafes so they can purchase surplus food. Both apps, which were launched in fall 2019, benefit consumer and retailer alike.

Why it's interesting:

By creating apps and platforms which utilize existing food and delivery systems, businesses are helping consumers to easily and conveniently adopt greener practices. Brands have a huge opportunity here to provide innovations, drive consumer momentum and support the move towards sustainable living.

Complex cocktails

More is more at these bars slinging drinks with 20-plus ingredients.

he A-Z Cocktail, conceptualized by Bompas & Parr and available at W Hotel in Times Square during January 2019, boasts one gredient for every letter of the alphabet.

t would be all too easy to randomly combine a minibar's worth of gredients and make something undrinkable. The challenge here as to create something beyond novelty for its own sake and end p with a balanced drink," says Harry Parr, cofounder of Bompas & arr and the cocktail's creator.

he ingredient list includes eight types of rum, three types of ognac, one of mezcal, one of gin, six liqueurs and two types of itters, as well as vermouth and other aperitif wines from around e globe.

he objective? An unusual drinking experience—one that onsumers would be hard-pressed to create at home. "The idea vith mixing so many rums is to get a more intriguing flavor profile nan what you might be able to achieve with a simple serve," says arr.

The beverage program at upscale Mexican eatery Xixa in Brooklyn offers deconstructed takes on classic cocktails. These complex creations feature multi-ingredient ice cubes which are then dropped into the drinker's liquor of choice. The Old Fashioned Cube, for example, freezes together 23 ingredients to recreate the spicy, citrusy, smoky essence of the cocktail. The ice cube is added to a couple of ounces of alcohol, and the flavor profile evolves with each sip as the cube melts, for a progressive and unique drinking experience.

Why it's interesting:

With millennials and generation Z drinking less, it takes more for alcohol to grab their attention. Bars and restaurants are stepping up their game in response, leaning into sensational, compelling cocktails that pique drinkers' interest and offer a unique experience that can't be recreated at home.

Seesaw Coffee designed by Nota Architects. Photo by Shiyun Qian.

WUNDERMAN THOMPSON

FOOD & DRINK

45

Transportational interiors

Seeking an edge that goes beyond their menus, cafés and restaurants are conjuring up elaborate interiors that transport consumers to exotic locales.

Now getting a cup of coffee can involve a walk through a Zen-like garden and ordering a cocktail can propel you to outer space.

At a Beijing shopping mall branch of Shanghai chain Seesaw Coffee, Nota Architects has created a stone path through lush foliage and mossy boulders, with cherry blossoms overhead and occasional puffs of white fog to add to the atmosphere. Wooden decks and benches ring the space, with the coffee bar theatrically positioned on a softly lit stage.

At Shanghai tea house Icha Chateau, design studio Spacemen hung 35,000 meters of shimmering, layered gold chains from the ceiling, evoking traditional Chinese tea terraces. The opulent interior underlines the rising design stakes in a city that also houses the largest Starbucks in the world, where coffee is described as theater.

Tokyo also has its share of transportational interiors. Nikunotoriko serves Japanese-style barbecue, competing with countless other restaurants in the city. The difference here is that architect Ryoji Iedokoro has created a dining room in a cave, employing low

THE FUTURE 100

...D & DRINK

...ighting, walls of jagged rock and a translucent floor that resembles ...ater underfoot.

...hose wanting to be transported even further can head to Tokyo's ...Bar Planetaria, owned by Konica Minolta, which constructs and ...perates planetarium theaters. The planetarium hosts regular drink ...nd food evenings, where for a few hours, Tokyo denizens can kick ...ack on a circular sofa and drink among the stars. From August to ...November 2019, the domed theater offered views of the Hawaiian ...ight sky.

...A planetarium-like domed ceiling also features in upscale ...Copenhagen restaurant Alchemist. The domed area is one of ...several sections that diners experience on a visit that could last up ...o five hours. There might be images of jellyfish swimming among ...plastic bags overhead, to raise awareness of sea pollution, or a dark ...sky streaked with the northern lights. Rasmus Munk, the chef and ...ounder of Alchemist, told *Food & Wine* magazine the restaurant is ...designed to make you feel "as though you've left the outside world ...and arrived somewhere new." Hence it may not, as its website ...warns, be ideal for business discussions or nervous first dates.

Why It's Interesting:

...transportational interiors are emerging at a time when competition ...s heating up among cafés and restaurants. This is particularly true ...when it comes to capturing generation Z, which prizes experience ...and yearns for a story behind every cup of tea or coffee. These ...cafés and restaurants provide brief moments of escape from busy ...cities, without having to board a train, a plane—or a rocket ship.

46

Biodiverse dining

Chefs are cooking up biodiverse menus that cater to climate-conscious diners.

The United States has lost 90% of native fruit and vegetable varieties since the 1900s. Today, just 12 plant sources and five animal sources make up 75% of the food we consume, according to the Food and Agriculture Organization of the United Nations, despite the fact that t here are approximately 300,000 edible plant species globally. And just three crops—wheat, corn and rice —make up almost 60% of plant-based calories in most modern diets.

This reliance on a handful of species poses a serious threat to ecosystems and food security. Biodiversity is crucial for ensuring everything from human health to ecological stability to wildlife protection, as the World Wide Fund for Nature (WWF) attests. The wildlife conservation organization's March 2019 "Future 50 Foods" campaign, in collaboration with Knorr, hopes to encourage people to diversify their diets in an effort to protect endangered species.

The "Future 50 Foods" report includes a list of 50 plant-based ingredients consumers and chefs can incorporate into meals. "Diversified diets not only benefit human health but benefit the environment through diversified production systems that encourage wildlife and more sustainable use of resources," explains Peter

Gregory, research advisor at Crops For the Future, which contributed to the WWF campaign.

At Teranga, a West African eatery that opened in New York City in February 2019, chef and owner Pierre Thiam emphasizes ingredients that expand today's limited diet. "By supporting underutilized crops in my menus, I contribute to saving our planet's biodiversity," Thiam told *Forbes.com*. "In the current context, designing a menu should be a conscious and responsible act."

Teranga's menu features ingredients like baobab, moringa and fonio, overlooked in the West, which are not only central to West African cuisine but also support biodiversity. Take the ancient grain fonio. "It's a grain that's great for the planet," said Thiam. "It's drought resistant; it grows in two months; it scores low on the glycemic index, so it's great for your health too."

Lou, which opened in Nashville in September 2019, substitutes more conventional processed sugars and flour with ingredients such as coconut sugar and buckwheat to achieve a more diverse diet.

"By actively championing biodiversity inside and outside the kitchen, chefs can play a key role in creating interest in and a market for more diverse ingredients, helping to support farmers' livelihoods, improve diets and strengthen our food systems," Marie Haga, executive director of the Global Crop Diversity Trust, which supports crop diversity to protect global food security, told *Forbes.com*.

Why it's interesting:

As examples such as the recent surge in veganism and the sweeping renouncement of plastic straws illustrate, diners are shifting their eating habits to support environmental efforts. Diversified diets offer another avenue for environmental activism—and a tastier meal.

> By supporting underutilized crops in my menus, I contribute to saving our planet's biodiversity. In the current context, designing a menu should be a conscious and responsible act.
>
> **Pierre Thiam, chef and owner, Teranga**

47

Co-cooking kitchens

Cooking is getting communal.

Dense urbanization is creating a need for smarter use of spaces, while budding culinary entrepreneurs are looking for more cost-effective options when it comes to getting started in the business. Taking cues from the explosion of coworking offices, co-cooking spaces are opening up around the world to cater to the growing desire for a place in which to not only innovate and network but also cook and socialize.

In July 2019, Samia Bingham, founder and CEO of culinary services startup Flavors Culinary Group, won the Small Biz Challenge in Los Angeles, hosted by the UPS Store and *Inc* magazine. The Maryland-based winner is using her prize money to launch Flavors, The Culinary Complex, a kitchen incubator where chefs and culinary specialists can innovate and network with other members of the culinary community. The hub is set to open in summer 2020.

WeWork launched WeWork Food Labs in spring 2019 in Manhattan, initially as a membership-based scheme. The WeWork Food Labs New York flagship and its first accelerator program both launched in October.

Menachem Katz, head of operations at WeWork Food Labs, tells Wunderman Thompson Intelligence, "WeWork Food Labs aims to empower innovators across the food and agricultural space, giving them the tools and resources they need to create sustainable solutions that address challenges both within our own community and on a global scale." Accepted startups receive investment from WeWork, and access to industry experts, investors and VCs, as well as workshops and events, not to mention space in the R&D kitchen.

Mission Kitchen will open its first two London co-cooking facilities in 2020. These also offer mentorship opportunities, events and professional kitchens for their members.

Co-cooking isn't just for professionals, however. Communal kitchens are opening up in countries like Japan where apartment space is limited. Kitchen Studio Suiba in Tokyo was designed as a rental space where users can cook for each other, as well as a place where food and drinks businesses can interact with their customers.

Why it's interesting:

With space at a premium and costs for kitchen equipment prohibitive for many, co-cooking kitchens are a practical and sociable solution for home chefs and culinary specialists alike.

Sober bars

A wave of restaurants and bars are dedicating themselves to alcohol-free service.

According to the World Health Organization, between 2000 and 2016 the number of drinkers in the world decreased by 5%. Accompanying this shift, consumers opting for teetotal lifestyles—or simply cutting down on booze—are looking beyond simple juices and soft drinks as alcohol alternatives, and are in search of new concoctions to satisfy elevated palates. As a result, restaurants and bars are creating teetotal environments, and curating non-alcoholic drinks menus.

Getaway opened in April 2019, providing a swanky social hang-out for Brooklyn teetotalers. The menu boasts a list of sophisticated beverages, each containing a complex blend of flavors, including quirky ingredients such as pink peppercorn, juniper and fennel—without a single drop of alcohol on site.

In New York, Listen Bar has been creating teetotal buzz since it opened in October 2018. Proving it is possible to have a good night without alcohol, it hosts themed party nights once a month where visitors can enjoy an array of non-alcoholic cocktails and craft beers while taking part in activities such as karaoke, astrology readings, a sex-toy version of truth or dare and even live tattooing.

NDERMAN
OMPSON   Listen Bar in New York City. Photo by Tonje Thilesen

The Virgin Mary opened in Dublin in May 2019, claiming to be the first permanent alcohol-free bar in Ireland that follows standard pub opening times and contains all the traditional vibes of a regular pub. It offers carefully hand-crafted cocktails with additional twists, and even a brew that mimics the texture and appearance of Guinness, made with chilled nitro coffee served from a stout tap.

Choosing to focus on the health-conscious client, London's Redemption bar serves nourishing booze-free alternatives, drawing on ingredients like activated charcoal, CBD cannabidiol extract in its lager, and kombucha on tap, all claiming a ream of health benefits.

For bars that want to delve into the teetotal space, non-alcoholic contenders like Seedlip are making it easier. Seedlip's beverages, made using a variety of herbs and spices, provide an alternative to spirits in more than 300 Michelin-starred restaurants and are served in more than 25 countries. Aecorn's non-alcoholic aperitifs, made from Pinot Noir, Meunier and Chardonnay grapes, are designed to be served as a spritz or mixed in a cocktail.

Why it's interesting:

As consumers shift towards healthier lifestyles, bars and drinks brands are catering to this shift without making clients feel that they are missing out on social experiences.

WUNDERMAN THOMPSON   Top left: Redemption bar, London. Photo by Jessica Allegretti
Top right and bottom: The Virgin Mary bar, Dublin

NDERMAN
OMPSON   Getaway bar, Brooklyn

49

Regenerative farming revolution

Food brands are tackling climate change through regenerative farming.

Intensive farming has so depleted the world's soils that the United Nations has warned we could have just 60 harvests left. In response, some food brands are asking producers to transition to regenerative agriculture. This term covers a raft of techniques that actively restore soil quality, with the added benefit of sequestering carbon and reducing greenhouse gases, thus delivering a win–win– food that's better for the planet and for people too.

In an interview with *Pebble* magazine, Guy Singh-Watson, founder of the UK's Riverford Organic Farmers, explained that "food grown in healthy soil is healthier. It's better balanced nutritionally, with fewer toxins. If you're growing your own food that's the reason you want to get to grips with the soil near you. I've met farmers who won't eat the produce that's grown on their own farms."

Danone is now leading a coalition of 19 major companies, including Nestlé, Unilever and Kellogg Company, to push for regenerative agriculture, aiming to reinvent our food system and restore diversity. According to the Food and Agriculture Organization of the United

> **Food grown in healthy soil is healthier. It's better balanced nutritionally, with fewer toxins.**
>
> **Guy Singh-Watson, founder, Riverford Organic Farmers**

Nations, just nine plants account for two-thirds of the world's crop production, a key factor in the depletion of soil quality.

General Mills has also announced a major commitment to regenerative agriculture, promising to adopt the techniques on a million acres of farmland in the United States by 2030. The company has also donated $650,000 to Kiss the Ground, a non-profit organization that trains farmers to use soil health practices to make land more resilient. General Mills brand Annie's Homegrown is also helping to raise awareness of soil health via its Soil Matters campaign, which has featured on limited-edition packs of products made with ingredients grown using regenerative practices.

The opportunity to combat climate change has led outdoor brand Patagonia to partner with Hopworks Urban Brewery in Oregon and launch its own Long Root beer brand. The beer is brewed with a trademarked novel grain called Kernza that removes more carbon from the atmosphere than other grains, requires less water and pesticides, and helps prevent soil erosion, thanks to those eponymous long roots.

Why it's interesting:
In the future, food brands that adopt regenerative agriculture practices can be a powerful force in the fight against climate change, combating greenhouse gases and restoring soil quality.

Hot new ingredients

Mounting climate concerns are inspiring a new look at ingredients that have previously flown under the radar.

Solein powder

A Finnish company called Solar Foods is developing a protein powder from nothing more than air, water and electricity. Solein powder, estimated to hit the market in 2021, is about 65% protein, on par with soy and algae. It is, the company website declares, "an entirely new kind of food that is both natural, and free from the burdens of agriculture and aquaculture."

With viable farmland diminishing and ethical questions arising around eating animals, there's been a flood of research globally into future sources of protein, from culturing meat in labs to frying up crickets and blending mealworms. Each has its downside. Lab-grown meat is hugely expensive and the thought of eating bugs and insects makes many people queasy.

Solein powder doesn't have any of those issues. It uses a fermentation process similar to that used for making wine or beer, however, instead of putting yeast into a sugary liquid, Solar's microbes are nourished by small bubbles of hydrogen and carbon dioxide, producing a fine powder that looks and tastes like wheat flour and can be used as an ingredient for food such as yoghurt, shakes or pasta.

Solar Foods' technology is sparking interest from those with an interest in making food in places where arable land and sunlight is scarce—in some cases, very scarce. Solar is working with the European Space Agency to develop the technology for Mars missions, CEO Pasi Vainikka told BNN Bloomberg.

Watermelon seeds

Watermelon seeds, a traditional snack for guests at Chinese New Year and other festivals around Asia, are getting a modern makeover in the global health food market.

The world watermelon seed market is expected to grow to $751 million in 2025, according to Grand View Research, Inc. The bulk of the market is composed of raw seeds, a nutritious vegan alternative to other fats.

Watermelon seeds are also showing up in some novel applications. Atomo, a Seattle-based startup is reverse-engineering coffee, aiming for a more sustainable version of the brew without using actual coffee beans.

Climate change is expected to reduce the land suitable for coffee production by as much as half by 2050, according to the Climate Institute. By 2080, wild coffee—a key genetic resource for coffee farmers—could be extinct, say the institute's researchers. Atomo's brew uses a combination of watermelon seeds, sunflower seed husks, acacia gum and yerba mate caffeine. The goal, cofounder Jarret Stopforth told CNBC, is to re-create the "core components of coffee—the body, the mouth feel, the aroma and flavor." The company hopes to ship its first batch of cold brew to its Kickstarter backers in 2020 and to start retailing by mid-year.

Sustainability and climate concerns are driving innovation in the food and drink category—and fostering a newfound appreciation for previously overloooked ingredients.

Watermelon seeds also appear in not one but two of Whole Foods' top 10 trends for 2020—as a new plant-based alternative to soy in supplements and as a spread in the form of watermelon seed butter.

Butterfly pea flower

Chefs and mixologists on multiple continents are experimenting with the vibrant indigo and color-changing properties of the butterfly pea flower. The flower—long used in Southeast Asian cakes and rice dishes—is now showing up around the globe, its popularity fueled as much by its health benefits as by its distinctive color.

Thirsty mag ran a piece in May 2019 featuring eight different blue pea flower cocktails served across the United States, from the Little Violeta at Geist in Nashville (other ingredients include gin, pineapple and aloe) to the Purple Rain at Madison on Park, San Diego (peach liqueur, lemon, egg white and a few drops of CBD oil). *Food & Drink* magazine featured three butterfly pea flower drinks to make for summer 2019, using citric acid to turn the hue from blue to purple.

Butterfly pea flower is used to tinge lobster linguine at the Woodside Inn in Colaba, Mumbai. In Australia, the Hunter Distillery makes a butterfly pea liqueur.

Why it's interesting:

Sustainability and climate concerns are driving innovation in the food and drink category—and fostering a newfound appreciation for previously overlooked ingredients.

51

Beauty

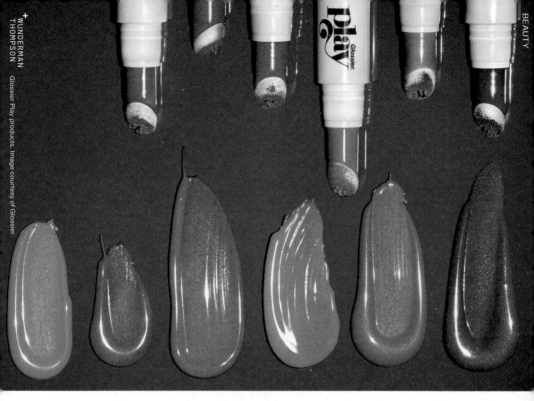

51

Euphoric makeovers

Make way for maximalist beauty.

Shimmering streams of glitter tears, unabashed multicolored eyeshadows and a glistening constellation of rhinestones are just a few of the eye-catching looks that define HBO's coming-of-age hit series *Euphoria*. The show took to the screens in June 2019 and has sparked a makeup frenzy on social media.

Vogue published an article in November 2019 titled "Why the fashion world can't get enough of *Euphoria* makeup" and Instagram now offers *Euphoria* filters created by Igor Saringer. Why the hype? Because the dazzling, attention-grabbing looks in the show fully capture the characters' self-expression—an aesthetic espoused by generation Z.

"Gen Z is completely redefining what makeup can and should be used to do, by embracing a total freedom in expression and defying beauty and makeup norms," the show's makeup artist Doniella Davy told the *Hollywood Reporter*, "I love seeing how these young artists and humans are flipping the whole idea of beauty and makeup on its ass."

Glossier launched the Glossier Play collection of "dialed-up beauty extras" in March 2019. This playground of possibilities promotes

BEAUTY

Gen Z is completely redefining what makeup can and should be used to do, by embracing a total freedom in expression and defying beauty and makeup norms.

Doniella Davy, makeup artist

bold and dramatic looks, with products such as Vinylic Lip and Glitter Gelée offering ultra-shiny lacquered lips and jeweled-effect eyes—essentials to building a *Euphoria*-inspired look.

The expressive and maximalist makeovers that once felt exclusive to high fashion are now being democratized thanks to *Euphoria*. Davy said the show's creator Sam Levinson encouraged her to "introduce a new makeup language," and with that she has opened new possibilities of makeup experimentation for gen Z and beyond.

Why it's interesting:

Euphoria has tapped into gen Zers' desire for makeup with meaning and the notion that the beauty brush can paint a story. Brands should rethink their makeup tools as a channel for capturing a generation of self-expressive youth wanting to break stereotypes, convey how they feel and be fueled by creative inspiration to experiment—and, more importantly, have fun.

ANDERMAN
OMPSON   Euphoria. Images courtesy of HBO

52

Molecular spas

Luxury skincare brands are diving into DNA analysis for the ultimate in bespoke beauty.

EpigenCare, a winner of Johnson & Johnson Innovation's contest for biotech beauty companies in 2018, piloted Skintelli in February 2019 with plans for a full rollout in 2020. Skintelli leverages epigenetics to analyze skin. The personalized, direct-to-consumer service uses next-generation DNA sequencing to offer consumers deep insight into their skin's genetic condition and predisposition.

British luxury retailer Harrods incorporates DNA analysis into its beauty services at the Wellness Clinic, an integrative beauty spa opened in 2018. For the Gen Identity service, guests give a saliva sample and complete a lifestyle assessment and these are used for skin diagnosis and the preparation of a treatment plan. "We have developed a unique, personalized cosmetic treatment for the skin based on the analysis of the DNA of each person," explains the clinic's José Maria Garcia Antón. The results are used to craft a tailored skincare regimen and to create a bespoke facial cream that targets the individual's specific needs and genetics.

Cult beauty brand Biologique Recherche is leveraging DNA for its latest luxury offering. The My Beauty DNA kit offers a full analysis of

+WUNDERMAN THOMPSON

Harrods Wellness Clinic. Photo by Jack Hobhouse

UTY

genetic data by analyzing cheek swabs to assess an individual's genetic predisposition to skin concerns such as collagen breakdown, glycation (an excess of sugars that causes deep wrinkling), inflammation, sensitivity, free radical damage and pigmentation.

"Understanding your genetic predispositions helps both the patient and the dermatologist to better understand an individual skin's inherited needs and can explain up to 60% of factors affecting your

skin's condition," says Raphaëlle Faure, Biologique Recherche brand manager.

Why it's interesting:
Services such as 23andMe have democratized DNA testing, and consumers are looking for new ways to integrate genetic analysis into their daily routines, revolutionizing everything from diets to beauty habits.

NDERMAN
OMPSON   Biologique Recherche

33

Transhuman beauty

Designers are looking beyond traditional beauty standards, experimenting with transhumanist looks that will evolve beauty as we know it.

"A revolution is unfolding in operating rooms, labs, artist and designer studios across the world," wrote trend forecaster and designer Geraldine Wharry in her article "The transhuman future is here" for *Dazed Beauty*. Wharry depicted a landscape where science, technology and design come together to exalt a transhuman aesthetic. "New beauty standards will emerge out of this transhumanist scenario in which mutant creations would colonize our current traditional sense of reality," she predicts.

As science steadily merges human and machine, the beauty and fashion industry borrows this concept to create forms and features that transcend traditional beauty standards. In fall 2019, Balenciaga sent models down the runway with dysmorphic features, sporting exaggerated, sculpted cheek bones and overly plumped lips for its spring/summer 2020 collection at Paris Fashion Week. The luxury fashion brand explained that the looks aim to "play on beauty standards of today, the past and the future."

Rick Owens replaced traditional makeup aesthetics with prosthetic

A revolution is unfolding in operating rooms, labs, artist and designer studios across the world. The transhuman future is here.

Geraldine Wharry, trend forecaster and designer

horns, bulging black eyes and other face-altering features in the show for his fall/winter 2019 collection. In October 2018, *Vogue* featured the self-described "transhuman" Instagram-famed duo Fecal Matter, and also showcased the pair's extreme three-hour beauty routine on *Vogue.com* in March 2019. The artists have created a pair of $10,000 boots that blend into human skin, replacing conventional stilettos with skin heels, and plan to release a cheaper and more accessible version.

Why it's interesting:

Transhuman beauty marks a further step toward the uprooting of conventional beauty standards, an evolution of the 2018 Grotesque Beauty anti-beauty movement. Anticipating a future where natural ecosystems and human existence may be fundamentally altered, consumers and designers are beginning to re-evaluate the definition of beauty.

54

Skintellectuals

Skincare devotees are turning to experts in scientific fields to deliver technical, precise products.

Launched in October 2019, Noble Panacea is a luxury skincare line developed by Sir Fraser Stoddart, the 2016 Nobel laureate in chemistry. The trademarked Organic Molecular Vessels derived from his research are 10,000 times smaller than skin cells, and offer a new product delivery system which enables improved product penetration and absorption. "The precise selection and encapsulation of active ingredients aims to deliver unprecedented results," says the scientist.

Atolla launched in August 2019 with a mission to make consumers experts on their own skin. Founded by graduates of the Massachusetts Institute of Technology (MIT), Atolla leverages machine learning and data analysis for precise and hyper-personalized product formulations that take into account everything from medications and diet to local air quality and pollution, and also the oil, moisture and pH levels of each individual's skin. Each month users take a skin test and receive an updated serum. The formulas are accompanied by a precise breakdown of ingredients and a detailed explanation of what each component does. So, just as Atolla's algorithm learns from the data, subscribers' knowledge of their skin health improves with each use.Maelove is another skincare line founded by MIT graduates—a roster of cancer and brain researchers, chemical engineers and medical doctors. "We start by looking at proven clinical research in peer-reviewed journals and collaborate with brilliant chemists, dermatologists, plastic surgeons and medical researchers to create formula blueprints," the brand explains.

Why it's interesting:

Scientific skincare is raising the bar for a growing class of educated consumers. Offering scientific levels of expertise and insight into skin, these new brands are answering demand for education and deep insight into skin health.

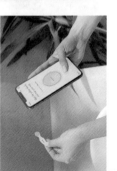

ENDERMAN Above: Atolla skincare
OMPSON Right: Noble Panacea skincare

55

Menopause beauty

The beauty industry is catching on to a powerful group of consumers: women experiencing menopause.

"After a few million years, we figured it was time," says Kindra, a new brand backed by Procter & Gamble. It offers a beauty and wellbeing range for women experiencing menopause and is just one of a wave of brands that is waking up to a major opportunity.

According to the North American Menopause Society, more than a billion women around the world will be experiencing menopause in 2025. While menopause is nothing new, the way women approach this phase of their life is changing. As our report "Elastic generation: the female edit" revealed, a new generation is ripping up the rules and reinventing life past 50.

Fay Reid (@9to5menopause), a London-based blogger aiming to take the stigma out of menopause, wants brands to acknowledge this shift. "What I want brands to realize," she tells Wunderman Thompson Intelligence, "is that women like me in their 40s and 50s still like makeup and fashion, just like they did in their 30s. I still want to look and feel good."

Menopause brings a host of changes for women. Alongside hot flashes, they can experience dry, dull or dehydrated skin, reduced

skin elasticity and even breakouts. At a time when women are turning away from anti-aging messaging (68% of UK women aged 53-72 use beauty products to look and feel their best, rather than look younger, according to Wunderman Thompson Intelligence research), there is potential for brands that can offer targeted, effective solutions.

In addition to Kindra, several other meno-friendly brands were launched in 2019. Pause Well-aging is a US startup founded by Rochelle Weitzner, a beauty industry veteran who reached menopause and realized there was a dearth of suitable skincare products. Better Not Younger, a US brand tackling menopause-

related hair issues such as thinning and brittleness, was founded by women in the industry who also spotted a gap. Alongside the startups, big players such as Vichy are dipping their toes in the water.

Why it's interesting:

Currently these brands are targeting an affluent audience. There's a broader opportunity to cater widely to women, offering more affordable price points as well as more inclusive solutions that meet the needs of all ethnicities. "The brand that delivers something that's inclusive will clean up, I promise you," says Reid.

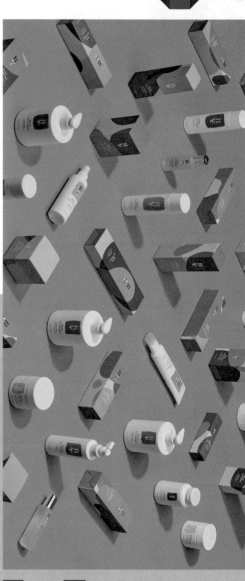

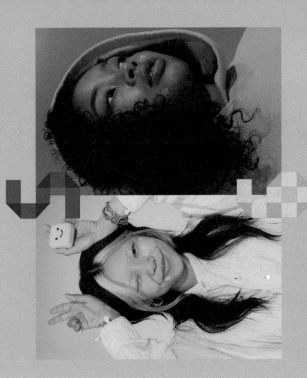

IRL filters

The digital overlay has given beauty consumers a new lens to push experimentation with new looks.

From inspirational to real life, these beauty filters are reimaging contemporary trends that can live both online and offline.

New skincare brand Starface launched a collection of star-shaped pimple patches called Hydro-Stars in September 2019, bringing the emoji aesthetic into the real world. The playful acne stickers are akin to star emojis and make for a great Instagram-worthy portrait; the remedy for a zit has never looked so fun. "It's a subtle accessory—a little accent piece that you see when you're face to face with somebody—and it's super-photogenic and cute," cofounder Julie Schott told *Vogue*.

A recent movement on TikTok is driving what *Dazed Beauty* described as "a roulette of body mods." From temporary facial stickers to permanent piercings, the trending #piercingchallenge hashtag on TikTok sees users cycle through Snapchat's series of digital facial piercings with their eyes closed. The challenge is to then get a real-life version of whatever piercing they randomly land on. As of mid January 2020, the hashtag had over 98 million views,

with some users taking up the challenge and others donning fake piercings instead.

Why it's interesting:
Driven by the playfulness with online filters of generation Zers and younger millennials, and their drive to push beauty boundaries, digital filters are inflecting a direct and very real influence on physical beauty looks.

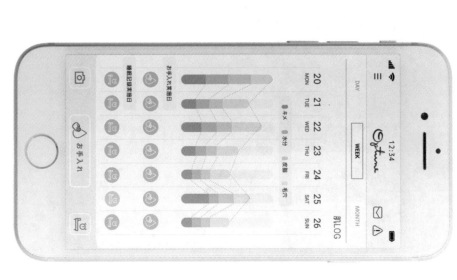

57

Skincare 2.0

Growing demand for hyper-personalization is driving innovation in product dosage and application.

In July 2019, Japanese luxury beauty brand Shiseido unveiled Optune, an IoT personalized skincare system. The system combines a dedicated app, where users can track skin conditions, sleep patterns, hormone levels and environmental factors, with a proprietary countertop dispenser which includes five serum cartridges. Informed by daily—or even hourly—skin analysis via the app, a combination of serums is formulated to address the user's needs that day and doled directly into their hand for application.

Neutrogena is also rethinking how skincare products are formulated and applied for hyper-personalized results. Unveiled at the CES 2019 tech show, Neutrogena MaskiD is a 3D-printed face mask crafted specifically for each individual's unique face shape and skin needs. The hyper-personalized, on-demand production means that the mask not only delivers active ingredients specific to the user's needs, but also helps ensure that those ingredients are properly aligned on the user's face.

"Using micro 3D-printing, we can actually get your exact eye alignment, your nose, your mouth, how high your forehead is," Michael Southall, research director and global lead of beauty tech

way to apply skincare products. Revealed at CES 2019, the Opté Precision Skincare System incorporates a wand that digitally scans the user's skin, analyzes their complexion using LED lights and an integrated digital camera to detect spots in real time, and delivers targeted serum to treat and correct the skin.

Why It's Interesting:

Technology is paving the way for a reconsidered skincare regime, ushering in a new frontier of product creation and application.

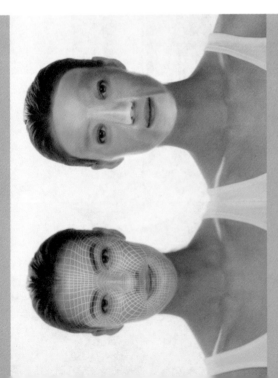

at Neutrogena, explained to *Allure*.

"The key with 3D printing is that we can put the active ingredient you want just where you need it, anywhere on the mask, as opposed to one product that you're trying to use all over the face."

Opté is also leveraging 3D printing to reimagine how consumers apply skincare. One of the first brands to emerge from P&G Ventures, Procter & Gamble's innovation arm, Opté combines optics, proprietary algorithms and printing technology for a new

NDERMAN   Above: Neutrogena's MaskID
OMPSON   Right: Opté Precision Skincare System by Procter & Gamble

UTY

Lash out

While brows might have been the major canvas for beauty experimentation in 2019, it looks as if the lash is set to take over for 2020.

Master makeup artist Pat McGrath, whose creations are harbingers of beauty trends, executed a number of inventive lash looks at the spring 2020 shows. The 61 different makeup looks that McGrath created for the Marc Jacobs show—nodding to what she calls "an idealized interpretation of real life"—included spidery false lashes for an exaggerated, artsy take on 1960s chic. For Valentino, McGrath crafted lashes from gold in a look she dubbed Opulent Obsession. But the concept can also take an underground turn. At Gucci, makeup artist Thomas de Kluyver, who's known for a leftfield beauty aesthetic, positioned false lashes on the brows and under the eyes, while Isamaya Ffrench, another artist renowned for experimentation, worked up punkish, clumped-together lashes for Olivier Theyskens that she refers to as "spider legs."

This focus on lashes on the runway comes against a background of growth for the false eyelashes market. According to an October 2019 report by Grand View Research, the global false eyelashes market is set to reach $1.6 billion by 2025, representing a CAGR of 5.4%. The report added that the false lash market in the United

+
WUNDERMAN
THOMPSON

Pat McGrath for Marc Jacobs

BEAUTY

...States was valued at over $400 million in 2018, and that growth of the false lash market in the Asia Pacific region is set to achieve a CAGR of 6.6% by 2025.

Why it's interesting:

Lashes offer a way of highlighting the eye that contrasts with the recent focus on brows. McGrath told *Fashionista* in a 2019 interview that "brows have taken a back seat a little bit—it's all about the lashes." And this focus on lashes could translate into more experimentation in the mascara category, which has been somewhat subdued in recent years, with the *Business of Fashion* wondering in 2019 whether mascara was "losing its relevance." Could a renaissance be on the way?

DERMAN
MPSON   Pat McGrath for Valentino

59

Microbiome beauty

Beauty gets biological: a swathe of beauty brands are bridging biology and skincare, turning their attention to the skin's microbiome, the bacterial barrier that protects the skin.

Kinship, launched in November 2019, is the latest beauty brand to address the skin's microbiome. Kinship's products are formulated with Kinbiome, a trademarked plant-based prebiotic that supports the skin's natural barrier, developed using proprietary microbiome technology.

In the same month, SL&Co—launched by Susanne Langmuir, the founder of Bite Beauty—hit the market with a product formulated to balance the skin's microbiome. Released in November 2019, The Powder of Youth No 1 is the first product in the brand's lineup and the powder cleanser, exfoliator and mask features Lactobacillus ferment to protect good bacteria on the skin.

Nimble indie brands are not alone in driving this shift; legacy beauty companies are also throwing their weight behind microbiome research and products.

Estée Lauder has partnered with leading microbiome research company Nizo, and released findings in November 2019 that correlated skin aging with microbial composition of the skin. "The Estée Lauder Companies has been working with a probiotic culture of Lactobacillus plantarum and has identified several positive benefits in topical application of Lactobacillus extract," says Steve Schnittger, vice president of global microbiology and fermentation research and development at Estée Lauder.

In March 2019, L'Oréal announced a new partnership with microbial genetics company Ubiome to advance microbiome research and better understand the interplay between bacterial diversity and skin health," Guive Balooch, global vice president of the L'Oréal Technology Incubator, tells Wunderman Thompson Intelligence. L'Oréal previously partnered with Epicore Biosystems, a startup specializing in microfluidic platforms and wearable sensors. At the CES 2019 tech show, L'Oréal debuted My Skin Track pH by La Roche-Posay, a wearable sensor that measures skin pH levels using microfluid technology developed in collaboration with Epicore Biosystems. Balooch notes that although "the scientific and medical communities have long known the link between skin pH levels and common skin concerns," the My Skin Track pH concept takes this a step further to "empower consumers with meaningful information about their skin, so that they can find the products that are right for their individual needs."

Why it's interesting:

"Biology could bring skincare to a new level," says Balooch. And as consumers demonstrate a growing appetite for a biological approach to beauty, established legacy brands and emerging startups alike are turning their attention to microbiome beauty.

60

Blue beauty

Cosmetics brands are turning to the oceans as their latest source of natural ingredients.

Naturally derived, sustainable skincare is increasingly popular. According to research by Hamacher Resource Group released in March 2019, 30% of skincare consumers—a percentage that skewed female and younger—had increased their natural purchases in the last year, *Global Cosmetic Industry* magazine reported. The seas are now proving a rich source of natural elements.

With part of its mission to conserve the oceans, One Ocean Beauty creates products formulated with marine-based ingredients. Founder Marcella Cacci told *Well & Good* that the process involves taking "a single cell or micro-organism out of nature, and then we regrow it in the lab through biotechnology, so it's completely sustainable production." Among the brand's products are Marine Collagen capsules, made from hydrolyzed marine collagen sourced from deep-water fish, and Replenishing Deep Sea Moisturizer, with algae extract from the Sea of Japan that will "soothe inflammation and brighten the complexion," the brand says.

Launched in August 2019, British skincare brand Freya & Bailey uses seaweed in its anti-pollution cosmetics products as an

WUNDERMAN THOMPSON

Freya & Bailey skincare

> **Mindfully sourced marine-based ingredients are powerful, natural and sustainable.**

Why it's interesting:

Infusing skincare products with mindfully sourced marine-based ingredients unites consumers' desire for natural and sustainable products with a unique source of powerful actives—and each one has a captivating story behind it.

...alternative way to boost collagen. Its Sail! Marine Eye Gel is formulated with seaweed algae, fruit extracts and vitamins, which support the production of collagen, the brand says.

At the ingredients level, In-Cosmetics North America 2019 saw several marine-based actives on show, as *CosmeticsDesign USA* pointed out. These included Seadermium, a skin-plumping marine active produced by LipoTrue and sourced from Réunion island in the Indian Ocean. The Creanatural range by French brand The Innovation Company offers natural ingredients based on marine and plant extracts that include caviar extract and squid ink.

One Ocean Beauty packaging designed by Fabien Baron of Baron & Baron

Retail

61

Ethical edits

Online luxury marketplaces are elevating ethics as well as aesthetics when curating their collections.

Consumers are purchasing for values more than ever. "The New Sustainability: Regeneration," a Wunderman Thompson report published in fall 2018, finds that 83% of consumers say that, when deciding between brands, they'll always pick the one with a better sustainability record, and 70% are willing to pay more for products and services that help protect the environment or don't infringe on human rights. To help cater to this conscious shopping movement, a host of retailers are curating ethically driven collections.

Launched in July 2019, Buho is an ethical e-commerce hub offering a curated selection of brands that prioritize sustainable practices, gender equality and fair trade. Buho works with carbon-neutral shipping partners, and uses fully compostable packaging and plantable seed tags for its consciously crafted homeware and products for men, women and kids.

In June 2019, luxury fashion online retailer Net-a-Porter launched Net Sustain, a new vertical dedicated to sustainable brands. The 26 brands and over 500 products in the edit meet at least one of five sustainability related requirements set out by the retailer—these

cover human, animal and environmental welfare.

"Our sustainable edit provides our customers with the knowledge they need, understanding that they can trust that these brands have been carefully reviewed and meet our criteria for inclusion," says Elizabeth von der Goltz, Net-a-Porter's global buying director. "Our aim is to give a voice to the brands that are truly making positive changes by providing them with a platform to highlight their best practice."

In June 2019, luxury fashion veterans Dexter and Byron Peart launched Goodee, a luxury marketplace that refines sustainable retail with a principled and story-forward approach. "We don't just want people to shop, we want to cultivate a purpose-driven conversation," Dexter Peart tells Wunderman Thompson Intelligence. "People now want to make better choices in their lives and we have created an opportunity for people to engage."

Goodee's goal is to show consumers that sustainable and design-forward don't have to be mutually exclusive terms. "We want to change the narrative of organic and sustainable consumer purchases as being a trade-off against owning beautiful things. We felt like there needed to be a more modern approach to sustainability, to present it in a more appealing, digestible way," Byron Peart explains to Wunderman Thompson Intelligence.

Why it's interesting:
Consumer are increasingly seeking out brands whose values align with their own. In response, retailers are tailoring their products and platforms to showcase ethics and help consumers shop purposefully.

Anti-excess consumerism

As skepticism about influencers and awareness of environmental damage rise, shoppers are consciously stepping back from the ledge of excess consumer culture.

Beauty bloggers, whose very existence and success has previously hinged on reviewing the latest products and releases, are starting to actively denounce the beauty industry's endless cycle of new products. One beauty YouTuber is taking a radical stance; Samantha Ravndahl, who as of January 2020 had amassed 976,000 subscribers, has asked brands to stop sending her PR packages and free products to review. "Every time a new product was sent to me, I'd look at it and think, 'Well, it's here, it's new, I might as well review it,'" Ravndahl explained to the *Cut*. "I wouldn't want to be told to buy something new when just last week, I'd been told to buy something else that was really similar. That's not realistic, and that's not how people buy makeup. It's certainly not how I'd buy makeup."

Review culture is not only impractical, short-sighted and even anxiety-inducing—beauty consumers are also increasingly uncomfortable with the excessive waste it generates. "What pushed it over the edge," said Ravndahl, "was the physical waste. I live in a household of eight people, and the waste that I alone created was more than the others combined."

NDERMAN
MPSON   Depop peer-to-peer second-hand marketplace

The beauty community is echoing this sentiment. Ravndahl received overwhelmingly positive feedback on her decision to cut back, with one viewer commenting, "Thank you SO much for this.Unfortunately the beauty community thrives on buying more, more, more and it's not a healthy trend."

Elsewhere on the internet, beauty junkies are flocking to popular online community Reddit to support each other in the decision to purchase less. The thread r/MakeupRehab, which had over 75,000 members as of January 2020, sees many former members of the thread r/MakeupAddiction banding together to encourage conscious consumption.

The anti-excess movement is also taking root in the fashion industry. The secondhand clothing market is on track to reach sales of $43 billion by 2022, according to the "ThredUp 2019 Resale Report" compiled for ThredUp by Global Data, and is particularly strong among the key millennial and generation Z markets, which are adopting secondhand apparel two and a half times as fast as other age groups. The secondhand luxury goods market is even growing faster than the primary market; the 2019 BCG-Altagamma "True-Luxury Global Consumer Insight" study estimates that luxury resale will grow at an average annual rate of 12% through 2021, compared to the 3% growth rate for the primary market over the same period.

Brands and retailers are pivoting in response: in November 2019, Selfridges opened a permanent space for luxury clothing resale platform Vestiaire Collective, following a pop-up for Depop, the peer-to-peer second-hand marketplace, from August through October 2019.

"We have had the most insane excess," Orsola de Castro, cofounder and creative director of Fashion Revolution, a British non-profit that campaigns for global supply chain transparency and responsibility, tells Wunderman Thompson Intelligence, "so it makes sense that we're questioning it."

Why it's interesting:

The archetypal insatiable consumer is becoming an outdated relic of the 20th century as consumers turn a more discerning eye on purchasing. "Millennials and gen Z are disrupting the market and placing greater importance on the social and environmental impact of their purchases than previous generations," notes Vestiare. Rising generations are buying with less frequency and more mindfulness, creating a better model for consumerism, so brands should be cautious of pushing products mindlessly—they risk appearing blindly greedy and out of touch.

63

(AR)etail

Retail experiences are being reimagined by advances in augmented reality (AR), creating new windows for discovery.

More brands are investing in AR's boundless potential for creating immersive shopping landscapes. In New York City, Italian furniture house Natuzzi has followed Ikea's lead and opened a showroom where shoppers can wear Microsoft's HoloLens 2 headset to enter an augmented version of their own home. They can fill this virtual version with Natuzzi pieces, easily customizing patterns and colors.

"It gives them a sense of place and mood that's almost as real as a physical furniture display, and the experience helps them form an emotional connection to their choices," creative director Pasquale Junior Natuzzi told *Dezeen*.

Kohl's is the latest in a line of brands, from Gucci to Gatorade, to harness Snapchat's Portal AR Lens. For a limited time in November 2019, customers could access the retailer's virtual holiday pop-up boutique and shop labels like Jason Wu, Vera Wang and Lauren Conrad by clicking on the merchandise to access Kohl's online store.

Then there's Obsess, a dynamic online shopping platform

In the long-term future of AR glasses—and later contact lenses—our eye view will become our screen.

Neha Singh, founder, Obsess

RETAIL

WUNDERMAN
THOMPSON

WUNDERMAN
THOMPSON

Natuzzi showroom

developed by *Vogue*'s former head of product Neha Singh. Obsess ditches the 2D thumbnail images featured on most online shops. Its multiple CGI-powered, 3D virtual worlds range from luxurious apartments to natural landscapes, each containing themed shoppable product lines.

In China, Armani has become the first global luxury brand to employ AR on a mass scale via a WeChat Mini Program. Through a partnership that draws on L'Oréal's ModiFace technology, Armani's cosmetic customers can use their WeChat app to virtually try on makeup at home and make immediate purchases. Alibaba has also heavily invested in AR for its beauty consumers on the Tmall e-commerce portal, giving brands like Tom Ford Beauty and MAC the tools to help online shoppers virtually test out makeup products in their online flagship stores.

Offline, Swarovski brought its AR try-on experience to Chinese customers in its Chengdu store in spring 2019, following its London

debut. Shoppers entering the boutique encounter multiple mirror-like interactive screens that let them virtually wear crystal-encrusted jewelry, in a similar vein to Sephora's AR-powered makeup counters.

In June 2019, Shenzhen-based tech startup Coolhobo demonstrated just how the future of AR-powered retail could look. Its winning concept for Google and JD.com's China AR competition showed how customers at Walmart's bricks-and-mortar store could use AR navigation to pick up everything on their shopping lists by following floating arrows that point the way to each item. Along the way, they encounter product information and friends' recommendations in real time, and interact with brands via fun, immersive games.

Coolhobo founder and CEO Loïc Kobes tells Wunderman Thompson Intelligence that investment, research and development that takes new AR to the next level would mean "giving the camera the ability to understand our physical world, like a 3D GPS, accurate within centimeters." The camera, he explains, would know what it was looking at, just as humans do. "That will massively impact retail, especially physical stores."

Why it's interesting:

Right now, most retailers are experimenting with AR in one-off projects, but with the rollout of 5G, AR shopping experiences could reach uncharted levels of immersion, giving new depth and meaning to the merging of the online shopping experience with IRL. Singh told *Vogue* her predictions: "In the long-term future of AR glasses—and later contact lenses—our eye view will become our screen. Digital information and objects will often be indistinguishable from physical objects, and a new layer of digital fashion will emerge where items won't need to be manufactured physically, but will be 'worn' in this AR realm virtually."

64

Subscription goes east

Subscriptions are no longer just for news and gyms.

The ecosystem for a subscribed life may be most advanced in Japan, where you can now subscribe to everything from bar drinks to hair and beauty treatments, cars, suits and even stays in charming rural homes.

Subscription used to mean committing to pay in advance for an agreed number of uniform products, in exchange for convenience and bulk savings over time. Now more imaginative subscription models are building variety into their packages, in some cases blurring the lines between purchase and rental.

In Japan, Toyota launched a car subscription service called Kinto in February 2019. Kinto One, the basic plan, lets consumers "own" a Toyota for three years and then return it, for a single price that includes insurance and maintenance. The premium Kinto Select plan, aimed at younger drivers looking for variety, lets subscribers "own" and "try" six Lexus cars over three years.

In Japan's famously formal work culture, a subscription service called Kirudake offers fuss-free working wardrobes for corporate clients. The plan starts at 4,800 yen a month (around $40), which

Kinto by Toyota

WUNDERMAN
THOMPSON

A new generation is embracing subscriptions, even for big-ticket items, to achieve convenience and affordability.

covers two suits, one for summer and one for winter. Garments are individually hemmed and adjusted to fit each member, and shirts and ties can also be included.

The subscription world has mushroomed to a point where Kirudake, along with some 100 other subscription services, is part of an umbrella super-subscription service called Oyo Passport, which offers an added layer of savings for dedicated subscribers.

Another recent entrant to the subscription game is responding to problems associated with Japan's super-aging population. Almost a third of the country's population is over 65, according to 2018 government figures cited by the World Economic Forum, and 2.3 million Japanese people are aged 90 or older.

When old people die, their homes are often left vacant, especially in rural areas. ADDress, a subscription service version of Airbnb launched in April 2019, is one answer to rural depopulation. Users sign a one-year contract and pay a fixed monthly rate of 40,000 yen (around $360) to live in any listed property (a single month's

subscription is available for 50,000 yen, or around $450). The homes are often in bucolic locations, and come with a local "guardian" who imparts living and sightseeing tips, and keeps common areas in the homes clean.

ADDress president Takashi Sabetto writes on the company website that he believes having just one address is "a thing of the past," adding: "I hope you will work together to create a society that protects and takes advantage of the rich nature of Japan, old houses and local goodness." The service, with its community-building aspect, has gained the attention of big brands. All Nippon Airways recently announced a collaboration where the airline offers low airfares to ADDress members.

Why it's interesting:

A new generation is embracing subscriptions, even for big-ticket items, to achieve convenience and affordability. This new iteration of subscriptions differs from previous models in that it's flexible enough to allow consumers all the variety they seek.

65

New shopping worlds

From streaming channels to virtual landscapes and games, immersive retail has reached new heights for the next generation of shoppers.

E-commerce platforms are exploring innovative ways to make their content enticing and their products come to life. In China in October 2019, Alibaba's Taobao Life launched a 3D avatar game aimed at generation Z. Users can customize their character's outfits with luxury streetwear apparel and accessories that are also available for purchase on the platform. Soon after the launch, Chinese pop idol Dong Youlin posted photos of himself on social media wearing the same MSGM sweatshirt and Iceberg pants as his Taobao avatar, kicking off a viral frenzy on Weibo.

"The market is going to continue to get younger and these young consumers are inundated with brand messaging," China social media and marketing expert Lauren Hallanan tells Wunderman Thompson Intelligence, describing the future of social gaming and commerce as a retail channel. "Games are a way to draw them in and keep them engaged."

Popular PC video game *The Sims* inspired Moschino's creative director Jeremy Scott to create a ready-to-wear line. Featuring

prints based on the game's Plumbob symbol, denim wear, and a hoodie branded with the Freezer Bunny character, the collection was released in spring 2019 and was available both IRL and digitally within the game, as part of the avatars' wardrobe.

Streaming experiences have also expanded into uncharted spaces. Just months before Victoria's Secret announced it was canceling its annual live fashion show, Rihanna's Savage X Fenty brand collaborated with Amazon to stream its New York Fashion Week runway on Amazon Prime, giving the video service's members the opportunity to shop the lingerie collection without leaving the platform.

Why it's interesting:

Global brands are embarking on unconventional partnerships that blend worlds to create innovative retail discovery experiences for a young cohort of mobile-first and digital-native shoppers. Successful retailers will meet gen Zers and millennials wherever they are, whether it's in a virtual game or on new streaming platforms.

99

New beauty playgrounds

As experience culture cuts a swathe through retail, there's perhaps no sector better suited to a hands-on moment than beauty.

No matter how alluring a product might appear online, there's no substitute for consumers being able to test out shades or try a new texture IRL. In April 2019 the *Business of Fashion* cited research from Piper Jaffray that showed around 90% of American teenagers still preferred to buy cosmetics in stores. While e-commerce sales account for an ever greater share of consumer purchases, "beauty is the only category where bricks-and-mortar's share hasn't fallen," says Erinn Murphy, principal and senior research analyst at Piper Jaffray.

With that in mind, brands are ramping up their in-store beauty experiences, and reimagining them as veritable playgrounds.

In October 2019, Harrods announced the launch of its H Beauty standalone beauty concept, with the first store set to open at the UK's Intu Lakeside shopping center in Essex in April 2020. *Retail Gazette* reported that the store will span 23,000 square feet and offer services such as a "coffee-to-cocktail" bar, and blow dry and facial treatments. Brands will include Chanel, Dior, Huda Beauty, and others new to the retailer. "H Beauty is an opportunity to bring our mission to more beauty lovers across the UK," says Annalise

AIL

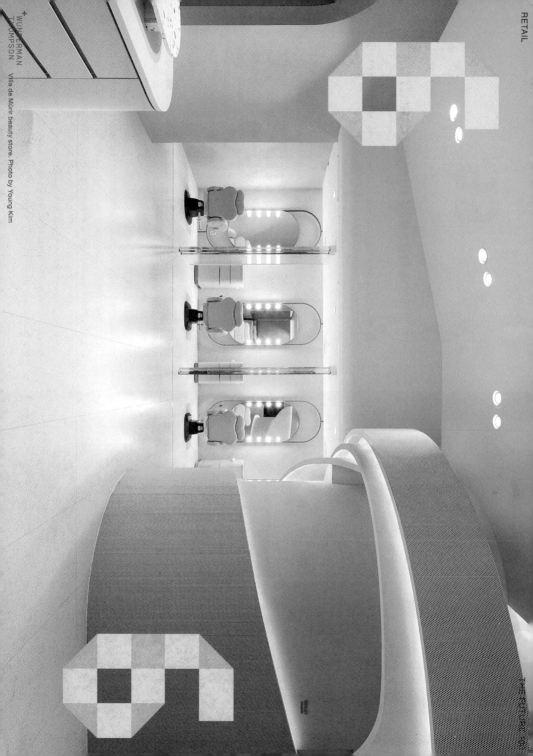

AIL

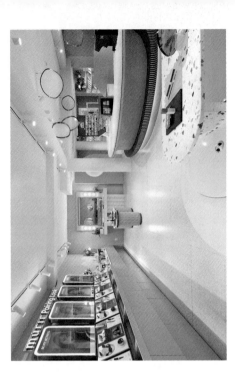

Fard, Harrods home and beauty director. "We are on a mission to show the world the art of what is truly possible in the world of beauty today." Harrods has also announced it will open its second UK H Beauty store in Milton Keynes.

After Beauty, which opened in fall 2019 on London's bustling Piccadilly, describes itself as a "beauty playhouse." The extensive three-story space carries 140 brands, including SkinCeuticals, Dermalogica, Holika Holika, and Patchology. "After Beauty was founded to bring fun and excitement back to the beauty industry," cofounder Zanelle Lim told *Get the Gloss*. "We wanted to create a destination for beauty obsessives to lose themselves in a world of products, color and creativity. Customers have a better understanding of products now than ever before, so we want them to throw out the rulebook and discover new things."

The trend is taking hold globally. In October 2019, e-commerce platform Grove Collaborative launched clean beauty concept store Roven on Abbot Kinney Boulevard in Los Angeles, as a sub-brand to its core natural home products business. *Beauty Independent* described the store's design as "a study in pastels enhanced by soft edges" that incorporates "a lot of good vibes, and eye-catching colors and curves." Roven cofounder Nicole Farb told *Beauty Independent* that "the ability to touch and feel the brand is more powerful than we would have expected."

In Seoul, Villa de Mûrir is described by Collective B, the design studio behind the concept, as a "beauty curation brand." The store is at once futuristic and cocooning, decked out in millennial pink and terrazzo stone, and offers Villa de Mûrir's own line as well as products from other leading beauty brands. The space also includes

a production studio "for YouTube and social media content creators," the *Coolhunter* reported, alongside treatment rooms and a café.

Why it's interesting:
Beauty retailers are clearly listening to research that points to generation Z's love of IRL shopping. According to data released by AT Kearney in September 2019, 81% of 14-24-year-olds surveyed preferred to shop in stores, with some using it as a way to disconnect from social media and the digital world, while 73% said they liked to discover new products in stores. These new beauty environments are being conceived as welcoming, warm spaces that invite the consumer to play, experience and, of course, buy new products.

NDERMAN
OMPSON   Villa de Mûrir beauty store. Photo by Young Kim

51

Uninterrupted commerce

From social media to search engines, consumers can shop just about anywhere online and the process is becoming more seamless than ever before.

Instagram is on its way to becoming a one-stop shop for brands thanks to the launch of Checkout in spring 2019, and enthusiasm around native commerce on the platform only seems to be accelerating. *Glossy* reported in November 2019 that brands such as Joe's Jeans and SoulCycle are working with Instagram influencers and collaborators to sell their apparel through the Checkout feature, and have achieved overwhelmingly positive results so far.

Hot on Instagram's heels, Google introduced an update in October 2019 that allows users to shop and make purchases from thousands of vendors directly through its search engine. Consumers can also use Google Shopping to locate an item they're looking for at a nearby store, track the price of a product, and receive personalized shopping recommendations.

With extensive e-commerce capabilities already in place in China, TikTok is experimenting with in-app e-commerce in the United States. In China, brands can link to stores both inside and outside of the short video platform, and nearly every other Chinese social

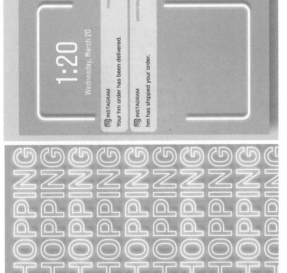

media site has its own built-in e-commerce platform, from Xiaohongshu to generation Z favorite Bilibili.

"This state of affairs in China is very advanced," Elijah Whaley, a brand growth and influencer marketing expert in China, tells Wunderman Thompson Intelligence, adding that consumer sentiment towards online shopping as entertainment will continue to fuel a completely integrated content to commerce experience.

"Sixteen-year-old girls aren't going to the mall necessarily anymore, but sitting on their phones and flicking through online stores or watching e-commerce live streams or direct to commerce content,"

he says. "For the right demographic, online shopping is the new going to the mall for entertainment and hanging out."

Why it's interesting:

According to Instagram data, 130 million users tap on shopping posts every month. Consumers are undoubtedly using Instagram and other online content spaces for product discovery, and brands can leverage this by working with influencers to remove the pain points in the purchasing experience.

Death of the luxury department store

A string of long-established big-name department stores has folded under staggering levels of debt and bankruptcy, which begs the question: what does the future of luxury retail look like?

Business Insider has calculated that more than 9,000 individual stores closed in the United States in 2019. This is unsurprising given that bricks-and-mortar retail revenue is plummeting across the world. US department stores experienced a dramatic 30% drop in sales between 2007 and 2017, according to US Census Department retail figures, and Morgan Stanley has predicted that department stores will account for just 8% of the apparel market by 2022, down from 24% in 2016.

Barneys declared bankruptcy in August 2019 and in November 2019 announced that it would officially close. "The entire industry is in survival mode," Daniella Vitale, then Barneys CEO, told employees earlier in the year, according to a recording obtained by CNBC. "The model is not working," she said, adding that it's not working for Neiman Marcus, "it's not working for Saks, it's not working for us, it's not working for Nordstrom."

In November 2019, LVMH purchased renowned but diminished

Tiffany & Co, whose prestige and Hollywood heritage were no longer enough to keep it afloat on its own.

In January 2019, Lord & Taylor's Fifth Avenue flagship—which first opened in 1914—shut its doors for good. The store had completed a $12 million renovation just over 18 months before. Struggling parent company Hudson Bay, which also owns Saks Fifth Avenue, then sold the retailer to Le Tote in November 2019.

Henri Bendel officially shut down in January 2019 after 123 years in business, and bankruptcy could be looming for Neiman Marcus, which in March 2019 reached a deal with creditors to restructure its $5 million debt.

These struggles are symptomatic of a larger shift in the luxury retail landscape. According to research from Expedia and the Center for Generational Kinetics, 74% of Americans value experience over products. Legacy retailers such as Nordstrom and Selfridges are pivoting to the experience economy with workshops, cultural programming and pop-ups, while newcomers like Showfields are blurring the lines between art, commerce and experience, turning shopping into an immersive and multisensory experience.

When they do shop for products, idealistic and principled generation Zers and millennials are looking for brands that align with their beliefs. According to research by Bain, this group is driving 85% of luxury sales growth globally and is expected to constitute 45% of luxury shoppers by 2025. A survey by SONAR™, Wunderman Thompson's proprietary research tool, found that 83% of consumers always pick the brand with the better sustainability record, and 70% are willing to pay more for products and services if they protect the environment or don't infringe human rights.

> **The entire industry is in survival mode. The model is not working. It's not working for Saks, it's not working for us, it's not working for Nordstrom.**
>
> **Danielle Vitale, former CEO, Barneys**

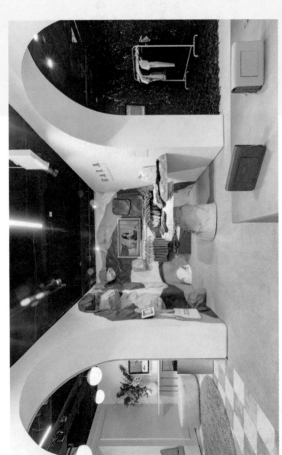

"It's very hard now for a company not to stand for something," said Vanessa Friedman, *New York Times* fashion director and host of the newspaper's international luxury conference. "People buy things not just because they are pretty but because they represent something more."

Byron Peart, cocreator of e-commerce platform Goodee and cofounder of luxury accessories brand Want Les Essentiels, echoes this sentiment. "The brands of the future will be rooted in purpose," Peart tells Wunderman Thompson Intelligence. "There is a change in real time about how luxury is defined. Whereas it previously fell under a price and exclusivity matrix, we think it will shift towards drive and purpose."

Why it's interesting:

In a climate where status is increasingly cued by values and purpose in place of price and prestige, the luxury retail category is undergoing a seismic shift. Luxury department stores of yore no longer resonate with modern consumers, who are willing to pay for experiences and ethics. As Peart says, "good design and purpose will become the arithmetic to luxury."

69

Next-gen retail spaces

With much of their lives spent on social media, millennials regard design values as being of paramount importance—and they have high design expectations on behalf of their offspring too.

In major cities across the globe, various aspirational children's spaces have been devised in striking contrast to the primary colors and wipe-clean surfaces that have long dominated play areas.

In China, the Loong Swim Club in Suzhou is a soothing space designed by Shanghai architecture firm X + Living. It has been imagined in soft tones of pink and blue, and has circular lighting fixtures that emit a pleasant, diffused glow. It's more than just a pool: a library space is decked out with inviting, lozenge-shaped curved seating, and its café borders on the fantastical, with ornate, egg-shaped domes, a mirrored ceiling and polka-dot floors. It's a space that's equally appealing to parents and children—a rarity in design aimed primarily at kids.

In New York, the Wonder is a family members' club that opened in the Tribeca district in 2019. Its interiors are bold—tones of red, yellow and blue abound—and carefully designed, with a café and a coworking space for parents alongside play and activity areas. "Our

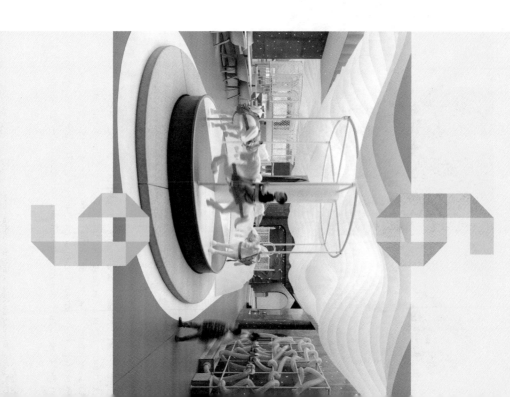

NDERMAN
OMPSON

AIL

Lolly-Laputan café, Dalian. Image courtesy of Wutopia Lab. Photo by CreatAR Images

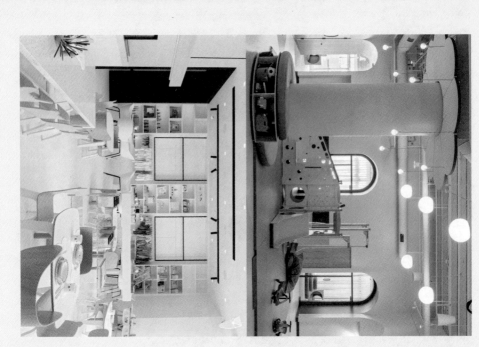

Top: Brella childcare center, Los Angeles
Bottom: White and the Bear restaurant for children, Dubai

vision, ultimately, is to be that voice for a new generation of parents," cofounder Noria Morales told media company PSFK. "The whole idea or perception around parents is so outdated. It's more diverse. We're interacting with our kids in different ways. We're spending more time with our kids than ever."

Restaurants for children are taking on a chic identity. In Dubai, White and the Bear is a children's eatery imagined in black and white, with pale wood furniture and fixtures. Sneha Divias Atelier, which designed the space, told *Dezeen* that it chose a palette that would not "overstimulate the senses," adding that "the color scheme promotes creativity, imagination, and learning."

In Dalian, China, Wutopia Labs devised Lolly-Laputan café as "an imaginary fairyland," *Dezeen* writes. The design is fantastical and playful, yet with a hushed, vrefined color palette. A steel slide sits over a pit filled with white balls, there's a carousel in stark white and gold, and there's a café with pale, Scandinavian-style wood tones.

Why it's interesting:

These design-led spaces appeal to the exacting tastes of millennial parents, whose children are part of generation alpha. Born between 2010 and 2025, this emerging generation is driving its parents' purchases: according to a July 2018 Wunderman Thompson Intelligence study of gen alpha parents, 81% of US millennial parents say the habits of their children influenced their last purchase. These children value time spent in physical spaces as much as in the digital world. In a 2019 report on gen alpha, Hugh Fletcher, head of thought leadership (EMEA) and UK marketing at Wunderman Thompson Commerce, advised that whatever brands start doing now "needs to be built around what gen alpha customers expect."

70

The super-convenient superstore

Chinese grocery giants are diversifying, developing a hybrid retail model to appeal to a wider range of lifestyles.

Hema Fresh, the supermarket from China's Alibaba, opened in 2017, targeting smartphone-savvy young shoppers with a gamechanging blend of digital commerce and bricks and mortar. By July 2019 the fresh food retailer had 160 stores across 21 cities in China. According to NACS, it aims to penetrate yet more locales and to deepen its online-to-offline ecosystem. Part of this strategy includes developing new sub-brands that are tailored to specific consumer groups in different regions.

At the end of 2019 there were four Hema sub-brands. The original high-tech Hema is aimed at convenience-seeking millennials in first-tier cities. In July 2019, Alibaba launched sub-brand Hema Mini, which sells unpackaged fresh produce in a format catering to older, price-sensitive, suburban shoppers—the parents and grandparents of Hema's original target customers—who would otherwise shop at their neighborhood vegetable market. Hema F2 stores stock ready-to-eat deli items and snacks geared toward office workers in business districts. Hema Market, positioned near large residential communities, offers daily staple foods. Hema Station is a delivery-

NDERMAN
OMPSON   Hema by Alibaba. Images courtesy of Alibaba

To achieve a truly seamless online-to-offline experience, big chains are adapting their business models across different locations to cater to specific communities.

only hub located mainly in areas that lack a physical Hema retail store.

Other chains are developing similar models. In September 2019, electronics retail giant Suning acquired an 80% stake in supermarket chain Carrefour China; that month it announced plans to transform Carrefour stores into integrated online-to-offline supermarkets and to introduce smaller versions of its electronics stores in 200 of the supermarkets, based on each outlet's location and customer profile. Café chains Luckin and HeyTea offer several online-to-offline formats tailored to different lifestyles, from pick-up only spots to more upscale coffee and tea bars.

Tencent-backed Yonghui Superstores launched its Super Species brand in 2017, a high-end offering with a cook-to-order service. This was followed in June 2018 with opening of a Guangzhou Super Species outlet with fresh food delivery by drone.

Why it's interesting:

Retail expansion in China used to depend on targeting the booming smaller cities. Yet digitized customers and supply chains have changed the retail landscape. To achieve a truly seamless online-to-offline experience, big chains are adapting their business models across different locations to cater to specific communities.

Luxury

11

Retro gaming retail

Luxury brands are tapping into millennials' affinity for nostalgia and adventure by borrowing from vintage video games.

Louis Vuitton, never shy of dabbling in the world of games, released a retro-inspired, 16-bit video game called *Endless Runner* in July 2019. Inspired by Virgil Abloh's fall/winter 2019 collection, the game is free to play via the Louis Vuitton website and harks back to a 1980s lo-fi blocky aesthetic with simple gameplay. There are no product pushes or redirects to shop embedded into the game; first and foremost, it is intended to entertain. The game is familiar, accessible and, like most video games, extremely addictive.

Earlier in July 2019, Gucci introduced the vintage-inspired Gucci Arcade gaming feature on its mobile app. It currently features four titles: *Gucci Lips*, *Gucci Grip*, *Gucci Ace* and *Gucci Bee*. The latter is a maze game reminiscent of Pac-Man, where players have to navigate a bee (a popular motif for the brand) through different levels while collecting tokens and unlocking special elements.

These launches follow in the footsteps of Chanel's Coco Game Center, a pop-up beauty arcade experience. The 1990s-themed

video game arcade toured Asia in spring 2018 and incorporated the brand's products and identity. In 2017, Cartier launched a Pac-Man-style game on WeChat to promote its Amulette de Cartier range.

Why it's interesting:

Millennial shoppers are expected to account for 50% of spending in the personal luxury market by 2025, according to a 2019 report from Boston Consulting Group and Altagamma. Looking to stay relevant with younger consumers, luxury labels are embracing gaming culture and refining the image of the stereotypical gamer.

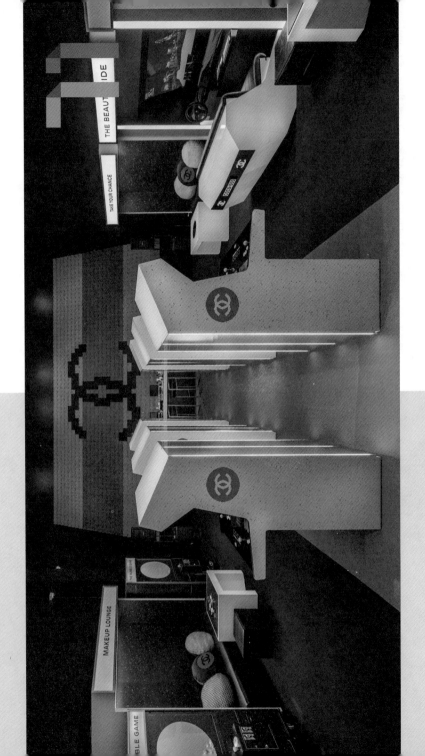

Coco Game Center by Chanel. Image courtesy of Chanel

72

Haute horticulture

A groundswell of designers, celebrities and retailers are featuring florals in brand activations, elevating flowers to a mark of luxury.

As an evolution of the elaborate floral headpieces that dominated the SS19 runways, brands and retailers are turning to florals to reference high-fashion opulence.

In September 2019, high-end department store Selfridges tapped "imaginative and flamboyant" floral studio Rebel Rebel for the launch of Kate Hudson's sustainable clothing collection HappyxNature. Elegantly overgrown pedestals and flower crowns were chosen to complement the fashion line. The floral design house was also responsible for the flowery backdrops and floral arrangements featured in haute-couture fashion house Giambattista Valli's fall/winter 2020 campaign for H&M.

Retailers are also putting fresh blooms front and center. As part of Neiman Marcus's March 2019 grand opening of its first New York City retail location, PopUp Florist opened a semi-permanent flower cart offering its beautiful bouquets. And luxury consignment retailer The RealReal has a flower stand stocked by Fox Fodder Farm—

WUNDERMAN
THOMPSON

Princess Nokia with gypsophila, anthuriums and orchids.
Photo by Petra Collins for Office Magazine. Image courtesy of Phaidon Press

THE FUTURE 100 173

Floral artistry by London-based Harriet Parry Flowers

rated top florist by *Vogue* and *Harper's Bazaar*—at the entrance of its Manhattan flagship boutique.

The art of floristry has been further established in Phaidon's 2019 book *Blooms: Contemporary Floral Design*, which celebrates this craft across disciplines, from haute couture to music videos. "Together, these floral creatives are reinvigorating the world of floristry," Claire Coulson, *Blooms* contributing author, tells

Floral creatives are reinvigorating floristry-and having a profound effect on visual culture and design.

Claire Coulson, contributing author, Blooms

Wunderman Thompson Intelligence, "pushing the boundaries of artistic expression with flowers and plants and having a profound effect on visual culture and design."

Why it's interesting:

Flowers have evolved from pretty to provocative thanks to a visionary class of creatives who are elevating avant-garde and unexpected floral designs into a luxury cue for brands.

73

Jet-setting pets

Pets are increasingly being treated as members of the family, including tagging along on luxury holidays, and some hotels and airlines are bending over backwards to make them feel welcome.

At VistaJet, a private jet charter company based in Malta, the number of animals on board has increased by 104% since 2017, with one in four VistaJet members flying regularly with a pet. The jet travel company's VistaPet pet flyer program, introduced in April 2019, offers four-legged travelers care kits, handmade sleep mats, rope toys and bio-organic menus.

Prior to their holiday, nervous pets can undergo a four-week pre-flight course to counter their fear of flying, helping to desensitize them to things like the smell of fuel, the roar of jet engines, cabin air pressure and turbulence. Once your pet is on board, flight attendants offer natural flower essences to mix in pets' drinking water to further help relaxation. The airline can also recommend pet-friendly hotels, salons, walkers and even photographers at your destination.

In November 2019, Canopy by Hilton, a boutique hotel-style chain in North America, introduced its partnership with Bark, makers of the BarkBox monthly customized subscription box of themed dog toys

DERMAN
MPSON   VistaPet service at VistaJet

URY

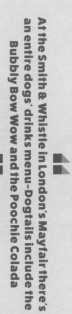

At the Smith & Whistle in London's Mayfair there's an entire dogs' drinks menu—Dogtails include the Bubbly Bow Wow and the Poochie Colada

and treats. Canopy's emphasis is on a local experience and dogs are no exception. In addition to a snuggly toy and all-natural treats, it also offers a neighborhood guide of dog hot spots for Fido to visit.

At the Smith & Whistle in London's Mayfair there's an entire dogs' drinks menu, with Dogtails including the Bubbly Bow Wow (dog-friendly prosecco and liquidized blueberries) and the Poochie Colada (kale, broccoli and coconut water).

The trend for luxury holidays for pets is prevalent in Asia too. Hotel W Shanghai The Bund is among many in the Marriott group to join the Pets Are Welcome (PAW) program, with special treats, toys and dog walks.

Why it's interesting:

Luxury for pets is being bolstered by the singledom trend, particularly in China. Singles are lavishing their disposable income on dogs and cats instead of kids. Nearly 40% of Chinese pet owners are single and they're contributing to a pet economy that's more than tripled from 2013 to 2018, reaching almost $25 billion, according to a 2019 report by Frost & Sullivan.

74

Health concierges

High-end destinations are catering to wellness-minded travelers with tailored health services.

In October 2019, Four Seasons launched a new wellness retreat in Hawaii. The all-inclusive destination was created specifically to provide "what today's luxury traveler wants: an exclusive and differentiated wellness travel experience," says Christian Clerc, president of global operations at Four Seasons Hotels and Resorts.

Guests are matched with a personal wellness guide who helps craft a bespoke health program incorporating nutrition, fitness and holistic spa treatments. The experience also includes one-on-one sessions with wellness practitioners and makes use of tech-enhanced services, such as thermal body mapping, for deeper health insights.

Equinox Hotel, which opened in New York City in July 2019, also features individual health concierge services. To ensure a good night's sleep, the hotel offers on-call sleep coaches to analyze guests' circadian rhythms, and it provides in-house services such as jet-lag tonics and cryotherapy chambers.

Four Seasons has a fresh focus on wellness

Combining tailored services with expert insight, health concierges are shaping up to be the next evolution of the global wellness tourism industry.

This follows the success of The Benjamin hotel's Rest & Renew program, developed by sleep expert Rebecca Robbins. "We've designed a series of products and services that improve the sleep experience," she tells Wunderman Thompson Intelligence. These range from a pillow menu segmented by sleeper type to a "power down" call (the opposite of a wake-up call) where "the staff will come up to your hotel room and share some good sleep strategies," she explains.

Why it's interesting:

Combining tailored services with expert insight, health concierges are shaping up to be the next evolution of the global wellness tourism industry, worth in excess of $639 billion according to the Global Wellness Institute.

15

Wellness architecture

Architects are constructing a healthier living environment, further cementing the wellness movement.

More and more architects, interior designers and engineers are working together with scientists for healthy design," says Xue Ya, president of architecture firm Delos Asia and part of the team behind the Well Living Lab. She adds that they aim to make spaces more like human beings' natural life."

Delos collaborated with the Mayo Clinic on the Well Living Lab, which investigates the health implications of indoor environments. The lab, which opened its second location, in Beijing, in 2019, is dedicated to identifying how buildings—and everything that goes in them—impacts human health and wellbeing."

As well as its work on the lab, Delos has devised multiple projects pioneering healthy home design. It has created what it identifies as the healthiest condo in New York City, incorporating amenities such as antimicrobial surfaces, showers dispensing filtered water infused with vitamin C, in-duct aromatherapy and individually calibrated circadian lighting systems.

At the 2019 CES tech show, Delos unveiled Darwin, a smart-home system that certifies a healthy indoor environment. It adds "a layer of wellness intelligence to the smart-home landscape," says Delos CEO and founder Paul Scialla. The system integrates features such as indoor air and water purification and light and temperature optimization throughout the day to support natural sleep cycles.

The need to create healthy indoor retreats will become a necessity as people spend more time indoors. Research by the US Environmental Protection Agency has found that Americans spend approximately 90% of their time inside, meaning a lucrative market in interiors that prioritize wellbeing.

Why it's interesting:

Sustainable building practices—which show no signs of slowing down—focus on the health of the environment, and they prioritize the health of the occupant. "The spaces that we inhabit influence and partially shape who we are and how we are feeling," designer Jenny Sabin tells Wunderman Thompson Intelligence. As nearly every aspect of modern life gets the wellness treatment, architects are drawing this attention to the built environment, turning wellness-infused living spaces into the latest luxury.

> # Your senses are connected so strongly to experience. We are at a point where clients are looking for bespoke stuff.
>
> **Errol Capel, creative director, SynerG**

Sensory travel

In an era of mass distraction, luxury travel is using all five senses to imprint experiences.

Hotels and airlines are diffusing signature scents; spas are offering chime and gong baths; and nature is being welcomed in rather than shut out.

For some brands, it's simply a question of pointing out and making time for what's already on their doorstep. Luxury travel company Belmond offers First Light nature walks in partnership with Leica Sport Optics at its hotels in Botswana, Mallorca, Cape Town and Iguazú Falls, on the Argentina/Brazil border. Guests head out at dawn with Leica binoculars to spot flora and fauna in the surrounding area. The soft light and quiet help deepen guests' appreciation for local natural beauty, and the brand draws on nature to differentiate it in a memorable way.

At downtown Kuala Lumpur's EQ, the new flagship of the Hotel Equatorial chain, ambient music is played through underwater speakers in the 29th-floor infinity pool and its Japanese restaurant Kampachi boasts a sushi counter made of fragrant hinoki wood, a type of cypress used to make incense.

EQ also employs scent in the lobby, ballroom and lounges to evoke a sense of luxury. Scent consultant AllSense worked with EQ to pick a

Why It's Interesting:

There's increasing awareness of the importance of being present in the moment. Luxury travel has long focused on sight, taste and touch to create evocative experiences and memories, and is increasingly expanding its tool kit to also include smell and sound.

...cent called Black Orchid, with floral and lemony top notes and a ...oody base that includes sandalwood and musk.

...nother client of AllSense, and of sound specialist SynerG, ...ingapore's Changi Airport plays music carefully selected to help ...ith traffic flow. At all four terminals at Changi, voted the world's best ...irport by Skytrax for seven years in a row, music has a faster tempo ...t peak hours and is slower at off-peak times—a subtle way of ...fluencing the speed at which travelers walk. "Your senses are ...onnected so strongly to experience," Errol Capel, creative director at ...ynerG, tells Wunderman Thompson Intelligence. "We are at a point ...here clients are looking for bespoke stuff."

NDERMAN   Above: EQ's sushi counter
OMPSON   Right: EQ's infinity pool

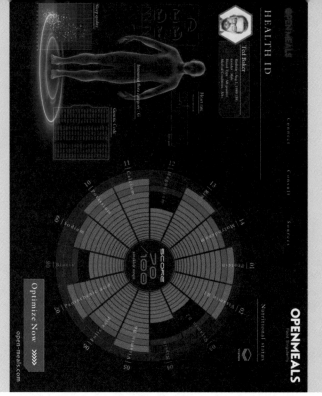

OPENMEALS
Food Singularity

Biodata services

Advances in speedy, sophisticated DNA analysis are paving the way for lifestyle experiences that elevate the hyper-personalized offerings already saturating the luxury space.

Set to open in Tokyo in 2020, restaurant Sushi Singularity will collect bio samples from guests to create bespoke, 3D-printed sushi tailored to diners' nutritional needs. Daniel del Olmo, founding partner of the Passionality Group, has called it the next era of dining. "We believe hyper-personalization will become commonplace in the future," he said at the Restaurant Finance & Development Conference in Las Vegas in November 2019.

Another sushi dining experience assesses a person's DNA information to curate a menu suited to their specific nutritional needs. London's Yo! Sushi partnered with at-home genetic testing company DNAFit in February 2019 for the Yo! Dinner, Yo! Way scheme, and offered free personalized meals to a select number of customers who mailed in a saliva sample.

DNA matchmaking is also turning the search for love into a science. Tokyo-based Gene Partner Japan uses DNA samples to analyze a person's human leucocyte antigen (HLA) genes. The theory is that the bigger the difference between two people's HLA makeup, the

...more likely they'll find each other attractive. Competing Tokyo firm Gene Future offers a similar service to future couples at a more affordable price. In Singapore, GeneMate, which launched in June 2019, offers customers the chance to find their life partner using biodata and the firm's own unique algorithm. Companies in both Japan and Singapore have received government support for DNA matchmaking services as they battle dropping birthrates.

In travel, biotechnology is taking already unique Airbnb experiences to a transformative level. Airbnb partnered with 23andMe in spring 2019 in a bid to help customers tailor their activities around their ancestral heritage, revealed through taking one of 23andMe's DNA testing kits. "Someone with Mexican roots could find an experience in Mexico City to learn ancient techniques of natural dye as part of their heritage vacation," Airbnb suggests.

Why it's interesting:

Despite continued debate over whether genetic testing can accurately and conclusively predict factors like compatibility or even heritage, consumer DNA services aren't going anywhere anytime soon. As testing kits become more streamlined and advanced, applications will likely continue to expand into new territories that add value beyond basic wellness reports and assessments.

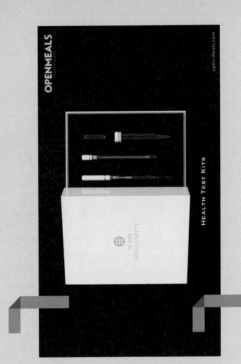

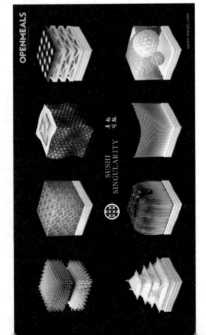

Sushi Singularity. Image courtesy of Open Meals

We believe hyper-personalization will become commonplace in the future.

Daniel del Olmo, founding partner, Passionality Group

Cannabis consultants

As cannabis culture becomes increasingly refined, experts are offering connoisseurship services to discerning customers.

Cannabidiol, one of the active but non-psychoactive ingredients in cannabis, is now universally known as CBD and is increasingly widely available, in increasingly sophisticated formats.

In May 2019, CBD retailer Standard Dose expanded from an online shop to a bricks-and-mortar wellness haven in New York City. In-store "educators" are on hand to walk visitors through the products and find ones that "suit their individual needs, since CBD affects everyone very differently," Standard Dose founder Anthony Saniger told *Coveteur*. The guidance complements a range of curated experiences, from meditation workshops to a tea bar with hemp-infused drinks.

On an even more exclusive level, California-based cannabis consultant Amy Robertson provides ultra-personalized experiences and advice to help her clients sift through the hype and find the high-quality, artisanal cannabis that can fulfil their unique needs. The high-end market—they can have anything," Robertson told *Vice*. "clients aren't looking to solve a medical issue, "it's about what kind of mind-shifting experience can they have," said Robertson. A growing number of luxury consumers are looking for education and guidance for navigating the cannabis market and business ethos, as

ENDERMAN OMPSON Standard Dose CBD retailer, New York City

claims and products become subject to more intense scrutiny. According to Arcview Market Research, the market could exceed $23 billion by 2022.

"It is in part due to consumers becoming more conscious in general," Emma Chasen, cofounder of cannabis education firm Eminent Consulting, tells Wunderman Thompson Intelligence. "If you care about the food you put in your body and take time to source organic, local produce then you should absolutely care about the cannabis you are consuming."

New festivals and immersive events are bringing together brands, experts, first-timers, and seasoned enthusiasts for education, entertainment and networking. *Broccoli* magazine's In Bloom festival kicked off in May 2019 in Portland, Oregon, with cannabis-themed art and musical performances, workshops, panel discussions and tastings. A few months later in Los Angeles, the Weedmaps Museum of Weed took guests on a cultural and political journey, shedding light on common misconceptions of cannabis.

"I think the next step in education will be targeting healthcare professionals and physicians," says Chasen. "To best help their patients, they need the education more than any other demographic. Therefore, I predict we will start to see more degree programs and accreditations coming from universities and community colleges in the near future."

Why it's interesting:

The CBD market swarms with countless brands aimed at the cannabis curious. Those that take the extra step to enlighten customers on the many facets of cannabis consumption, from strains to dosage to formulation, will stand out. High-end consumers in this space are seeking an experience crafted exclusively to them.

19

The new-age explorer

In an era of political and economic unease, people are turning to travel as a respite and as a tool for happiness.

A survey conducted by the Travelzoo members' travel site found that 70% of respondents polled across Australia, Canada, China, France, Germany, Hong Kong, Spain, the United Kingdom and the United States planned on incorporating wellness activities into their travel plans for 2019—and 83% of respondents said that taking a holiday has a positive effect on their mental health.

In response, Travelzoo launched its spring 2019 "May is for Me" campaign. The campaign's online hub offered dedicated travel packages specifically focused on wellness, along with wellness travel tips. Travelzoo defined wellness holidays as breaks tailored to improving mental or physical health, and the May for Me site included packages for yoga in Nepal, health farms in Portugal, and spa days across the United Kingdom and United States, all aiming to meet the growing demand for wellness travel.

In October 2019, luxury travel site Black Tomato kicked off the Every Cloud contest. Acknowledging that "the world can feel like a dark and dreary place; our feeds filled with bad news, uncertainty and

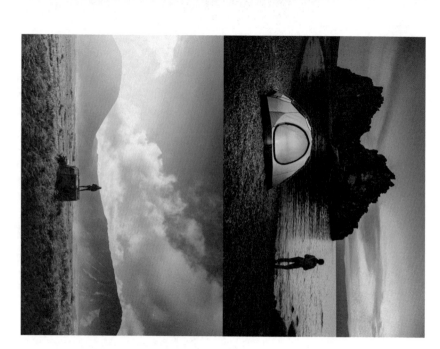

The world can feel like a dark and dreary place; our feeds filled with bad news, uncertainty and stress. Every Cloud goes in search of silver linings.

Black Tomato

stress," Every Cloud goes "in search of silver linings." The winner will travel the world over the course of 2020 in search of joyful experiences, while creating content alongside Black Tomato, leaning into the widespread belief that travel experiences are universally uplifting.

According to the Black Tomato site, the traveler will document "encounters with some of the world's most unique—and unquestionably positive—people, places and experiences" and the year-long campaign will be shared with the Black Tomato audience, turning one person's individual journey into inspiration for many.

Why it's interesting:

As consumers try to embrace a more optimistic mindset, travel is evolving from an escape into a meditation on positivity and happiness, and a channel for wellbeing.

Black Tomato Every Cloud inspirational travel program

Vegan hotels

High-end travelers get the vegan treatment thanks to luxury hotels providing an ethical and sustainable experience.

In a Victorian village in the Scottish Highlands is a hotel that showcases "ethical luxury." Saorsa 1875 opened in June 2019 and every aspect of a stay here is steeped in its thoroughly thought-through vegan philosophy. From staff uniforms to cleaning products to minibar snacks to electricity—which is provided by vegan-certified green energy company Ecotricity—every detail, from check in to check out, is vegan, ethically sourced and free of animal byproducts.

"We want to show people that veganism isn't just a compassionate, ethical choice; it's also an exciting, vibrant way of life," says Saorsa 1875 cofounder and head of lifestyle Jack McLaren-Stewart.

Saorsa 1875 is a timely opening, as more Britons adopt a vegan lifestyle. According to the Vegan Society, the number of vegans in the United Kingdom quadrupled between 2014 and 2019. Mintel research released in 2019 found that 34% of British meat eaters had taken a flexitarian approach and actively reduced their meat consumption in the six months to July 2018.

WUNDERMAN THOMPSON   Vegan suite at Hilton London Bankside. Image courtesy of Hilton

URY

Reflecting this growing market, Hilton unveiled "the world's first vegan suite" in January 2019 at its London Bankside location, created in collaboration with design duo Bompas & Parr and the Vegan Society. The suite's soft furnishings are exclusively made from plant-based fabrics, including organic cotton carpets, soybean-silk curtains and buckwheat-stuffed pillows. Fittings, right down to the key cards issued at the dedicated check-in desk, draw on Piñatex, a material made from pineapple leaves that resembles leather.

"While the suite is primarily designed for the sustainable traveler, we hope that everyone can enjoy it—not just those who enjoy a vegan lifestyle," general manager James B Clarke told CNN, also revealing that the suite has attracted high-profile attention, with "inquiries from celebrity athletes, among others."

Why it's interesting:

Veganism, which once called to mind an ascetic, puritan lifestyle, is being elevated to a covetable luxury amenity driven by ethical consumers. While the food industry is responding en masse to this market, luxury brands are ushering in the next evolution of vegan lifestyles by transforming destinations into sanctuaries free of animal-derived products.

WUNDERMAN
THOMPSON

Health

HEALTH

81

Healing festivals

Music has the power to transport us and it seems a natural step for musicians to embrace the wellness wave.

Icelandic band Sigur Rós, renowned for creating ambient, otherworldly music, held a series of sound baths to enable fans to experience the playlist *Liminal* "in a live arena with other human beings." The band describes each sound bath as a blend of "soaring live vocals and mesmeric, sound-reactive lights to bliss you out. Everyone surrenders to the stillness and, if it's been done right, gets to go away feeling like they might just have seen everything from a slightly different angle." The events took place between 2017 and 2019 at venues ranging from the Natural History Museum of Los Angeles County to the Days Off festival in Paris and London's British Summer Time Hyde Park festival.

Glastonbury Festival launched the Humblewell area in 2019, which the organizer describes as encompassing "the physical, emotional, and social dimensions of wellness." The program of events included Breathbeats, a fusion of "breathwork and psycho-acoustic sound," created by DJ Tom Middleton and Richie Bostock—otherwise known as the Breath Guy.

NDERMAN
MPSON   Newcastle wellness installation at Pharos festival, New Zealand. Photo by Superimpose

Charting the rise of the wellness trend at festivals, the *Guardian* pointed to Love Trails Festival, which fuses running with music. The festival says that from its main stage, "an eclectic mix of iconic and new artists soundtrack three jam-packed days featuring trail running adventures of various distances." Theo Larn-Jones, cofounder and director of Love Trails, told the *Guardian* that "the crux of the festival is tapping into the desire from especially younger people—so those in their 20s and 30s—to live fuller and healthier lives and feel good. I am part of that group: we still want to get off our faces and get drunk and party but don't necessarily want to get off our faces and get drunk in the process. It's like the runner's high; that endorphin hit from a run is replacing other kinds of highs you might get at festivals."

There were a host of wellness activities at Childish Gambino's Pharos event in New Zealand in 2018, including "sound baths, cosmic humming, truth connection booths, and enlightenment exercises," *Dezeen* reported. "Pharos is meant to be a communal space—a place that evolves and reacts to the culture," the rapper, whose real name is Donald Glover, told *Dezeen*. "We are selling real intimacy. We protect the experience and it becomes something you genuinely share with the people around you and you take away something special."

Why it's interesting:

For millennials and generation Zers, a music festival experience isn't necessarily synonymous with unbridled hedonism. Instead, they're looking to expand their minds in ways that enhance their wellbeing, with forward-thinking musicians and festival organizers tapping into this nascent movement.

02

Psychedelic health

As cannabis moves smoothly into the mainstream, psychedelic drugs are coming to the fore as the next generation of therapeutics.

Research within the scientific community points to the potential for psilocybin—the psychoactive compound in magic mushrooms—to treat depression by taking users deeper into their consciousness.

In September 2019, Florida-based John Hopkins Medicine launched the Center for Psychedelic and Consciousness Research after receiving $17 million from private donors. The lab says it will use psychedelics "to study the mind and identify therapies for diseases such as addiction, PTSD and Alzheimer's." Its program includes research into psilocybin mushrooms.

Imperial College London opened the Centre for Psychedelic Research in April 2019 to study the action of psychedelic drugs, with a particular focus on researching the treatment of depression. Dr Robin Carhart-Harris, the head of the center, says that the opening "represents a watershed moment for psychedelic science; symbolic of its now mainstream recognition. Psychedelics are set to have a major impact on neuroscience and psychiatry in the coming years."

INDERMAN
HOMPSON   Wavepaths psychedelic experiences without drugs

As more research points to the benefits of psychedelics, US lawmakers are paving the way for its integration into the mainstream. Denver, Colorado and Oakland have decriminalized the possession of psilocybin products, with Santa Cruz potentially following in the same footsteps.

Further legitimizing the halogenic substance, the Food and Drug Administration (FDA) granted Breakthrough Therapy designation to Compass Pathways in October 2018 and, more recently, to Usona Institute in November 2019. Both companies are conducting clinical trials into psilocybin's potential to treat severe depression. According to the Anxiety and Depression Association of America (ADAA), 16.1 million Americans suffer from major depressive disorder (MDD)—if the research proves correct, psilocybin could become a treatment option.

Health benefits aside, consumers are also tapping into psychedelics to explore their mind and consciousness in a deeper way, and psychedelic retreats are growing as a result. Britain's Psychedelic Society offers psilocybin retreats in Europe, and says they are "aimed at people in good mental and physical health wanting to explore the nature of reality and the mind."

Synthesis is a retreat center in the Netherlands that pioneers "transformative wellness." Launched in April 2018, it offers core three-day events at £1,640 ($2,148), aimed at "curious individuals who want to utilize moderate-to-high doses of psilocybin truffles to catalyze creative breakthrough, explore consciousness, find meaning, improve confidence and search for mystical experience."

Achieving a psychedelic experience without drugs is becoming a viable option thanks to startup Wavepaths. Led by a team of scientists, technologists, psychotherapists and artists, its mission is to make "transformative experiences widely accessible." Combining music, light and input from psychotherapists, Wavepaths' immersive experience will guide participants either towards "stillness and calm," or on a "journey inwards, connecting to deeper emotional states," the company says.

Why it's interesting:

Psilocybin could be the new cannabis. Growing research into psychedelics points to its therapeutic benefits for mental health and, with the legal process slowly trudging along, consumers are turning to retreats to tap into psychedelics and open up a new wellbeing experience.

As more research points to the benefits of psychedelics, US lawmakers are paving the way for its integration into the mainstream.

NDERMAN
OMPSON   Synthesis wellness retreat, the Netherlands. Image courtesy of Synthesis

Fast healing spaces

Self-care as a concept might be front and center in consumers' minds, but how many city dwellers can take time out for a spa day or lengthy treatment?

Enter a crop of fast healing spaces, offering doses of peace and calm squeezed into convenient time slots for stressed urbanites.

3Den describes itself as an "urban lounge," located in New York's new Hudson Yards development. Alongside places to work, it also offers "quiet zones, nap pods, and generously stocked showers" that provide its clientele with the opportunity to recharge while they're in the city. "We're an aggregate of the best parts of the coffee shop, the hotel lobby, elements of a gym and various other resources," 3Den founder and CEO Ben Silver tells Wunderman Thompson Intelligence. "We're not reinventing the wheel when it comes to consumer behavior; these are things that people are already doing, but they're doing them in a very disparate and dysfunctional manner. We're aggregating them into a much better consumer experience." Entry to 3Den is affordable, starting at $6 for 30 minutes.

Thinx, known for its period-proof underwear, created a wellness experience around its products with the opening of the Rest Room, a pop-up space on Elizabeth Street in New York's SoHo that ran

> The pace of life might be faster than ever, but consumers are increasingly conscious of the mental and physical toll a non-stop lifestyle can take.

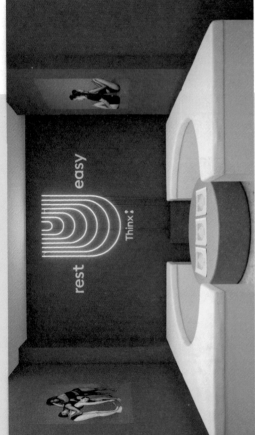

from October 28, 2019 to January 1, 2020. Customers could purchase Thinx products, relax in the drop-in lounge area and enjoy a program of events that spanned OB/GYN fertility consultations and educational sessions on how Thinx products work.

The concept is taking hold in London too. With branches in the city's Holborn and Shoreditch neighborhoods, Pop & Rest offers nap and meditation pods from £8 (around $10) for 30 minutes. Inhere currently rents outs and sells its chic wooden meditation pods to businesses, with a permanent location set to open in spring 2020.

These western takes on fast, functional healing follow in the footsteps of established healing cafés in South Korea. Chains

include Shim Story, a "public convenience lounge" that offers heated beds, massage chairs and video games, and Mr Healing, which provides massage chairs and eye masks in an atmosphere scented with essential oils. Writing in the *Atlantic*, Uri Friedman called the cafés "a balm for a sleep-deprived population that works some of the longest hours in the developed world."

Why it's interesting:

The pace of life might be faster than ever, but consumers are increasingly conscious of the mental and physical toll a non-stop lifestyle can take. These "walk-thru" healing spaces are tailoring mindful wellness to suit the breakneck speed of the modern world, allowing patrons a moment of contemplation and respite in their hectic days.

84

Digital spas

Social media and technology are frequently blamed for mental illness and poor health habits. Forward-thinking digital apps and platforms are now leveraging technology to encourage mindfulness and foster wellbeing.

In May 2019, *Dazed* launched the Dazed Beauty Digital Spa, which it describes as "an immersive space designed to make you feel healthier and happier away from the stresses of everyday life." Reimagining the traditional spa, the initiative falls somewhere between an online community and a digitally guided wellness practice. The week-long program includes live-streamed yoga and breathwork classes, and a range of think pieces, quizzes and meditative podcasts that cover everything from color therapy to positive affirmations.

Other digital platforms are also being designed to help users find respite, relaxation and mental balance. Meditation app Headspace is working on the world's first prescription-grade meditation app, specifically designed to treat a range of stress-related chronic diseases.

Even the Pokémon Company is turning its attention to wellbeing with the Pokémon Sleep gamified app. Announced in May 2019 and

launching for mobile devices in 2020, Pokémon Sleep aims to "reward good sleep habits as part of a healthy lifestyle."

"The future is about integrating digital health tools like therapy apps with standard healthcare treatment," Daniel Månsson, cofounder of Flow, tells Wunderman Thompson Intelligence. Launched at the beginning of June 2019, the Swedish startup is creating a medication-free digital treatment for depression.

Why it's interesting:

Tech and smartphones have been blamed for a host of health problems, from poor mental health to sleep disruption. These new apps and platforms, however, are working to change that, paving the way for optimal wellbeing.

WUNDERMAN THOMPSON   Opposite left and top right: Headspace.
Bottom right: Pokémon Sleep. Image courtesy of Nintendo

> The terms "feminine care" and "feminine hygiene" will be made redundant as society moves towards an inclusive future.

meet the needs of transmasculine customers," while in 2017 Pyramid Seven created "underwear for periods, not gender," and Aunt Flow is actively changing language to be more gender inclusive.

Why it's interesting:

The terms "feminine care" and "feminine hygiene" will be made redundant as society moves towards an inclusive future. Brands in this space need to rethink language and products—replacing "feminine products" with "menstrual products," for example, or positioning themselves in the wellness sector, rather than women's health, will allow everyone who has periods to identify.

#5

Genderless periods

As society moves towards a more inclusive future, gender norms are being re-evaluated and period brands, once exclusively marketed to girls and women, are rethinking their audience.

In fall 2019, Always made the decision to stop using the Venus symbol on its packaging, in a bid to be more inclusive of trans and non-binary consumers. "For over 35 years Always has championed girls and women, and we will continue to do so," says Procter & Gamble. "We're also committed to diversity and inclusion, and are on a continual journey to understand the needs of all of our consumers."

New York-based company Thinx is taking a much more definitive stance. It first featured a transgender model in a campaign in 2016, and released a commercial called "MENstruation" in October 2019 that portrays a world where both men and women have periods. It ends with the tag line, "If we all had them, maybe we'd be more comfortable with them."

Changes in language and marketing to be more gender inclusive have been adopted by brands over the past few years. Lunapads released a period boxer brief in 2016 which has been "designed to

NDERMAN
OMPSON

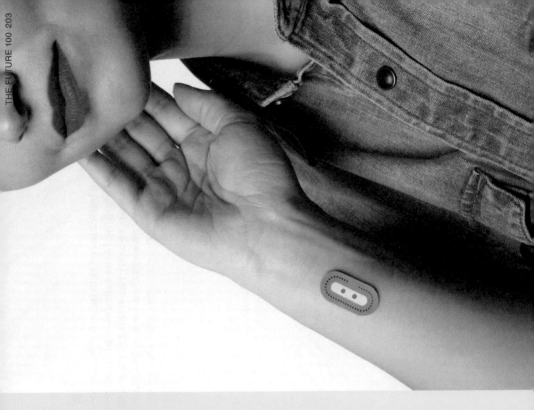

PH-balanced everything

Could pH levels be the next port of call in gaining a deeper understanding of skin and health concerns?

L'Oréal's My Skin Track pH launched as a prototype in June 2019, under the personal care giant's La Roche-Posay brand. This microfluidic sensor captures trace amounts of sweat from pores through a network of micro-channels, "providing an accurate pH reading within 15 minutes," L'Oréal said at the time of the product's reveal at the 2019 CES tech show.

When pH balance is compromised, L'Oréal explains, it can trigger inflammatory responses, which could exacerbate conditions such as skin dryness, eczema and atopic dermatitis. The skin's acidity balance can be affected by environmental factors or individual underlying conditions, for example.

"PH is a leading indicator of skin health," says Professor Thomas Luger, head of the department of dermatology, University of Münster, Germany, in L'Oréal's statement. "It is something my patients ask about, but until now it has been very challenging to measure skin pH outside of a clinical setting. This tool has the potential to inspire consumers to adopt healthier skincare habits and empower medical professionals with an entirely new way to

NDERMAN
OMPSON   My Skin Track pH by La Roche-Posay. Image courtesy of L'Oréal

recommend skincare regimens."

My Skin Track pH is being tested through La Roche-Posay dermatologists in the United States, with the aim of eventually launching a direct-to-consumer product.

Vaginal health is also affected by pH balance, and a number of underwear brands have launched claiming to balance pH levels in that area. Among them is Huha, infused with zinc "to prevent infection and odor-causing bacteria." Pure 5.5 says its breathable underwear helps to prevent infections and odor by keeping the vagina's pH balanced. However, obstetrician and gynecologist Dr Sherry A Ross told *Well & Good* that she doesn't believe pH-balanced underwear is "any safer than other vagina-friendly fabrics like cotton."

Alkaline water is on the rise, too. Citing data from Spins, a data firm with a focus on wellness, *Bloomberg* reported that the alkaline water category, which is still a fraction of the massive bottled water

PH is a leading indicator of skin health. It is something my patients ask about, but until now it has been very challenging to measure skin pH outside of a clinical setting. This tool has the potential to inspire consumers to adopt healthier skincare habits and empower medical professionals with an entirely new way to recommend skincare regimens.

Professor Thomas Luger, dermatology department head, University of Münster

industry, grew 36% to nearly $270 million in the United States in the year to April 2019. Claims for alkaline water include that it offers "better hydration," with market-leader Essentia saying it offers "supercharged hydration so you can do that thing," while Flow, promoted by Gwyneth Paltrow's *Goop*, offers what it calls "naturally alkaline water" in cartons, rather than plastic bottles, to underline its sustainable ethos.

Why it's interesting:

While pH levels are linked to skin health, the jury's out on the efficacy of alkaline waters—in August 2019, *Forbes.com* ran an article titled "Seven reasons why alkaline water is basically a waste of money." But the rise in this market illustrates the ongoing interest among consumers in the next big wellness-enhancing thing that they can fit seamlessly into their hectic lives. As Kara Nielsen, vice-president of trend insights at CCD Helmsman, told *Bloomberg*: "We're demanding more from everything—it has to have a purpose. This is how the younger generation thinks about nutrients."

07

Engineering companionship

Loneliness is not just a social issue. It's a public health problem too.

As the population's overall lifespan continues to extend, more of today's elderly population is facing aging alone and a number of new services and innovative tech brands are addressing this problem.

Research published in the *Wall Street Journal* suggests that eight million Americans over 50 years old have no spouse, partner or living child, according to sources including the US Census, and data from the Amsterdam Study of the Elderly published in the *Journal of Neurology, Neurosurgery and Psychiatry* shows that those who are lonely are more susceptible to depression, heart disease and dementia.

Japanese robotics startup Groove X unveiled Lovot at the CES 2019 tech show. An appealing robot, Lovot offers companionship and affection. Its many sensors allow it to interact with its user, responding to cuddles, squeezes and strokes. Lovot was designed by Kaname Hayashi, creator of pioneer robot Pepper. As he explained to *CNET*, the point is not to replace human relationships, but to preserve the capacity to engage emotionally. "If you love

something every day, then you have the power of love," Hayashi said.

Also featured at CES 2019, ElliQ is a voice-activated companion robot that, after several years in development, is now available for pre-order. The multifunctional device helps older people stay connected to family and serves as an in-home companion, responding to voice, touch and even gaze. It can also act as entertainer, as well as supply helpful, proactive reminders to drink water and take exercise or medication.

Why it's interesting:

Projections by the US Census Bureau show that by 2030 there will be more Americans aged 65 and older than aged 18 and younger, for the first time in US history. With older generations set to outnumber their younger counterparts, this growing consumer group is not to be ignored.

Big Tech health

Big Tech's next frontier? Taking on the labyrinthine US healthcare system.

Several tech giants have dived into health in recent months, with mixed reactions given tech's growing monopoly on society's infrastructure.

Apple announced in November 2019 that its Research app is partnering in three health studies that it describes as "landmark": the Apple Women's Health Study, the Apple Heart and Movement Study, and the Apple Hearing Study. The multiyear, longitudinal studies are being conducted in partnership with academic and research institutions—for example, the Harvard TH Chan School of Public Health and the NIH's National Institute of Environmental Health Sciences are partnering Apple for the Women's Health Study, and the Brigham and Women's Hospital and the American Heart Association are participating in the Heart and Movement Study. Participants can enroll in the studies via the Research app. Apple says that they "can contribute to potentially groundbreaking medical discoveries with iPhone and Apple Watch, and help create the next generation of innovative health products."

However, writing in the *New York Times*, Natasha Singer mused that, alongside the fact that Apple's products tend to be owned by

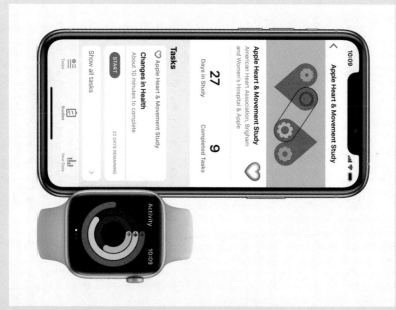

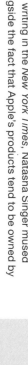WUNDERMAN THOMPSON   Apple's Heart and Movement Study. Image courtesy of Apple

higher-earning consumers, potentially skewing the results of the studies, "there are also some concerns that Apple, which has already reshaped how people live, communicate and entertain themselves, is pursuing yet another way to influence society, this time through health."

Google is targeting the health market, too. In November 2019, fitness wearables company Fitbit announced that it had agreed to be acquired by Google, in a deal that valued the company at $2.1 billion, with the transaction expected to complete in 2020. "Google is an ideal partner to advance our mission. With Google's resources and global platform, Fitbit will be able to accelerate innovation in the wearables category, scale faster, and make health even more accessible to everyone," says James Park, cofounder and CEO of Fitbit.

Analyzing why Fitbit's healthcare connections are likely to have attracted Google, Patrick Lucas Austin wrote in *Time* that Fitbit already works with "insurance companies, other firms and even the government of Singapore to provide customers, employees, and citizens with fitness trackers in what are likely lucrative deals," adding that, "for Google, Fitbit's healthcare ties, along with its established base of users, might be exactly what it needs to give its wearable device strategy a shot in the arm." The *Time* article also points out that, according a Statista estimate, "the healthcare tech space could be worth $24 billion by 2020."

Not to be left behind, Amazon has launched Amazon Care, which the company bills as "the best of both virtual and in-person care." Currently being piloted for Amazon's own employees in the Seattle area, the service provides general healthcare services, such as help with colds, allergies and infections, contraceptive consultations and STI testing, and prescriptions delivered to the door, with both in-person visits at the home or office and remote consultations.

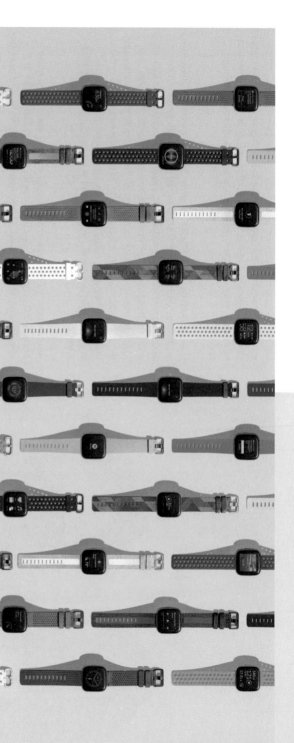

TechCrunch observes that, while Apple also offers remote and on-premises healthcare for its employees, Amazon Care is notable given that it's "much more external-facing than those offered by its peers in Silicon Valley, with a brand identity and presentation that strongly suggests the company is thinking about more than its own workforce when it comes to a future potential addressable market for Care." Pointing out that Amazon acquired Health Navigator, an online symptom-checking and triage tool, in October 2019, CNBC wrote that "if Amazon Care succeeds among employees, the company could someday sell it to millions of people who already rely on Amazon for their groceries, entertainment, and more."

Why It's interesting:

Having overhauled almost every aspect of human existence, Big Tech is now setting its sights on the healthcare market. While there's no doubt that these tech giants' prowess in creating seamless interfaces could positively impact the often difficult-to-navigate US healthcare system, questions over privacy and the use of customers' data loom. Fitbit says that, following the Google acquisition, data will not be sold or used for ads, while Apple says that consumers can tailor the data they share with its studies. However its moves are viewed, it's clear that Silicon Valley is firmly staking its claim in the healthcare market.

89

Beyond cars

America, the country that pioneered mass production of the automobile and created a car culture of road trips and drive-in restaurants, is seeing the development of its first purpose-built car-free neighborhood.

Culdesac Tempe is a new neighborhood in Arizona that broke ground in late 2019. It is set to open in fall 2020 to 1,000 renters who must agree not to own a car. Culdesac bills itself as "the world's first post-car real estate developer," and its $140 million project will boast a dog park, market hall, grocery store, gym and restaurants.

Culdesac aims to promote a lifestyle that's both good for the environment and good for people, with an abundance of shaded paths to encourage walking, scootering and biking. There are plans for light rail to connect it to downtown Tempe, Arizona State University and the airport. Emergency vehicles and delivery services can still get in, as well as a small fleet of shared cars.

This resonates with a clutch of other cities around the world which, for health reasons, have banished cars from their centers. These include Oslo—which early in 2019 removed 700 parking spots downtown to discourage driving—Madrid and Fazilka, India.

In 2011 an article in the *Journal of Public Health*, published by Oxford University Press, mused "Are cars the new tobacco?" and drew a direct link between car culture and physical inactivity, obesity, cardio-vascular disease from air pollution, death and injury from crashes, and climate change. Since then, there have been renewed efforts around the world, mostly by governments, to curb air pollution from vehicles and get people walking and pedaling.

In 2021, New York will become the first US city to impose a congestion charge for driving downtown at peak hours, following cities such as London and Singapore. Beijing holds a lottery for new car license plates, with more slots for electric vehicles than conventional ones, and requires every gas-powered vehicle to remain idle one day a week, with the day determined by the last digits of its license plate.

In 2019, New Delhi began restricting cars to alternate days on the road, also based on license plate numbers, after toxic pollution left people with smarting eyes and resulted in schools being closed. In Singapore, the government is heavily subsidizing workplace showers and changing rooms so people who walk, run or cycle to work can freshen up before clocking in.

Why it's interesting:

For decades, urban design has been dictated by automobiles, with space set aside for street parking and with the development of ever more sprawling suburbs. But the growing realization of the ill effects of too many vehicles has brought a tipping point. Young people are less interested in owning cars, partly because of cost and partly because of the ease of ride-hailing, preferring to spend their money on experiences and travel. For Culdesac's founders, the car-free experiment in the college town of Tempe is just a start. Ultimately, the company hopes to build the first car-free city in the United States.

90

Death doulas

A swathe of innovative services is driving a wellness-centric and eco-friendly approach to death.

According to Statista, in 2019 funeral homes in the United States alone generated revenue of $17 billion. The industry, which has seen little innovation over the past century, is primed for an overhaul. From new-age funeral homes to end-of-life coaches, newcomers are shaking up the sector and re-examining taboos and traditions surrounding the end of life.

Death doulas, also referred to as death midwives, are increasingly recognized as modern care practitioners, driving a raft of official training and certification programs. In 2019, the University of Vermont's College of Medicine became the first university department to offer an end-of-life doula professional certificate program, becoming part of a roster of global organizations including the International End of Life Doula Association (INELDA), the Art of Dying Institute, the Conscious Dying Institute and End of Life Doula UK.

Recompose is a new kind of after-death facility, slated to open in spring 2021 in Seattle. It will be the first facility to offer a sustainable option to traditional burial and cremation. Recompose will offer a proprietary system for corporeal composting, which "gently convert human remains into soil, so that we can nourish new life after we die," says the Recompose website.

started looking at the sort of relationship we have to death in this society," Recompose CEO and founder Katrina Spade told WBUR radio station, "and I started to think about whether we could have places in our cities where we had a more conscious relationship with death and could think more about our mortality and our place in the natural cycles."

Exit Here opened in London in October 2019. It is a nouveau funeral parlor overhauling the funeral planning process. Founded by restaurateur Oliver Peyton, it offers "a previously unavailable level of service, choice, flexibility and attention to detail." Exit Here was created to put the individual first, with a full service experienced in a polished, dignified and ultra-modern package—including caskets and urns designed in house. "From religious beliefs to the environment, today we have a much more individual and informed view on life," says the parlor's website. "Exit Here has been created to reflect that individuality and offer choices that weren't there before."

Why it's interesting:

The growing interest in dying well is giving rise to this death-positive movement, ushering in new end-of-life services. As the Global Wellness Institute notes in its 2019 trends report, "finally, a 'better death' is becoming integral to a 'well life.'"

NDERMAN   Above: Exit Here funeral parlor, London
OMPSON   Right: Better Place Forests natural alternative to cemeteries, US

Finance

New faces of finance

Fintech is reinvigorating the stuffy financial sector with new branding that taps into pop culture and has unlikely brand ambassadors.

Klarna, the Swedish online payments company famed for its disruptive "shop now, pay later" business model, is on a mission to remove financial friction for consumers—or, in the brand's words, "make shopping smoooth" (yes, the third "o" is intentional). In January 2019, Klarna doubled down on this sentiment with an unconventional and provocative move, announcing rapper Snoop Dogg as brand ambassador and minor shareholder.

Snoop Dogg is "arguably the smoothest man alive," and is a great match for the company, says Daniel Jontén, VP marketing at Klarna, adding that "he allows us to convey our mission in a new and creative way." Together they devised the campaign "Get Smoooth" and consequently rebranded Snoop Dogg as Smooth Dogg. The rapper is put into unique (and sometimes cheekily outlandish) scenarios that emphasize the smoothness of making online payments with Klarna—think pink silk robes, glossy Afghan hounds and golden peanut butter. "Klarna and Snoop's smooothness, as well as quirky worlds and visual expressions, harmonize perfectly," says Jontén. "It is a great way for Klarna to plunge into pop culture, becoming a global topic of conversation."

NDERMAN
OMPSON   Klarna's "Get Smoooth" campaign featuring Snoop Dogg as Smooth Dogg

The "Get Smoooth" campaign led to the March 2019 launch of products that are featured in the ads, including a silky bed set, cashmere toilet paper and a "smoooth robe." From the marketing language to the payment model, Klarna has gained popularity among millennials and generation Z, who value convenience, flexibility and financial control.

Launched in 2005, Klarna went through a radical rebrand in 2017, stripping away its early visual identity and communication, which was "closely aligned with the vast majority of the financial industry—blue and monotonous," says Jontén. The strategy has paid off. Klarna is now the largest private fintech company in Europe and is

valued at $5.5 billion. It has 70 million shoppers, and partners with 170,000 retailers to offer seamless purchasing.

Why it's interesting:
Even as lifestyle and culture evolve, little has changed in traditional banking to keep up with consumer trends. Fintech companies such as Klarna have found success by revitalizing conventional payment models while referencing pop culture to become a consumer-led brand.

Carbon credit

Imagine a world where every transaction impacts on an individual's carbon footprint score.

That vision is not too far off, as new systems are being implemented to heighten consumer awareness and shift a sustainable mindset to one that is actionable.

Consumers say they want to live more sustainably and do less harm to the planet. But acting on that desire can be difficult. For instance, 89% of US and UK consumers say they recycle at home yet only 52% always do so, and 85% say they avoid single-use plastics but only 20% do so on every occasion, according to SONAR™ research in Wunderman Thompson's "New Sustainability: Regeneration" report. Now businesses and governments are coming up with tools to nudge consumers to do the right thing.

In spring 2019 Swedish fintech company Doconomy introduced a no-nonsense credit card that cuts off spending when you reach a carbon limit, rather than a financial limit. The Do Black credit card tracks the carbon footprint of each purchase and stops working when a user is deemed to have hit their monthly limit. Calculations for the limit are based on the United Nations' 2030 carbon reduction target, and the amount of a user's limit is roughly half of the per capita carbon dioxide currently emitted by citizens of developed countries.

Doconomy also offers a way for users to purchase additional credit by buying units in climate-friendly projects in developing countries. But this "should not be used as an indulgence for further consumption," its website says. The startup, which bills itself as the "world's first mobile banking service for everyday climate action," also offers a Do White credit card that simply tracks a user's carbon footprint without imposing a carbon limit.

Governments are also facilitating sustainability. Helsinki, Finland, launched the Think Sustainably platform in mid 2019 to give residents, visitors and business owners tools to assess their daily behavior and make greener choices. From a think tank called Demos Helsinki, the platform rates local restaurants, galleries and attractions according to criteria including their greenhouse emissions. It also takes into account waste management, protecting biodiversity, accessibility and employment and preventing discrimination.

Other cities that are taking significant action on sustainability include Copenhagen, Denmark, where planners envision a city that is carbon neutral by 2025. The former industrial neighborhood of Nordhavn is being transformed into a "five-minute city" in which getting anywhere—to school or shops, for example—should be no more than a five-minute walk, to discourage driving. Oslo, Norway, is aiming to become carbon neutral by 2050 and Stockholm, Sweden, intends to be fossil-fuel free by 2040.

Why it's interesting:

According to SONAR™, Wunderman Thompson's proprietary research tool, 92% of consumers are trying to live more sustainably and 79% are conscious of their personal impact on the planet. But knowing how to put this into action can be a challenge. These new tools—from credit cards to sustainable city guides—can be useful for turning green intentions into actual green behavior.

Data: the new currency

Consumers are recognizing the value of their data—and rebelling against brands that harvest it for free.

"Data has become the most valuable asset on planet Earth, yet all of us as individuals, the people that produce that asset, have no rights to its value at the moment," data transparency advocate Brittany Kaiser, former Cambridge Analytica business development director and author of a whistleblower book about the company, tells Wunderman Thompson Intelligence.

Historically, brands relied heavily on data to learn about their consumers, and to date it's been freely collected. Recently, consumers have been starting to realize the value of what they're providing—and are pushing back. Asked to value on the information they're giving brands, US consumers priced demographics at $87 per month, digital behavior at $105 per month, purchase data at $200 per month, location data at $375 per month and biometrics at $550 per month, according to SONAR™ research conducted in September 2019 by Wunderman Thompson. The research reveals that 91% of consumers wish companies were more explicit about how they use consumer data and 89% think that companies are deliberately vague about data exchange terms.

If you own your data like your property, you have all the legal recourse to protect your property.

Brittany Kaiser, data transparency advocate

Kaiser believes a property rights framework is required to regulate data usage and incentivization. "If you own your data like your property, you have all the legal recourse to protect your property. And if anybody wants to use your property—be it the government or a corporation—you should get to know what they're using it for, how they're using it and be compensated for that," she says. "The right to property is a basic human right."

Why it's interesting:

As data complexity increases, so too does the need to provide greater oversight and regulation around managing and maintaining that data—marking a momentous shift in the traditional brand-consumer value exchange.

94

Biometric payments

Cash in hand takes on new meaning with the rise of biometric payments.

In 2018 consulting company Goode Intelligence predicted that more than 1.2 billion people would be using biometric payments by 2020. Advances in technology are allowing biometric scanning to be rolled out around the world, leading to increased payment security and more seamless transactions.

In April 2019, NatWest bank in the United Kingdom ran a pilot with 200 customers to test its new biometric fingerprint card. Customers register their fingerprint on their card and the fingerprint is stored locally so no biometric data is held by the bank. The card can then be used at any till with contactless payments, including purchases over £30, the usual contactless limit. By continuing to use cards for each payment, stores will not have to update their contactless-enabled card machines.

Getting rid of the card altogether, in September 2019 Fingopay launched its new finger vein ID recognition payment system at Copenhagen Business School's Spisestuerne café. Fingopay spent a year trialing the technology, and its payment system allows students and staff to register their Dankort, Visa or Mastercard with

their fingertip at the till and then pay seamlessly going forward.

"As vein patterns leave no trace and cannot be copied, it has been hailed as the ideal biometric for high-security authentication such as payments and identification," Simon Binns, CMO of Fingopay, tells Wunderman Thompson Intelligence.

San Francisco-based Incode is looking to make online payments more secure using facial recognition. Through its Incode Check product, launched in October 2019, consumers can use their face to

verify online payments. This helps to secure transactions that credit card companies could potentially deem fraudulent.

Why it's interesting:

As more and more consumers expect seamless transactions across all touchpoints, biometric payments will deliver both on ease and security.

> As vein patterns leave no trace and cannot be copied, it has been hailed as the ideal biometric for high-security authentication such as payments and identification.
>
> Simon Binns, CMO, Fingopay

UNDERMAN Left: Fingopay finger-vein payment system
THOMPSON Right: NatWest biometric fingerprint card

Financial therapy

95

Increasing financial insecurity is leading to a rise in financial therapy, which helps people get to grips with the emotional issues linked to money worries.

According to a Gallup poll released in April 2019, 25% of Americans worry "all" or "most" of the time that their family income will not meet their expenses, while 26% say they are "just making ends meet."

In November 2019 in the United Kingdom, the Money and Mental Health Policy Institute launched the Money and Mental Health Manifesto 2019. It was a call to politicians ahead of the UK's December 2019 general election to address issues such as "the link between suicide and financial difficulty," and recommends making money-related advice available as part of the mental health services provided by the British National Health Service.

Research psychologist Dr Galen Buckwalter spoke to *Goop* about the issue of financial post-traumatic stress disorder (PTSD), which he defined as "the physical, emotional and cognitive deficits people experience when they cannot cope with either abrupt financial loss or the chronic stress of having inadequate financial resources."

Amid these feelings of financial insecurity, financial therapy is on the rise. This growing field helps people to untangle the emotional issues that lie beneath their financial decisions. Nicolle Osequeda, a Chicago-based financial therapist, told *Fast Company* that "there is a lot of emotional, historical value tied into money and our relationship with money, and we need to talk about those things before someone can make changes or follow a plan."

In tandem with this more holistic approach to financial advice, financial services that take into account the emotional aspects of money are launching, too. Buckwalter in *Goop* points to Happy Money (in which he is an investor). The company says it "helps borrowers become savers." Following Happy Money's $70 million funding round in September 2019, the company's founder and CEO, Scott Saunders, told *Cheddar* that its research found "about a third of millennials have the equivalent of PTSD-like symptoms from their finances."

Saunders explained that the company makes loans at low interest rates "to help people eliminate high-interest credit-card debt faster and cheaper," working with "a national network of credit union partners." He added that Happy Money is "in business to take debt out of the world."

Why it's interesting:

Emotional and mental health remain at the forefront of national conversations, so it's no surprise that the thorny subject of financial health is getting more attention, with specialist financial therapists increasingly untangling financial and emotional issues. Services such as Happy Money illustrate a shift in corporate stance that, rather than profiting from keeping consumers stuck in debt, recognizes its emotionally debilitating effect and helps them break free.

96

Gen Z finances

Teaching financial literacy to a digital-native generation.

As Wunderman Thompson Intelligence reports in its "Into Z Future" study, even the youngest members of generation Z are entrepreneurial and many are earning big bucks. In the United Kingdom in 2018, children aged between six and 18 earned £4.5 billion, and have savings of over £550 million, according to the GoHenry "Youth Economy Report."

Startups, many backed by large financial institutions, are stepping in to teach young adults to be financially savvy in a digital-first way.

Greenlight is a US-based debit card and app which aims to teach kids and teens about financial literacy. Parents can monitor kids' spending through the app, adding money when needed and limiting the venues where it can be spent. "In the near future, I hope that this generation of kids grow up to spend wisely, learn the importance of saving and feel confident investing to build wealth over the long term," says Tim Sheehan, Greenlight CEO and cofounder.

Other fintech companies are expanding their offerings into the teen and youth market. UK-based Revolut's Revolut Youth card was reportedly imminent when this report was written, along with a corresponding app. In 2018, Monzo launched a youth account for customers aged 16 and 17, with plans to expand to younger audiences currently in the works.

Why It's Interesting:

As financial transactions become increasingly digital and intangible, today's youth will need to learn the value of a dollar without ever having to touch one. Financial literacy apps can equip gen Z and those even younger with the tools to handle their digital financial futures.

NDERMAN   Above: Greenlight financial service for kids
OMPSON   Right: Monzo card

Single spending

With the increase in singles comes the rise of single spending.

For too long, marketers have focused on traditional life stages, with carefree youth followed swiftly by marriage and family life. That's no longer a reality for many. "Single people represent an economic powerhouse, a force that can reshape markets with new needs and new standards of living," declares "The Single Age," a recent report from Wunderman Thompson Intelligence.

Single people buy houses, spend significant amounts on travel and tend to be better educated than their married counterparts. The trend is especially pronounced among women, who are increasingly financially self-sufficient. According to the Harvard Joint Center for Housing Studies, women made up more than half the single population in 2015, while the National Association of Realtors showed single women bought homes at twice the rate of single men in 2017.

Singledom is also up globally. Eurostat figures show that in Sweden, Denmark, Finland and Germany, single households accounted for more than 40% of all households in 2016. In China, the percentage of single adults grew from 6% in 1990 to almost 15%, or 200 million

Businesses are finally starting to address the "single tax," the costs that come with not having a partner with whom to split bills.

people, in 2017, according to China's Ministry of Civil Affairs. In Hong Kong, single women are buying homes to the point where they are a primary driver of gentrification.

Perhaps the most overt commercial celebration of singles is Alibaba's Singles Day, held each year on November 11. It is now the world's biggest shopping festival, hitting sales worth a record $38 billion in 2019.

Still, the "single tax," a term coined to describe the costs that come with not having a partner with whom to split rent, a mortgage or a healthcare premium, remains a real problem—and businesses are finally starting to address it.

Apps are popping up in many cities to support single life; from food deliveries to services such as Laundrapp in the United Kingdom, which picks up and drops off laundry and dry cleaning, and TaskRabbit, which outsources household tasks.

A recent *Refinery29* article offered tips for avoiding the single tax, such as sharing Netflix, Spotify and other accounts with family; going on holiday with friends to split room costs; and batch-cooking and freezing to save on food bills.

Why it's interesting:

Singles today are not shy about wielding their financial power. According to a survey of 3,000 respondents across the United States, United Kingdom and China commissioned by SONAR™, Wunderman Thompson's proprietary research tool, over 80% of American singles enjoy the fact that they can make all of their own financial decisions, and over 85% agree that making their own financial decisions is empowering. Whether the offer is innovations in coliving, single dining or solo travel, businesses that recognize and cater to this economically powerful demographic will come up tops.

New payment gestures

New payment options are making checkout more frictionless than ever.

Amazon engineers are working on a card-free, phone-free biometric system code-named Orville that will let shoppers at Whole Foods settle their bills with a wave of the hand. Orville, currently still at the test stage, uses scanners designed to recognize an individual hand using computer vision and depth geometry—shoppers would not need to physically touch the device or use their fingerprint.

This means an ultrafast and consequently more pleasant in-store purchasing experience—an Orville transaction should take less than 300 milliseconds on average, compared to the three to four seconds it takes to use a card, the *New York Post* reported.

And frictionless payments will likely mean monetary perks for retailers as well. "People tend to spend more when they don't have the experience of touching something tangible like money," Majd Maksad, founder and CEO of Status Money, a personal finance site, told the *New York Post*. "The utility of money becomes more ephemeral."

While this kind of transaction could still involve a cashier, Amazon and a handful of other technology companies are in a race to

implement cashierless stores. Cashierless convenience store Amazon Go already operates in 21 locations around the United States and in November 2019 announced plans to open larger cashierless grocery stores—and potentially license the technology to other retailers.

In September 2019, technology startup Trigo raised $22 million for its checkout-free endeavors, which, like Amazon Go, use cameras and sensors that track shoppers as they move around the store. Trigo technology will first be used by Shufersal, Israel's largest supermarket chain. Supermarkets that use Trigo's technology will be able to implement cashierless payments and also use data aggregated from shoppers' in-store activities to create personalized experiences and loyalty programs.

Why it's interesting:

The leather wallet has seen better days. Advances in payments technology are giving retailers the tools to almost completely remove pain points in the in-store transaction experience for discerning digital natives. Companies now only need to get more customers and regulators completely on board with biometrics. In the meantime, less invasive alternatives to facial recognition, like hand-gesture payments or cashierless stores, might gain more traction.

Subscription-based insurance

The insurance industry, traditionally slow to change, is dipping a toe into the subscription model that has become the norm for millennials and generation Z.

The open-ended nature of accessing services by subscription, from Netflix to clothing to personal care products, has become the new norm for younger generations. Almost 33% of millennials are members of at least one retail subscription service, according to MarTech Advisor.

The insurance industry is starting to catch up. In the United Kingdom, HSBC introduced Select and Cover in November 2019. This subscription insurance service allows customers to select between three and seven different kinds of policy, including motor breakdown, mobile phone, home emergency, and gadget cover. Subscribers, who must be HSBC account holders, can change their options annually as their needs shift. The monthly fee starts at £19.50 (around $25) and can be canceled at any time, at no cost.

HSBC's Select and Cover launch follows AvivaPlus's UK debut in 2018, when _Which_, the impartial product-review platform of the UK's Consumers' Association, compared its monthly insurance payment model to that of a Netflix subscription. The monthly payments are

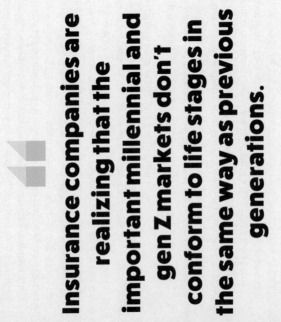

Insurance companies are realizing that the important millennial and gen Z markets don't conform to life stages in the same way as previous generations.

interest free, existing customers are guaranteed the same or a better price than an equivalent new customer when they renew, and the subscription can be canceled without incurring a fee.

AvivaPlus offers home or car insurance with three tiers of cover. "Like subscription services, it's designed to make it easy for customers to change their cover as often as they want without incurring charges," says Andy Briggs, Aviva's UK insurance CEO, adding that Aviva has "worked with thousands of customers to understand how insurance could better meet their needs and provide the flexibility they want for their modern lives."

In Brazil, São Paulo-based startup Kakau has launched a home insurance subscription service following a similar model.

British insurance company Urban Jungle focuses on renters' needs, offering what it describes as a flexible, pay-as-you-go monthly policy "designed specially for renters." Monthly contents cover starts at £5 (around $7). In May 2019, the company announced a £2.5 million ($3.2 million) seed funding round, stating that it had been "working closely with underwriters to remove many of the legacy home-owner questions renters are asked when taking out a policy," making its policies easier to understand and better suited to "generation rent." The company added that it intends to "stay with its customers as they grow and experience new life stages—many of which will happen while they're still renting" so it will further expand its insurance product in the future.

Why it's interesting:

Insurance companies are realizing that the important millennial and gen Z markets don't conform to life stages in the same way as previous generations. As a result, they're devising new products that are easier to understand and meet the ever-changing needs of young consumers who are reluctant to commit to long-term contracts. According to a 2019 First Insight report, "millennials continue to be the dominant force in retail both in the United States and the United Kingdom, as their shopping habits can be a deciding factor in what makes or breaks the success and longevity of retail models." With that in mind, insurance brands are shifting their focus to woo the vital younger generations.

FINANCE

Branded payments

Big Tech is looking to the world of finance—but trust remains an issue.

From transportation to entertainment, Big Tech has had its hand in almost all the cookie jars of consumerism, making its pervasive reach hard to ignore. Do consumers trust Big Tech enough to hand over their financial details?

In October 2019, Uber announced a new division: Uber Money. The banking initiative offers debit cards and improved payment options for drivers. A mobile banking account gives Uber drivers and couriers "real-time access to their earnings after every trip through the Uber Debit account," the company says, rather than having to wait for weekly payments. The move also offers a digital wallet so "earners and spenders will now be able to easily track their earning and spending history, manage and move their money, and discover new Uber financial products all in one place."

In August 2019, Apple released the Apple Card, a credit card backed by Goldman Sachs. The card is Apple's attempt to do for banking what it did for computers and smartphones: upend the status quo with innovative, simplified, streamlined technologies.

Apple positions the card as a simple, transparent way to bank, "designed to help customers lead a healthier financial life," according to Jennifer Bailey, vice president of Apple Pay.

Although the card has met gender discrimination issues, its release marks a significant step for Apple into the world of finance. Alongside the Apple Card, Apple Pay continues to make significant inroads in the financial realm, processing $1.8 billion in transactions in the first quarter of 2019.

And while Facebook Libra, the social media giant's foray into

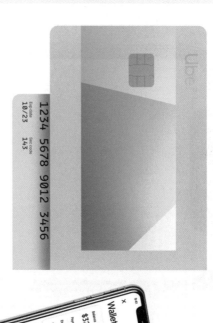

cryptocurrency, announced in June 2019, seems to be unraveling, it's another signifier of Big Tech's relentless push into the fintech space.

Why it's interesting:

After finding success in lifestyle brands, the world of finance is a natural next step for these tech leaders. Traditional banks, beware: despite hurdles, Big Tech brands are already starting to give the stodgy world of banking the Silicon Valley treatment.

After finding success in lifestyle brands, the world of finance is a natural next step for these tech leaders.

About the Wunderman Thompson Intelligence

Wunderman Thompson Intelligence is Wunderman Thompson's futurism, research and innovation unit. It charts emerging and future global trends, consumer change, and innovation patterns—translating these into insight for brands. It offers a suite of consultancy services, including bespoke research, presentations, co-branded reports and workshops. It is also active in innovation, partnering with brands to activate future trends within their framework and execute new products and concepts. It is led by Emma Chiu, Global Director of Wunderman Thompson Intelligence.

—

For more information visit: jwtintelligence.com

Contact:

Emma Chiu
Global Director of Wunderman Thompson Intelligence
emma.chiu@wundermanthompson.com

Wunderman Thompson Taipei
wt.taipei@wundermanthompson.com

Senior trends analyst

Emily Safian-Demers, Wunderman Thompson Intelligence

Contributors

MayYee Chen, Wunderman Thompson Intelligence
Marie Stafford, Wunderman Thompson Intelligence
Elizabeth Cherian, Wunderman Thompson Intelligence
Sarah Tilley, Wunderman Thompson Intelligence
Maeve Prendergast, Wunderman Thompson Intelligence
Nina Jones
Jessica Rapp

Sub editors

Hester Lacey
Katie Myers
Harriet O'Brien

Art director and designer

Shazia Chaudhry

Picture researcher

Farrah Zaman

Cover image: Still-life arrangement with flowers including sweet peas and clematis. Image courtesy of Phaidon Press

+ WUNDERMAN THOMPSON